Glenis Lucas has always had a great love of cooking, using fresh natural ingredients to produce varied and appetizing food. When she discovered that she was experiencing problems with gluten and dairy products, she began to experiment with a multitude of permitted ingredients and called upon all her experience to create a personal recipe collection which will appeal to all tastes.

THE COMPLETE GUIDE TO
GLUTEN-FREE AND
DAIRY-FREE COOKING

Over 200 Delicious Recipes

Glenis Lucas

WATKINS PUBLISHING

LONDON

This edition published in the UK in 2006 by
Watkins Publishing, Sixth Floor, Castle House, 75-76 Wells Street,
London W1T 3QH

© Glenis Lucas 2006

Glenis Lucas has asserted her right under the Copyright, Designs and
Patents Act, 1988, to be identified as the author of this work.

1 3 5 7 9 10 8 6 4 2

Designed and typeset by Jerry Goldie

Printed and bound in Great Britain

British Library Cataloguing in Publication data available

ISBN 1 84293 144 X
www.watkinspublishing.com

Contents

DISCLAIMER

Any information given in this book is not intended to be taken as a replacement for medical advice. Any person with a condition requiring medical attention should consult a qualified medical practitioner.

The recipes in this book are gluten free and dairy free unless stated otherwise.

The recipes are suitable for sufferers from the coeliac condition, wheat allergy, wheat intolerance, milk allergy and lactose intolerance. (Recipes containing oats have notes for coeliacs.)

Readers should ensure that they are not allergic or intolerant to any substances in the ingredients used in the recipes.

Dedicated to my husband Bernard
and my sons Richard and Ian

Acknowledgements

First and foremost I would like to thank my family for their continued support over the years; for their help in trying and testing the recipes many times. I would also like to thank everyone else who has helped make this book possible.

Foreword

Two major events, relevant to the allergy sufferer, have happened in recent months. Firstly, the Royal College of Physicians of England produced a report which stated there was a 'trebling of the prevalence of common allergic disease in the last twenty years in the UK, resulting in approximately one fifth of the UK population likely to be seeking treatment for allergy. Potentially life-threatening but previously rare allergies, such as peanut allergy, now affect approximately one in seventy children and are still increasing.'

Much more recently a House of Commons select committee report said that there were only six specialist full-time allergy clinics across the whole country and only six paediatric specialists compared with Germany's five hundred.

Allergy is an upcoming epidemic with little professional help available.

The problems of allergy are similar across the developed world and the eighteen million people estimated by the select committee to be affected in Great Britain increases to more than eighty million in the United States of America.

The treatment of allergy is avoidance of the allergen, as it has always been. Cure is not yet possible. Supermarket prepared meals contain all sorts of ingredients that may cause troubles, the source of which is not always clear. For example, whey powder may cause problems for milk allergic souls. This prevents the pre-prepared shop fare from being a sensible choice.

Allergy UK wholly supports any book that will help to free the allergy sufferer from the risks associated with their allergy.

This cookbook fulfils a true treatment option by allowing people to produce food that they can be certain about, and a real bonus – the meals from these recipes taste good.

Michael C Matthews MBBS
Chairman, Allergy UK

Introduction

This opening section is a necessarily brief thumbnail sketch about allergies. If you want more information please use the links in the book (*see Resource Guide*).

Allergies fall into two main categories: the classical allergy and the intolerance. The first is a clearly defined problem with a relatively well-known pathway. However, the symptoms that it causes are very varied. Even the existence of food intolerance is controversial in medical circles although a very definite and intractable problem amongst our patients. The differences are roughly as follows:

- Classical allergy involves a severe response to some substance which either has to be a protein or become bound to one. The response is an exaggeration of the normal, which tends to worsen each time it happens, and is sometimes fatal. It is triggered immediately on contact with the offending substance and often by just one substance (albeit a protein mixture), such as a bee or wasp sting.

- Intolerances are much slower in onset, tend to cover a range of foods and need repeated exposure to maintain the symptoms. They may start some days after contact with the offending substance and the symptoms may bear no relationship to the route of entry to the body.

Life is never simple, so there are a few conditions that seem to bridge the gap between allergy and intolerance. Both types of problem can coexist in one person making the picture even less clear.

To add to the confusion, some enzyme deficiencies are commonly known as intolerances. These may be either very rare or quite common, for example lactose intolerance which affects many millions worldwide.

Lastly, there are some substances that are, in their nature, irritant or toxic to anyone, but also are capable of causing allergies in susceptible people. Again the problems may be mixed with the more recognised forms of allergy.

Classical Allergy

Media and films usually portray classical allergy as a sudden severe anaphylactic reaction when someone is stung by an insect and within a few minutes or even seconds develops overall swelling, breathing difficulties, very rapid heart rate and eventually succumbs. Fortunately this is uncommon. Classical allergy can be a factor in many diseases, for example asthma and skin rashes (not necessarily eczema). Latex allergy is also an increasingly common problem especially in hospitals and more insidiously for surgical patients. It is important to note that although the symptoms may be related to one area of the body, such as the skin or lungs, it does not necessarily mean that the allergen has been either in contact with the skin or inhaled. This is an important factor and makes the proper detection of allergies necessary for their correct treatment.

Another concept worthy of mention is that similar allergens (substances causing allergies) fall into groups. For example, a person with a crab-meat allergy is likely to be allergic to lobster and, less comfortably, to cockroaches. Unlike the shellfish which are eaten, cockroaches cause problems by contamination of inhaled air with droppings and shell fragments. So the relevantly allergic person could have problems with a dusty house and the evening's crab salad. Just to confuse the issue further, the inhaled allergen could cause asthma, skin problems, bowel problems and so on while the ingested element could also produce a similar list of difficulties.

Milk and dairy products present a similar profile and people who have a reaction with cows' milk are more likely to have a problem with goats' and sheep's milk than those who have no such allergy. This makes their use as substitutes rather problematic.

Food Intolerance

Food intolerance is a factor in a whole range of conditions. Asthma, eczema, migraine and irritable bowel syndrome are the big four. Between them they affect a considerable section of the population and cause much suffering. Food intolerance is usually caused by a number of foods of which milk, egg white, yeast, cashew and almond are the major offenders, with gluten occupying a special place of its own. You may see that these all feature in baby foods and one hypothesis states that the baby's gut is unable to cope with these foods. It becomes leaky, allowing more toxic substances to cross from the bowel and cause problems in target organs; the skin in the case of eczema, the lungs in the case of asthma and so on. The effects remain local in the case of irritable bowel syndrome.

This is a very contentious area in medical circles and many physicians will disagree with these views, although supporting evidence is slowly accumulating.

Other Related Problems

A special place is reserved for bowel diseases and some physicians regard irritable bowel syndrome, coeliac disease, Crohn's disease and ulcerative colitis as worsening versions of the same problem – sensitivity to a fraction of grain called gluten. If you have been diagnosed with this problem, avoidance is mandatory for continued good health. The issue is under active investigation and this specific allergy may be only one factor.

Diagnosis and Treatment

This book is not a textbook of medicine, but of cooking. However a few things about diagnosis and treatment need to be stated.

Firstly, there is currently no cure for allergies and although some potential cures are in the pipeline they are some years away. Medicines only suppress the effects of allergies and they may be ineffective in the presence of severe anaphylaxis.

The only effective and foolproof way to avoid a classical allergy is to avoid the allergen, hence my support for this cookbook. This cannot be overemphasised.

The picture is a little brighter for food intolerance. It has been observed that those who rigorously exclude the offending food for a period of two years can sometimes reintroduce that food without the symptoms returning. This gives some support to the idea that the problem is caused by a leaky bowel wall that is sustained by repeated exposure to the offending food. The rest period may have allowed the bowel to recover and lose its leakiness. (*See Links for a fuller explanation.*)

Secondly, correct diagnosis is vital. You cannot avoid an allergen if you don't know what it is. The most important part that you can play in that detective job is to keep a truly comprehensive diary detailing everywhere you have been, everything that you have touched, eaten or inhaled in the six weeks prior to visiting your physician. While certain blood and skin-prick tests are useful, they are only helpful to confirm what the diary and consultations highlight as suspect substances. There are too many possibilities to allow an unfocused blood screen to be effective.

While there is access to the appropriate specialist in the USA, sadly the same cannot be said for Great Britain at the time of writing this introduction. This has led to many unproven tests being available on the high street and over the internet to exploit the gap between demand and services. Until and unless these are presented to scientific scrutiny, and proven safe and useful, they are best avoided.

Enzyme Deficiencies

There are many of these deficiencies and most will be well known to their sufferers, having been diagnosed early in life, but generally small numbers of people are affected. This is not the case with lactose intolerance (not in any way related to food intolerance) which is the lack of an enzyme necessary to digest lactose in milk. It is very common, especially in people of African and Oriental background (up to 95 per cent), less common in those of Mediterranean descent (50 per cent) and up to 15 per cent in western Europeans. It can cause stomach upset when milk is consumed. There is no cure and avoidance is again the only sure method of coping with the problem, despite some claims that lactobacillus-enriched foods will enable sufferers to eat milk products safely.

Chemical Sensitivities

The final category is that of chemical sensitivity. A good example is that of tyromine which can cause migraine attacks when present in foods such as: cheese, wine, peanut butter, chicken, onions, bananas, chocolate, vinegar and citrus fruits. As you can see, it is a very mixed selection of foods. True allergy to these foodstuffs may also be present in migraine, as can food intolerance, so identification of the root cause is complex.

Tyromine sensitivity represents a very specific chemical sensitivity for some people but other chemicals will have an adverse effect on everyone, to some degree. An example is that of chilli peppers. No one escapes the heat of that fruit. Whether it is regarded as enjoyable is another matter but the chemical effect on everyone is clear. Again, true allergies may also be present with their attending problems.

The Bottom Line

Correct identification of the allergen and its avoidance are the main, indeed only, pieces of advice that are needed and should be heeded.

Links

www.shared-care.com for helpful books and other allergy resources. The web publishing page (www.shared-care.com/WebPub) for free downloadable e-books with a fuller explanation of food intolerance theory.

www.allergyuk.org is the website of Allergy UK for comprehensive help and information.

Michael C Matthews MBBS
Chairman, Allergy UK

Information

Foods & Drinks to Avoid – Containing Gluten

This list is not exhaustive and labels should always be checked or food producers contacted for clarification.

Grains, flours and cereals

Wheat grain, wheat flour (strong flour has a high gluten content, spelt, kamut and triticale flours have a low gluten content), wheat flakes, cracked wheat, kibbled wheat, wheat berry, wholemeal, wholewheat, wheatmeal, wheat bran, durum wheat, wheat germ, porgouri, burghul, bulghar wheat, semolina, couscous.

Buckwheat is an exception – despite its name it is not from the wheat family.

Oat grain, oat flakes, oatmeal, oatbran, rolled oats, porridge oats, oat germ, pinhead oatmeal, oat cereal.

Oats need to be discussed with your GP or dietician if coeliac.

Rye grain, rye flour, rye flakes, rye meal.

Barley grain, barley flour, barley flakes, pearl barley, pot barley, barley meal.

Malt, malt flour, malt powder, malt extract/malt extract flavouring/malt vinegar.

Some gluten-free products contain small amounts of malt extract/malt extract flavouring/malt vinegar. The majority of coeliacs will not experience problems but coeliacs with a high level of sensitivity may.

Look out for rusks or plain flour, cereal binders, fillers, wheat proteins, proteins, wheat starch, starches – including modified starch, unless special wheat starch to Codex Alimentarius Standard. Some glucose syrups may be derived from wheat products. For most coeliacs this will pose no problem but for coeliacs with a high level of sensitivity it may.

Bread and baked foods

All loaves (including pumpernickel) and rolls unless specifically stated otherwise (many 'rye' and 'corn' loaves are 'lightened' with wheat).

Pitta, naan bread, crumpets, muffins, tortillas and tacos (which should really be corn usually contain some wheat in the UK).

Biscuits, breadcrumbs, cake mixes, scones, crispbreads, pie fillings, doughnuts, cookies, crackers, croutons, packet snacks, rusks, waffles, crepes, pizzas, pretzels, breadsticks, communion wafers, ice-cream wafers and cones.

Any breakfast cereals made using wheat, rye, barley and possibly oats. *If coeliac, oats need to be discussed with your GP or dietician.*

Pastry, pasta, noodles, batter, yorkshire pudding, suet, mincemeat, suet pudding, and many other puddings contain wheat.

Baking powder, bicarbonate of soda (baking soda) and cream of tartar may contain gluten.

Meat and fish

Prepared chilled meals, burgers, rissoles, salami, sausages, corned beef, luncheon meat, liver sausage, continental sausages, patés, ham, meat/fish pastes and spreads, meat/fish battered or crumbed (e.g. fish fingers, fish cakes), meat/fish in pastry, meat/fish soups, Scotch eggs coated with breadcrumbs, stuffed and processed products.

Vegetable products

Vegetable patés and spreads.

Vegetables coated with flour, batter or breadcrumbs (e.g. onion rings, vegetable tempura).

Vegetables canned in a sauce (e.g. creamed mushrooms), tinned beans, (also tinned spaghetti often grouped with vegetables), soups (including prepared chilled soups), tinned and packet snacks or ready prepared foods.

Desserts

Most puddings, pastry, pancakes, cheesecakes and others with biscuit base, yoghurts containing cereal, some ice cream.

Artificial cream, low-fat cheese spreads and prepacked grated cheese may contain wheat flour.

Seasonings, sauces and condiments

Gravy, sauces (packet, jar and bottled), casserole and 'ready-meal' mixes, some stock (bouillon) cubes and granules, some dressings, ready prepared and powdered mustard, stuffing, monosodium glutamate, some spice mixes (check labels).

Beverages

Barley water fruit squashes, malted milk, plain-chocolate and some instant coffee drinks, milk with added fibre, oat drinks (*if coeliac with a high level of sensitivity, oats need to be discussed with your GP or dietician*), and other powdered drinks.

Beer, ale, stout, lager, Pilsner lager, gin, some spirits and wines.

Confectionery

Sweets rolled in flour (e.g. liquorice and unwrapped sweets), seaside rock, chocolates. *Most chocolate is gluten free but may be made at the same premises as other wheat products with a risk of cross-contamination.*

Chocolate bars containing biscuit, other sweets (check labels).

Medication

Many prescribed and over-the-counter drugs contain wheat. Check with your pharmacist. Do not stop prescribed medication without discussing with your doctor.

Other

Margarine with wheat germ oil, glue on labels and postage stamps.

Gluten-free Foods & Drinks

This list is not exhaustive and labels should always be checked or food producers contacted for clarification.

Grains, flours and cereals

Arrowroot flour.

Buckwheat grain (natural unroasted/roasted), buckwheat flour, buckwheat pasta, buckwheat noodles.

Gram flour (chana dhal/yellow gram/chick pea).

Corn grain (maize/sweetcorn), cornflour (cornstarch), maize flour, cornmeal, polenta, cornflakes, corn pasta.

Lentil flour, lentils, split peas, chickpeas (garbanzo beans), pulses.

Soya beans, soya flour, tofu products.

Potato flour (farina).

Rice grain, rice flour (stoneground/brown/white), ground rice, rice flakes, rice bran, crisp rice cereal, rice pasta.

Sago grain, sago flour.

Tapioca grain, tapioca flour.

Special wheat starch (Codex Alimentarius Standard).

Maltodextrins can be produced from wheat, but the level of gluten contained in it is so low that it does not affect coeliacs.

Millet whole grain, millet flakes, millet pasta.

Quinoa whole grain, quinoa flakes, quinoa flour.

Amaranth.

Sorghum.

Bread and baked foods:
Gluten-free bread, cakes, biscuits, crispbreads, breakfast cereals, pasta, flours and flour mixes manufactured by specialist food companies.

Meat and fish:
All fresh and plain frozen meats and fish without wheat flour, batter or bread coatings, tinned fish in brine, oil or tomato sauce.

Vegetable products:
All fresh and plain cooked, tinned, dried or frozen vegetables, certain brands of baked beans and potato crisps, fresh and dried herbs.

Desserts:
Rice, sago and tapioca puddings, gluten-free cakes, scones, biscuits, pastries, sponge puddings manufactured by specialist food companies, jellies, sorbets, some gelatine-based desserts and custards.

Seasonings, sauces and condiments:
Gluten-free spice mixtures, salt, freshly ground pepper, some vegetable stock (bouillon)/stock (bouillon) cubes, yeast extract, French mustard, home-made mayonnaise and dressings. Sauces prepared with cornflour (cornstarch) or other gluten-free flours.

Fruit and nuts:
All fresh fruit and plain tinned fruit in natural juice or syrup, dried-fruit salad, dates, apricots etc. or frozen fruits, pure fruit juices, desiccated (shredded) coconut/fresh coconut, unprocessed nuts, fresh or shelled.

Beverages:
Tea/herb tea, pure coffee and cocoa, water (tap, spring, still, fizzy), fizzy drinks, most fruit squashes, cordials and fresh fruit juices, most wines, spirits, cider, sherry, port and liqueurs. *Whisky is made from barley but the gluten is removed during the distillation process.*

Confectionery:
Sugar, glucose, honey, jam, marmalade, treacle, many sweets and chocolates (check labels) plain ice lollies. *Most chocolate is gluten free*

but may be made at the same premises as other wheat products with a risk of cross-contamination.

Oils:

Olive, sunflower, safflower, rapeseed, grapeseed, soya, corn and nut oils.

Major supermarkets produce their own 'free from' (i.e. wheat-free/gluten-free) ranges of foods, in addition to those foods available from health-food shops.

Foods & Drinks to Avoid – Containing Dairy Products

This list is not exhaustive and labels should always be checked or food producers contacted for clarification.

Milk Produce

Cows' milk, condensed milk, evaporated milk, buttermilk, dried milk, powdered milk, coffee creamers and whiteners, malted milk, milk drinks, cream, ice cream, yoghurt, custards, creamed sauces.

Milk allergy sufferers must also avoid goats' and sheep's milk products but those with lactose intolerance may be able to tolerate these, depending on the severity of the condition.

Dairy Products

Cheese, cottage cheese, butter, ghee, most margarines, shortening, salad dressings and mousses.

Processed foods which may contain milk

Breakfast cereals (baby cereal made with milk), baked goods, e.g. milk rolls, some bread, cakes, biscuits, crackers and rusks containing milk.

Processed meat e.g. luncheon meat, chorizo, salami, sausages.

Pancakes, batters (including fish in batter) sauces and gravies.

Ready-made meals, puddings, instant desserts, instant mashed potato, pasta and pizzas, soups and baby foods.

Chocolate, toffee, fudge, confectionery and crisps.

Other Ingredients/Medication

Check food labels for the following ingredients which contain some cows' milk or milk products in them:

Casein, caseinates, hydrolysed casein, skimmed-milk powder, milk solids, non-fat milk solids, whey, whey syrup sweetener, milk sugar, lactose, lactic acid and lactal bumin.

A number of dry powder asthma inhalers contain lactose. Currently there are no lactose-free antihistamines in the UK except syrup formulations. Therefore, people with milk allergy need to check content with the Royal Pharmaceutical Society, 1 Lambeth High St, London SE1 7JW. Monosodium glutamate is naturally occuring in various high-protein foods, but is brewed commercially as an additive and probably rarely contains any lactose, but check with supplier. Most so-called MSG (monosodium glutamate) reactions are caused by other meal constituents.

Dairy-free Foods & Drinks

This list is not exhaustive and labels should always be checked or food producers contacted for clarification.

Soya milk (unsweetened and sweetened), fruit-flavoured and chocolate-flavoured soya and fruit smoothies, soya yoghurt, soya cream, soya ice cream.

Soya cheese, including processed 'cheese' slices and full-fat soft 'cheese'.

Rice milks.

Oat drinks. [*If coeliac with a high level of sensitivity, oats need to be discussed with your GP or dietician.*]

Other non-dairy milks such as almond, quinoa, pea protein and ground chufa (tigernut).

Potato milk (powder or liquid).

Fresh coconut milk, creamed coconut.

Dairy-free sunflower and soya margarines.

Cocoa powder.

Dairy-free plain chocolate.

Eggs (unless sensitive to the yolk or white).

Milk allergy sufferers must also avoid goats' and sheep's milk products but those with lactose intolerance may be able to tolerate these, depending on the severity of the condition.

Major supermarkets produce their own 'free from' (i.e. milk-free/dairy-free) ranges of foods, in addition to those foods available from health-food shops.

Calcium, Vitamins, Minerals, Bone Health & Exercise

Calcium, protein and other bone minerals and vitamins are required to build strong, healthy bones from an early age to maintain and protect against bone loss in later life. People with the coeliac condition may have poor absorbency of vitamins and minerals such as calcium and there may be an increased risk of developing osteoporosis (porous, brittle bones that fracture easily). Coeliac UK and The National Osteoporosis Society can be contacted for information (*see Resource Guide*).

Excluding dairy products from the diet eliminates a valuable source of calcium and vitamin D, so it is important to consume a wide range of bone-building vitamins and minerals, readily available from a well-balanced diet. To retain bone strength throughout life, appropriate, regular weight-bearing exercise also plays an important role as does a healthy lifestyle. Seek advice from your GP or other health professional.

Sources of Calcium

A varied, balanced diet will help provide essential bone-building nutrients and aid calcium absorption from food (*see above*). Do not make dietary changes without consulting your GP. Check labels to confirm that foods and drinks are gluten free and dairy free.

Calcium-enriched drinks: e.g. soya, rice milks.

Tinned fish with soft edible bones: e.g. sardines, salmon, pilchards, mackerel.

Fresh fish: e.g. fried whitebait.

Oysters, raw.

Green leafy vegetables: e.g. broccoli, cabbage, okra, spinach, spring greens, curly kale, watercress, young dandelion leaves.

Beans, green/French.

Sprouting seeds/beans: e.g. alfalfa/mung bean sprouts.

Sea vegetables: e.g. nori, dulse, wakami, kombu – fresh or dried seaweed.

Breads (gluten-free, dairy-free).

Freshly growing herbs.

Pulses: e.g. aduki, butter, chick, haricot, kidney, pinto, black, soya beans. Also split/whole dried peas/lentils.

Soya products: e.g. soya beans, soya milk/drinks, yoghurt, tofu (soya bean curd), soya cheese.

Baked beans (not all are gluten free).

Dried fruit: e.g. apricots, currants, figs, mixed peel.

Muesli (gluten-free).

Whole grain rice, cooked.

Tree nuts: e.g. almonds, brazil nuts, hazelnuts, walnuts.

Seeds: e.g. sesame, sunflower, quinoa, sprouted/cooked.

Tahini (sesame seed paste), black strap molasses.

Olives in brine.

Oranges, peeled.

Filtered tap water (some areas have a naturally high calcium content).

Mineral water (calcium content varies depending on source).

A Guide to Healthy Eating

Dietary changes should not be undertaken lightly, unnecessarily or without professional medical guidance to ensure that nutritional deficiencies are avoided.

When your diet is restricted due to wheat, gluten or dairy intolerances/allergies, it is important to eat a well-balanced, varied diet – not eating the same foods every day. Incorporate vitamins and minerals from the four main food groups, including:

Fruit and vegetables
Gluten-free/dairy-free bread, cereals and pasta, potatoes
Gluten-free/dairy-free milk products
Meat, fish, eggs, pulses, nuts and seeds

From the fifth group, choose economically – snack foods and drinks containing fats, oils and refined sugars.

Look for, use and eat foods in as natural, fresh and unrefined state as possible.

Eat at least five portions daily of raw/cooked fruit and vegetables, including freshly pressed fruit and vegetable juices (preferably organic) as these contain important enzymes, antioxidants and fibre to keep the body healthy.

Try 'living' salads, such as sprouting beans, seeds, mustard and cress. They contain all the nutrients and enzymes to mobilize and maintain essential health.

Use freshly growing herbs.

Try introducing sea vegetables into the diet. They are exceptionally mineral-rich. For example, dried green nori flakes can be used as a herb-like garnish for salads and soups.

Choose gluten-free and dairy-free bread, pastas, cereals, pizza bases etc.

Choose non-dairy alternative rice, soya and oat drinks. [*Oat drinks may need to be discussed with your GP or dietician if coeliac with a high level of sensitivity.*]

Drink 6–8 glasses of filtered/mineral water daily.

Eat less meat that is rich in protein and saturated fat
(especially red meats) in favour of poultry and turkey. Look
for free-range and organic processes, avoiding poultry fed with
growth hormones and chemicals. Eat lean meat or cut off the
fat. Avoid cooked meats processed with harmful chemicals.

Eat oily fish, such as sardines, salmon (wild or organically
farmed), swordfish, tuna, herring, mackerel or eel (including
tinned fish) at least two to three times weekly – these are rich
in omega-3 fatty acids. Select fish from sea or freshwater
sources free from pesticides and chemicals – small fish will
have had less time to absorb toxins. Do not eat fish skins as
poisonous chemicals may have been deposited there.

Eat organic free-range eggs produced from hens fed on a diet
free from pesticides, hormones and artificial colourants. To be
certified organic, the land on which they roam has not been
treated with chemical fertilisers.

Consider introducing complete proteins from plant sources in
the diet, for example soya products (e.g. tofu, tempeh and
TVP). Pulses, chickpeas (garbanzo beans), lentils, nuts and
seeds are also good sources of protein and fibre. They have
disease-fighting antioxidants and other valuable nutrients to
boost immune function.

Rotate your intake of soya products, gluten-free flours and
grains e.g. buckwheat, brown rice, tapioca, sago, gram, millet,
quinoa and potato to give the body a rest from eating the same
foods day in, day out.

Use a good quality sea salt, but not to excess.

Cut down on deep-fried chips or other foods, and fatty, high-
salt snacks such as crisps. Avoid hydrogenated, refined oils for
frying. Replace saturated and hydrogenated fats with

monounsaturated or polyunsaturated unhydrogenated fats such as olive oil, sunflower oil, corn oil and nut oils. Grill (broil) foods where possible or failing that, shallow-fry using a minimum of vegetable oil, draining well on absorbent kitchen paper.

Choose cold pressed olive oil for salads and cooking, also sunflower oil. Sunflower, corn and safflower oils are rich in omega-6 fatty acids. Linseed and rapeseed oils have a balance of omega-3 and omega-6 fatty acids. Dairy-free margarines are also good sources of omega-3 and omega-6 fatty acids.

Reduce the intake of white refined sugars in favour of good quality unrefined (and unbleached) sugars. These are minimally processed and retain the natural molasses. Their flavour is more subtle and less overpoweringly sweet and sickly. Bear in mind, all sugars are nutritionally 'empty' calories so aim to reduce consumption. Try sweetening with honey, apple juice, muscovado sugar or molasses.

Guidelines for Gluten-free Baking

Gluten-free baking is really rewarding. It produces lovely sponges, cakes, puddings and biscuits with good texture and flavour. As the sticky, glutenous component is missing from these specialist flours, the resulting bread, pastry, scones and pizza bases will be slightly different in texture – but still very acceptable.

Preferably cook only with gluten-free flours in order to avoid inhaling gluten.

Always keep gluten-free flours in a separate cupboard from gluten-containing flours to avoid cross-contamination.

Do your gluten-free baking first, to avoid the possibility of cross-contamination from airborne particles of gluten-containing flour.

If using gluten-containing flours before using gluten-free

flours, always wash utensils, sieves, weighing scoops, cooking
tins etc. Also, put away gluten-containing flours and
thoroughly clean work surfaces, hands and nails.

When trying your own gluten-free recipes (or adapting
existing gluten-containing recipes), slightly more liquid will
usually be required. It is absorbed quickly so it is best to have
ingredients weighed and cake tins greased in advance. The
oven should be preheated to the correct temperature.

As a general guide, one to two teaspoons of gluten-free baking
powder will be required to every 200–225g (7–8oz) (1½–1⅔
cups) of gluten-free flour.

About the Recipes

A wide range of gluten-free flours and grains are used.
The rice flour used is finely stoneground from brown and
white rice.
All margarines used are dairy-free soya or sunflower
margarines.
Almost all recipes use unrefined sugars.
All the recipes use large free-range eggs.
Cooking tins used are solid based where possible.
All recipes were made in a fan oven, which circulates heat
evenly throughout the oven.
All recipes use a teaspoon measure of 5ml and a tablespoon
measure of 20ml. If using a 15ml tablespoon for small
amounts of flour, cornflour (cornstarch) or other ingredients,
a further teaspoon per tablespoon may be required. UK fluid
ounces (20 fl oz = 1 pint) are used.
All tablespoon measures are level unless stated otherwise.
American cup measurements are used (1 cup = 8 US fluid
ounces).

The Recipes

Salads & Dressings

A 'Living' Salad

Consider incorporating sprouting seeds into your diet on a regular basis to provide a crisp, crunchy medley of flavours and textures. Ideal for using raw in salads and as garnishes. They can be steamed or stir-fried, although precious nutrients will be destroyed during cooking. They are extremely inexpensive to buy and easy to grow. Because 'living' salad is eaten raw and growing, it is highly nutritious. Proteins, vitamins, minerals, trace minerals, chlorophyll and enzymes are all available in an easily digestible form.

To Sprout

You will need glass jars, muslin to cover (or similar) and rubber bands to secure. The seeds should be fresh, whole and ideally organic. Place 1–2 tablespoons of seeds (depending on their size) in jars. Rinse the seeds well, cover with muslin and secure with a rubber band. Soak overnight in cold to tepid filtered, bottled spring water, or boiled and cooled tap water. Next day, drain, rinse in cold to tepid water and drain well. Leave in a dark, warm place to germinate, 15–24°C (60–75°F), rinsing and draining well, twice daily. Most of the seeds will start to sprout after about 1–3 days. Continue to rinse and drain twice daily whilst growing. For specific growing conditions and a guide to eating times and uses, see below.

Alfalfa:

2–3 days from germination, when sprouts are about 2.5cm (1") and yellowy leaves appear, bring into the light to 'green up'. Eat while crisp, within 6 days of germination. They have a fresh pea-like flavour and make a quick and easy garnish for salads and sandwiches. Avoid eating if suffering from lupus or other autoimmune conditions.

Broccoli:

Available from good seedsmen. Follow their instructions for growing and mix with other sprouting seeds or fresh salad vegetables. They have a pleasant, tangy flavour.

Chickpeas (garbanzo beans):

Eat from about 2 days after germination when sprouts are about 2–2.5cm (¾–1") long. Eat within a further 2–3 days, before leaf spikes appear and they become more fibrous. Use with other mixed sprouting seeds and beans, in salads or hummus.

Fenugreek:

Ready to eat for about 2–7 days after germination. They have a slightly spicy flavour and mix well with other salad sprouts for salads, sandwiches or garnishes for curries, etc. If you continue to grow them beyond this time, they become very 'leggy' and may be used in stir-fry dishes.

Lentils – Brown, Continental and Puy:

Ready to eat from about 2 days after germination and for a further 3 days. Sprout each variety separately or together. For easier digestion, the outer casings can be removed. Place the sprouts in a sieve under running water and squeeze off the casings.

Mung beans:

Harvest when sprouts are 2cm (¾") long onwards – about 2–3 days from germination. Continue to grow in the dark otherwise they will develop a bitter taste. Use for salads while sprouts are short and in stir-fry dishes when they are long enough. For easier digestion, the outer casings can be removed. Place the sprouts in a sieve under running water and squeeze off the casings. Eat within about 8 days from germination while fresh and crunchy.

Mustard and cress:

Grow according to instructions on seed-packet, sowing cress 3–4 days before the mustard so that both are ready for eating at the same time, or buy freshly growing mustard and cress. Use for garnishes and salads.

Quinoa:

The seeds have a bitter coating. This is easily removed by placing them in a fine-mesh sieve under cold running water and rinsing well, prior to soaking overnight. Eat within about 3–4 days from germination whilst crunchy, mixed with other sprouting seeds and beans.

Sunflower:

Eat on day of germination.

Aduki, flax (linseed), rice, sesame, soya beans and watercress are some of the many other seeds and beans that can be sprouted.

For recipes using sprouted seeds and beans see: *Avocado & Sprouting Bean Salad, Hummus, Roasted Buckwheat & Sardine Salad, Aduki Bean Soup, Miso Vegetable Soup, Duck Stir-fry with Plum & Orange Sauce, Lamb with Apricots, Chickpeas & Pilau Rice, Turkey & Ham Risotto, Kidney Bean & Vegetable Risotto, Quick Pepper & Tofu Stir-fry, Quinoa Porridge.*

Apple & Celery Salad with Hummus Dressing

This salad can be enjoyed for its beneficial cleansing effect on the body. It contains a form of fibre called pectin which can lower cholesterol and help regulate the digestive system improving absorption of nutrients.

SERVES 4 | PREPARATION TIME – 20 MINUTES

dressing:

2 rounded tablespoons hummus

1 tablespoon acacia/orange blossom honey

½ tablespoon apple juice

salad:

20g (¾ oz) lambs lettuce (mâche)

20g (¾ oz) mizuna

20g (¾ oz) frisée lettuce

10g (½ oz) lollo rosso lettuce/other red leaves

60g (2¼ oz) (½ cup) pecan nuts

85g (3 oz) (¾ cup) inner sticks celery, cut into 2.5cm (1")
  pieces

110g (4 oz) (½ cup) crisp eating apple, sliced

*Mizuna is of Chinese origin and cultivated in Japan for
centuries. It has a peppery, slightly mustardy flavour.
Available in prepacked mixed salad leaves, but if
unobtainable use rocket (arugula).*

Mix together the dressing ingredients until blended.

Arrange the salad leaves on plates or a large platter. Mix the
remaining ingredients and add to the salad.

Drizzle the dressing over the prepared salad. Eat immediately.

Avocado & Sprouted Bean Salad

Avocados are highly nutritious as they need no cooking and
retain their precious vitamins. The raw sprouted seeds, lentils,
beans and peas contain essential enzymes to aid digestion,
detoxification, immunity and all metabolic and regenerative
processes (*see 'Living' Salad on page 20 for sprouting
instructions*). Avoid eating alfalfa sprouts if suffering from
lupus or other autoimmune conditions.

SERVES 4 AS A SNACK OR STARTER | PREPARATION TIME – 40 MINUTES

soft green/mixed red and green lettuce leaves

4 rounded tablespoons sprouted and 'greened-up' alfalfa

2 tablespoons sprouted quinoa

2 tablespoons sprouted puy lentils

2 tablespoons sprouted brown lentils

4 rounded tablespoons sprouted mung beans

4 tablespoons sprouted chickpeas (garbanzo beans)

3 small spring onions (scallions), white and light green
   part only

5cm (2") piece cucumber

12 cherry tomatoes, halved

2 medium–large ripe avocado pears halved and stones
   removed (pitted)

a little lime juice

*To test if avocados are ripe, the skin should yield slightly
when pressed. To ripen avocados, put in a brown paper bag
with a banana.*

vinaigrette:
   2 teaspoons lime juice

   2 teaspoons white wine vinegar

   4 teaspoons olive oil

   ½ small clove garlic, crushed

   freshly ground black pepper

Arrange the lettuce leaves on medium-sized plates or large platter.
Scatter with mixed alfalfa, quinoa and the two varieties of lentils.
Finish on top with the mung beans then the chickpeas (garbanzo
beans).

Slice the spring onions (scallions) into 2.5cm (1") pieces then
shred lengthways into fine strips. Peel the cucumber, cut into 2.5cm
(1") pieces, then cut into fine slices lengthways then into thin match-
sticks. Mix together the spring onions (scallions) and cucumber and
scatter over the sprouts. Place the tomatoes around the edge of the
salad.

Cut through the avocado flesh to make large cubes, turn over and
push the skins inside out releasing the pieces. Sprinkle with a little
lime juice. Arrange the avocado over the spring onions (scallions) and
cucumber.

Mix the vinaigrette ingredients and sprinkle over the salad.

Chicory, Orange & Watercress Salad with Chorizo

Try this nutritious salad to boost the metabolism and detoxify the body. It provides stress-moderating B vitamins together with vitamins C, E and beta-carotene; also calcium, magnesium (aiding calcium absorption), iron, zinc, selenium, omega-3 and omega-6 fatty acids.

SERVES 5 | PREPARATION TIME – 10 MINUTES

½ tablespoon sunflower seeds

½ tablespoon pumpkin seeds

1 large head chicory (endive), sliced diagonally into 1cm (½") slices

½–1 bunch watercress, trimmed into sprigs

½ small fennel bulb with plenty of fresh feathery leaves, cored and sliced thinly

fennel leaves, cut finely

¾ large orange peeled, separated into segments and halved

thin slices of gluten-free, dairy-free chorizo/salami, skinned

Cheaper and some better quality chorizo/salami may contain gluten and/or milk products, so check labels carefully otherwise use home-roasted cooked meats.

dressing:

1 tablespoon extra virgin olive oil

½ tablespoon white wine vinegar

1 tablespoon orange juice

½ teaspoon raspberry vinegar

1 pinch white pepper

Preheat the grill (broiler) to high and lightly toast the seeds. Leave to cool.

Toss together the prepared chicory (endive), watercress, fennel, fennel leaves and orange segments in a serving bowl. Combine the dressing ingredients in a basin then mix vigorously. Sprinkle the seeds over the salad and pour over the dressing.

Arrange the meat slices on plates and serve with the salad.

Figs with Cream 'Cheese' & Parma Ham

SERVES 4 AS A STARTER | PREPARATION TIME – 15 MINUTES

few lettuce leaves, rinsed
4 ripe figs
2 rounded tablespoons non-dairy alternative to full-fat soft cheese
10 drops lemon juice plus the merest hint white pepper
2 rounded teaspoons lemon thyme, cut finely
4 thin slices Parma ham (prosciutto)
3 teaspoons olive oil
1 teaspoon lemon juice
2 teaspoons orange-blossom honey
freshly cut lemon thyme to garnish

Spanish Serrano ham is a good alternative to Parma ham.

Arrange the lettuce leaves on small plates or a large platter. Wipe the figs, cut off the stalks and cut a cross in the top of each to go just over three quarters way down. Spread almost open and place on the lettuce leaves.

Mix the soft cheese, lemon juice and pepper. Stir in the lemon thyme. Nestle the cheese mixture into the fig centres. Roughly tear each slice of Parma ham (prosciutto) in half and drape over the cheese – between the fig 'petals' and onto the lettuce to form a cross.

Mix the olive oil, lemon juice, honey and a merest hint of white

pepper. Drizzle the dressing over the salad. Garnish with a few finely snipped lemon thyme leaves and serve.

If you are able to obtain a less salty feta sheep's cheese, this can be tried instead of dairy-free, full-fat soft cheese, if tolerated as part of a low-lactose diet.

Hummus

This quick recipe uses tinned chickpeas. Hummus is a good source of calcium, magnesium, protein, B vitamins, iron, zinc and folic acid. Hummus can also be made from sprouted chickpeas enhancing its nutritional value (*see the instructions at the end of the recipe*). The flavour is equally good and it is almost as smooth. Hummus can also be used in Hummus Dressing (*see Apple & Celery Salad on page 22*).

SERVES 4–6 | PREPARATION TIME – 15 MINUTES

400g (14 oz) tin chickpeas, drained and rinsed
3 tablespoons light tahini (sesame-seed paste)
3 tablespoons lemon juice
1 clove garlic, flattened and peeled
½ teaspoon sea salt
2 pinches cayenne pepper
1 tablespoon olive oil
1 pinch paprika and freshly cut parsley to garnish

For a spicier hummus, chilli powder/turmeric can be added to taste.

Put the chickpeas, tahini, lemon juice, garlic, salt, cayenne and oil in a food processor. Blend until smooth. Adjust seasoning if necessary. Serve, sprinkled with a little paprika and finely cut parsley to garnish. Keep any unused hummus refrigerated.

SERVING SUGGESTION: Serve hummus with gluten-free toast, spread with
a dairy-free margarine and chopped raw vegetables with mixed salad
leaves. Alternatively, sprinkle hummus with a little more olive oil and
garnish with stoned (pitted) black olives and parsley. Serve with a raw
vegetable salad.

To make hummus from sprouted chickpeas:

Soak 110g (4 oz) (½ cup) dried chickpeas overnight in cold to tepid
water (in a large jar covered with muslin). Next day, drain, rinse well
and drain, leaving in a warm, dark place to germinate. Repeat the
draining and rinsing process twice daily. When sprouts are about 2cm
(¾") long (2–3 days from germination), use 240g (8½ oz) (1¾ cups)
for making the hummus, discarding any unsprouted ones.

Mango & Orange Quinoa Tabbouleh

Make this fresh-flavoured tabbouleh well ahead in order for the
cooked quinoa to cool. Quinoa is a useful addition to a
vegetarian or vegan diet because it is a complete protein,
containing all eight essential amino acids. It is vitamin and
mineral rich with a high calcium content, iron, B vitamins and
vitamin E. Combined with fruit, this dish supplies vitamin C
and beta-carotene (converted to vitamin A in the body).

SERVES 4 AS A STARTER OR SWEET
PREPARATION TIME – 15–20 MINUTES PLUS COOLING

100g (3½ oz) (½ cup) whole grain quinoa
1 pinch sea salt
400ml (14 fl oz) (1⅔ cups) boiling water
150g (5 oz) (¾ cup) peeled ripe mango, sliced thinly and chopped roughly (reserving 8 small slices for decoration)
100g (3½ oz) (generous ⅓ cup) fresh orange segments, cut roughly
1 small passion fruit, cut, fruit scooped out
16 medium mint leaves for decoration

½ teaspoon unrefined golden granulated sugar

A fruit combination of mango and pineapple also works well.

Place the grain in a sieve. Wash well under cold running water, separating the grains with fingers to remove the bitter coating. Drain well. In a small saucepan, add quinoa to the lightly salted boiling water. Return to the boil, cover and simmer for 12–15 minutes so that the germ separates and water is only just absorbed. Remove from the heat and leave to cool, covered. When cold, fork through to fluff up.

Mix in the mango pieces, orange segments and passion fruit. Serve into dishes. Garnish with the reserved mango and half of the mint leaves. Place the remaining leaves over the sugar and finely shred. Mix together and sprinkle over the fruit and grain. Serve immediately or chill.

Millet & Mixed Pepper Salad

Cooked millet has the texture and appearance of couscous. It can be sprouted for enhanced nutritional benefits and added cooked/sprouted to soups, stews or other salads. Millet supports the function of the digestive organs and is easy to digest. The peppers are rich in vitamin C (especially sweet red peppers) and a good source of vitamin A, B6, folic acid and fibre. Overall a good antioxidant salad.

SERVES 4 | PREPARATION TIME – 15 MINUTES

50g (1¾ oz) (3 tablespoons) whole grain millet

200ml (7 fl oz) (¾ cup) water

½ medium green pepper, sliced and diced

½ medium red pepper, sliced and diced

½ medium yellow pepper, sliced and diced

½ small red onion, sliced thinly and diced

1 tablespoon fresh mixed herbs/parsley, finely chopped

Try Spanish onion/chopped chives as alternative to red onion.

dressing:

¾ tablespoon olive oil

½ tablespoon white wine vinegar/cider vinegar

¼ teaspoon balsamic vinegar (optional)

sea salt and freshly ground black pepper

Rinse the millet in a sieve, drain well and add to a small saucepan with the water. Bring to the boil, cover and simmer for 14–17 minutes until water absorbed.

Whilst simmering the millet, prepare the vegetables, herbs and dressing. The millet may be added to the peppers, onions, herbs and dressing immediately or allowed to cool first. Mix well and serve.

Quinoa Tabbouleh with Cucumber, Spring Onions & Fresh Herbs

Quinoa seeds are fast and easy to cook. When combined with fresh herbs, the tabbouleh bursts with freshness and vitality. Try it to accompany dressed crab, lightly cooked fish or with an easy barbecue/buffet. Quinoa is rich in polyunsaturated oils, providing essential fatty acids. It is extremely nutritious and easily digested (both parsley and mint also promote digestion).

SERVES 4 | PREPARATION TIME – 15–20 MINUTES PLUS COOLING & 15 MINUTES TO PERMEATE FLAVOUR

100g (3½ oz) (½ cup) whole grain quinoa

1 pinch sea salt

400ml (14 fl oz) (1⅔ cups) boiling water

5cm (2") piece cucumber, cut into 8 slices, then cut into 5mm (¼") strips and diced

5–6 small spring onions (scallions), trimmed, cut into 5mm (¼") slices diagonally

2 tablespoons freshly cut mint

4 tablespoons freshly cut parsley

1 tablespoon lemon juice

¾ tablespoon olive oil

freshly ground black pepper

Place the grain in a sieve. Wash well under cold running water separating the grains with fingers to remove the bitter coating. Drain well.

In a small saucepan add quinoa to the lightly salted boiling water. Return to the boil, cover and simmer for 12–15 minutes so that the germ separates and the water is only just absorbed. Remove from the heat and leave to cool, covered. When cold, fork through to fluff up.

Mix in the cucumber, spring onions (scallions), mint, parsley, lemon juice, olive oil and season with pepper. Leave for at least 15 minutes for the flavours to permeate before serving.

SERVING SUGGESTION: serve simply with grilled (broiled) (or gluten-free floured and grilled [broiled]) fish or meat, perhaps with a few mixed salad leaves.

Roasted Buckwheat & Sardine Salad

This is a very quick, easy and nutritious snack and the mixed lentil sprouts look particularly attractive on the plate. Sardines are a rich source of omega-3 fatty acids, calcium and vitamin D (needed for absorption of calcium in the body for proper bone mineralisation). Buckwheat is high in fibre and protein and 'living' salad contains all the nutrients and enzymes essential for health.

SERVES 1 | PREPARATION TIME – 10–12 MINUTES

1 small tin sardines with bones in tomato sauce/oil

25g (1oz) (2 tablespoons) roasted/unroasted* (natural) buckwheat

| 5 tablespoons water |
| freshly ground black pepper |
| freshly cut salad leaves |
| sprouting whole puy, green and brown lentils (*see 'Living' Salad on page 20*) |
| freshly cut mustard and cress to garnish |

Tinned salmon, sild, skippers, pilchards, soft, hard or cod roes are also suitable alternatives to sardines. Try also fresh grilled (broiled) sardines drizzled with cold pressed olive oil, or other oily fish such as herring, kippers and mackerel.

Heat the sardines under the grill (broiler).

Add the roasted buckwheat and water to a small saucepan and bring to the boil. Simmer, stirring, until all water is absorbed and grain just tender – about 4 minutes. Season with a little pepper. Serve hot with the sardines, salad leaves and lentil sprouts. Garnish with mustard and cress.

Unroasted* (natural) buckwheat:

Put in a small saucepan with 7 tablespoons of water. Bring to the boil, cover and simmer, stirring occasionally, until just cooked and liquid absorbed – about 10–12 minutes. Unroasted (natural) buckwheat can also be sprouted.

Soup

Aduki Bean Soup

This is a robust-flavoured and substantial soup that satisfies the appetite. Savoury Herb Scones (*see page 118*) would be a natural choice to accompany the soup or home-made gluten-free bread. Beans provide protein, complex carbohydrates and are one of the best sources of vegetable fibre. Shitake mushrooms contain minerals and vitamins (also one of the few vegetable sources of vitamin D), essential amino acids and enzymes to boost immuniity. Both beans and shitake mushrooms are calcium rich.

SERVES 4 | PREPARATION TIME – 50 MINUTES PLUS 25 MINUTES FOR FINAL SIMMERINGS

60g (2¼ oz) (4 tablespoons) dried aduki beans, soaked overnight in plenty of water
1.135 litres (40 fl oz) (4¾ cups) boiling water
½ tablespoon olive oil
1 medium onion, sliced thinly and diced
1 stick celery, sliced thinly and diced
1 medium carrot peeled, sliced into 2.5cm (1") lengths and cut into thin matchsticks
1 clove garlic, crushed
½ gluten-free vegetable/beef stock (bouillon) cube
½ tablespoon tomato purée (paste)
3 medium vine plum tomatoes, skinned and chopped
5 sun-dried tomato pieces, cut finely

5 fresh medium shitake mushrooms, sliced thinly

2 pinches dried thyme

1 rounded tablespoon Atlantic sea salad

Atlantic sea salad is finely chopped dried seaweed, which is used here as a seasoning for the soup.

stock ingredients:
1 stick celery, sliced lengthways and quartered

2 bay leaves

½ carrot, sliced lengthways

Drain the soaked beans and rinse well. Place in a large saucepan and cover with fresh cold water. Bring to the boil and boil rapidly, uncovered, for 10 minutes. Drain the water and rinse well. Add the boiling water and stock ingredients to the saucepan, return to the boil, cover and simmer for 25 minutes.

Meanwhile, warm the oil in a large non-stick frying pan (skillet). Add the onion, celery, carrot and garlic. Cook together for 4–5 minutes without colouring. Add these to the cooked beans together with the stock (bouillon) cube, tomato purée (paste), tomatoes, sun-dried tomatoes, mushrooms and thyme. Return to the boil, cover and simmer gently for a further 15–20 minutes. Stir in the sea salad. Simmer for 2–3 minutes. Remove the stock ingredients and serve.

SERVING SUGGESTION: for an extra boost of B vitamins and minerals use sprouted aduki beans as a garnish for the soup.

Butternut Squash Soup

This soup is thick and warming, full of subtle flavours and goodness. It is extremely protective of the body being high in beta-carotene which is converted into the anti-viral immunity-boosting vitamin A. The squash seeds are, like all seeds, highly nutritious. Pumpkin can be used instead of squash in this recipe.

550g–650g (1 lb 4 oz–1 lb 7 oz) butternut squash, peeled
½ large red pepper, deseeded, cut into 3 strips
3 medium vine tomatoes, halved
1 tablespoon sunflower oil
1 medium onion, sliced
1 clove garlic, crushed
1 slightly rounded teaspoon gluten-free, dairy-free mild curry powder
1 heaped teaspoon tomato purée (paste)
540ml (19 fl oz) (2¼ cups) hot vegetable stock (bouillon)/water plus ½ gluten-free vegetable stock (bouillon) cube
sea salt and freshly ground black pepper
55g (2oz) creamed coconut dissolved in 140ml (5fl oz) (½ cup) hot water (*the coconut milk may be omitted but add a little more hot water to the soup*)

As a variation, 1 teaspoon of fresh grated ginger can be added with the curry powder if preferred.

Cut the squash in half, remove the seeds (reserving 1–2 tablespoons), then cut into 2.5cm (1") cubes. Lightly grill (broil) the squash seeds until lightly browned. Reserve.

Grill (broil) the pepper and tomatoes skin side up, until they blacken and blister. Place in a polythene bag, secure and leave until cool. Skin the tomatoes and peppers, cut tomatoes in half and remove the seeds. Chop the tomatoes and peppers roughly.

While the pepper and tomatoes are grilling (broiling), warm the oil in a large saucepan. Soften the onion and garlic for 4–5 minutes without colouring then stir in the curry powder and cook together for a further minute. Add the squash, tomato purée (paste), vegetable stock and seasoning. Bring to the boil, cover and simmer gently for 15 minutes.

Add the prepared peppers and tomatoes to the soup, stir and
continue to cook for a further 10–15 minutes until tender. Stir in the
dissolved coconut and water. Liquidize until smooth. Serve. Garnish
with the toasted squash seeds. [*Alternatively, garnish with chopped
coriander (cilantro) leaves or spring onions (scallions)*]

SERVING SUGGESTION: curry croutons, made using diced gluten-free
bread fried in a little dairy-free margarine and curry powder, are good
served with this soup.

Country Vegetable Soup

This soup is good accompanied by toasted gluten-free Crusty
White Bread (*see page 115*). As an alternative to baby corn, use
immature corn on the cob (cut into 1cm/½-inch slices) sold in
farmers markets when in season.

SERVES 4 | PREPARATION TIME – 30–45 MINUTES PLUS 45 MINUTES FOR
2 SIMMERINGS

110g (4 oz) (½ cup) chana dhal/yellow split peas

2 bay leaves

½ gluten-free vegetable stock (bouillon) cube

½ large red pepper, cut into 3 strips

3 large plum vine tomatoes, halved

2 sticks celery, sliced thickly

1 medium carrot, peeled and sliced thickly

125g (4½ oz) (1½ cups) leek, white and light green part
only, sliced

4 fresh baby corn, halved

1 clove garlic, crushed

sea salt and freshly ground black pepper

110g (4 oz) cooked and frozen butter beans (lima beans),
thawed* (*or a small tin*)

2 lean rashers rindless bacon, grilled (broiled) until crispy (*optional*)

To use dried butter beans, soak overnight in cold water. Drain and rinse well. Cover with water and bring back to boil, boil rapidly for 10 minutes, then simmer for 30–40 minutes until tender. Cool, measure into portions, approximately equivalent to a small tin of butter beans and freeze. Thaw as required and add to soups and casseroles.

Steep the chana dhal/split peas in boiling water for 15–30 minutes prior to cooking. Drain well. Bring 850ml (30 fl oz) (3⅔ cups) water to the boil, add chana dhal/split peas, bay leaves and stock (bouillon) cube. Cover and simmer for 30 minutes.

Meanwhile, grill (broil) the pepper and tomatoes, skin side up, until blackened. Place in a polythene bag, secure and leave to cool sufficiently to handle. Remove the skins, cut into thirds and add to the soup together with the celery, carrot, leek, baby corn and garlic. Return to the boil and simmer until vegetables are soft – about 10–15 minutes. Season well. Add the butter beans (lima beans) and heat through.

Discard the bay leaves. Remove the baby corn and a few pieces of red pepper. Liquidize half of the soup then remix both halves. Return baby corn and pepper to the soup. Serve and crumble the bacon over to garnish.

Courgette & Rosemary Soup

For this recipe, it is well worth looking for small to medium-sized organically grown courgettes (zucchini) for taste and because both the skin and flesh are eaten.

SERVES 2 | PREPARATION TIME – 25 MINUTES PLUS 15 MINUTES FOR SIMMERING

1 tablespoon dairy-free margarine

395g (14 oz) (3¾ cups) courgettes (zucchini), sliced thinly

½ small onion, sliced thinly

---

a good pinch celery seeds (*optional*)

1¼ teaspoons fresh rosemary (4 good pinches dried
   rosemary)

sea salt and freshly ground black pepper

370ml (13 fl oz) (1½ cups) boiling water

2 tablespoons soya cream

Melt half the margarine in a large non-stick frying pan (skillet). Stir-fry half the courgettes (zucchini) over a fairly high heat, turning them over from time to time until approximately a quarter are slightly coloured. Turn them into a large saucepan. Repeat with the remaining margarine and courgettes. Add the onion to the frying pan (skillet) for a minute with a little more margarine without browning.

Turn into the saucepan with the celery seeds, finely snipped rosemary, seasoning and boiling water. Return to the boil, cover and simmer over a very low heat for about 14–15 minutes until courgettes (zucchini) are tender. Liquidize the soup until smooth. Stir in the cream and serve. The soup freezes well without the cream. Thaw and reheat slowly, stirring in the cream before serving.

For a slightly better flavoured soup, 1 tablespoon butter can be used to colour the courgettes (zucchini) if this is well tolerated as part of a low-lactose diet.

Cream of Mushroom & Fennel Soup

This Italian-inspired soup will be lighter and creamier if the smallest and freshest closed-cap (button) mushrooms are chosen.

SERVES 4 | PREPARATION TIME – 25 MINUTES PLUS 10 MINUTES FOR
        FINAL SIMMERING

285g (10 oz) young fennel bulbs with leaves

2 tablespoons dairy-free margarine

600ml (21 fl oz) (2½ cups) hot water plus ½ gluten-free
   vegetable stock (bouillon) cube

sea salt and freshly ground black pepper

340g (12 oz) baby closed-cap (button) mushrooms

| 1 rounded teaspoon gluten-free cornflour (cornstarch) |
| ½ tablespoon fresh fennel leaves, cut finely |
| 3 tablespoons unsweetened soya milk |
| 3 tablespoons soya cream |
| fresh fennel leaves to garnish |

Trim the fennel, reserving the leaves. Cut in half and remove the triangular cores. Slice thinly. Melt half of the margarine in a large non-stick frying pan (skillet). Add the fennel and cook over a low heat without colouring for about 5 minutes. Turn into a large saucepan. Add the water, stock (bouillon) cube and seasoning. Bring to the boil then simmer for 10 minutes, covered.

Meanwhile, slice the mushrooms thinly. Melt the remaining margarine in the pan. Stir-fry the mushrooms over a high heat for a few minutes, until the juices start to run. Turn the heat to low and stir in the cornflour (cornstarch) stirring together for 1 minute. Add to the saucepan with the fennel leaves. Continue to simmer for a further 10 minutes. Remove from the heat. Reserve a few mushrooms from the soup then liquidize the remainder. Season to taste. Add the milk and cream. Serve. Garnish with reserved mushrooms and finely snipped fennel leaves.

A little blue/Roquefort sheep's cheese may be crumbled into the soup to garnish if a small amount is tolerated as part of a low-lactose diet.

Jerusalem Artichoke Soup

This is an unusual soup with a subtle, unique flavour. Jerusalem artichokes are in season from November to February. They have a reputation for being tough on the digestive system, producing gaseous side effects! If this is experienced, it may be reduced by adding a little asafoetida to the soup.

Serves 4 | Preparation time – 30 minutes plus 30 minutes for simmering

565g (1 lb 4 oz) Jerusalem artichokes
juice ¼ lemon
1 tablespoon dairy-free margarine
1 large onion, sliced
1 clove garlic, crushed
625ml (22 fl oz) (2⅔ cups) hot water plus ½ vegetable stock (bouillon) cube
1 teaspoon lemon juice
1 bay leaf
sea salt and freshly ground black pepper
1 tablespoon soya yoghurt
½ tablespoon soya cream
freshly cut parsley, coriander or tarragon to garnish

Peel and slice the artichokes into water with the lemon juice to prevent discolouration. Leave until required.

Melt the margarine in a large non-stick frying pan. Gently fry the onion and garlic for about 3–4 minutes until softening but not coloured. Drain the artichokes well and add to the onions. Mix and cook together for about 2–3 minutes without colouring. Turn into a large saucepan with the hot water, stock cube (bouillon), lemon juice, bay leaf and seasoning. Bring to the boil, cover and simmer for about 25–30 minutes until vegetables are tender. Remove the bay leaf and liquidize the soup.

Mix together the yoghurt and soya cream then stir into the soup. Serve. Sprinkle with parsley, coriander or tarragon to garnish.

Lightly Spiced Parsnip & Red Lentil Soup

SERVES 4 | PREPARATION TIME – 20 MINUTES PLUS 20 MINUTES FOR SIMMERING

2 tablespoons dairy-free margarine
1 large onion, sliced and diced

| 1 large clove garlic, crushed |
| 1 stick celery, sliced lengthways and chopped |
| 3 pinches aniseeds, partially ground |
| 2 cardamom pods, crushed, pods discarded |
| 3 pinches ground coriander (cilantro) |
| 3 pinches ground cinnamon |
| 3 pinches garam masala |
| 110g (4 oz) (⅔ cup) parsnip, peeled and sliced |
| 50g (2 oz) (generous ⅓ cup) swede, peeled, sliced and diced |
| 50g (2 oz) (⅓ cup) carrot, peeled and sliced |
| 175g (6¼ oz) (¾ cup plus 1 slightly rounded tablespoon) red lentils |
| 850ml (30 fl oz) (3⅔ cups) hot water plus ½ gluten-free vegetable stock (bouillon) cube |
| sea salt and freshly ground black pepper |

apple sauce:

| 60g (2½ oz) (3½ rounded tablespoons) cooking apple, peeled, sliced and finely diced |
| ¾ tablespoon water |

Melt the margarine in a large saucepan. Soften the onion, garlic and celery over a low heat for 5–6 minutes, stirring occasionally. Add the spices and cook together for a further 2 minutes. Toss the parsnip, swede and carrot into the spicy mixture and stir.

Add the lentils, water and stock (bouillon) cube. Bring to the boil, cover and simmer for 20 minutes stirring twice during that time, until tender. Season to taste, liquidize the soup until smooth.

While the soup is simmering, add the apple and water to a small saucepan. Simmer over a low heat until soft and pulpy, taking care not to burn the apple. Stir the apple sauce into the soup and serve.

Minestrone Soup with Fusilli

SERVES 4 | PREPARATION TIME – 30 MINUTES PLUS 15 MINUTES FOR
SIMMERING

2 medium tomatoes, halved
2 rashers streaky rindless bacon *(optional)*
1 tablespoon olive oil
1 small onion, sliced finely
1 small leek, sliced finely, the white and light green part only
1 clove garlic, crushed
1000ml (35 fl oz) (4 cups) vegetable stock (bouillon)/hot water plus 1 gluten-free vegetable stock (bouillon) cube
1 bay leaf
1 stick celery, sliced finely
1 medium carrot, peeled and sliced finely
1 small turnip, peeled, sliced finely and diced
1 tablespoon tomato purée (paste)
40g (1½ oz) (½ cup) fine corn and rice 'fusilli' pasta
sea salt and freshly ground black pepper
35g (1¼ oz) (½ cup) green cabbage, finely shredded
60g (2¼ oz) (¾ cup) fresh haricot beans, trimmed and cut into 4cm (1½") lengths
1 rounded tablespoon freshly cut parsley

Grill (broil) the tomatoes, skin side up, until cooked. When cool, skin the tomatoes, slice and dice finely. If using bacon, grill until crisp but not burnt. Leave to one side.

Warm the oil in a large saucepan. Add the onion, leek and garlic. Soften together for 3–4 minutes, stirring occasionally without colouring. Add the vegetable stock (bouillon), bay leaf, celery, carrot, turnip, tomato purée (paste), tomatoes, fusilli and seasoning. Return to the boil and simmer for 10 minutes.

Add the cabbage and beans and cook briefly – for about 3 minutes until cooked. Remove the bay leaf and stir in the parsley. Serve into dishes and sprinkle with the crumbled bacon.

Miso Vegetable Soup

This nutritious soup has a slightly oriental flavour and aids digestion. It is rich in beta-carotene, protein and vitamin C, with B vitamins and vitamin D. There is a good range of minerals, with high levels of calcium, iron, phosphorus and iodine. It is also rich in essential fatty acids and fibre. All these nutrients are important for normal function and maintainance of health in the body.

SERVES 4 | PREPARATION TIME – 15 MINUTES PLUS 15 MINUTES FOR SIMMERING

795ml (28 fl oz) (3⅓ cups) boiling water

250g (9 oz) (2 cups) sweet potato, peeled, sliced and large diced

200g (7 oz) (1½ cups) butternut squash, peeled, sliced and large diced

200g (7 oz) (generous 1¾ cups) celery, sliced

120g (4 oz) (1 cup) celeriac peeled, sliced and large diced

½ tablespoon brown rice miso

1 rounded teaspoon green nori flakes

1 pinch white pepper

freshly cut mustard and cress

Green nori flakes are traditional Japanese sea vegetables, dried and ready for use as a herb-like garnish for soups, batters and meals. They are available from health food shops. Half tablespoon of Atlantic sea salad makes a good alternative if nori flakes are unobtainable.

While preparing the vegetables, bring the water to the boil in a large saucepan. Add the prepared vegetables, miso, nori flakes and seasoning. Return to the boil then simmer for about 15 minutes until vegetables are tender. Liquidize the soup until smooth. Serve. Garnish with mustard and cress.

Nettle, Leek & Potato Soup

At a restaurant, many years ago, I tried nettle and potato soup (feeling rather adventurous). I've never forgotten that delicious soup, so please do try this as a spring tonic. Nettles have been used medicinally for centuries. They have a detoxifying action on the body and are iron rich. Their nutrients strengthen the immune system, aiding healing and health. They contain the trace mineral boron, also calcium, magnesium, phosphorus and good quality protein. Use protective gloves to pick the nettles from an unpolluted source. Nettle tea can also be made from the freshly picked leaves and, when cooked as a vegetable, nettles taste rather like spinach.

SERVES 2 | PREPARATION TIME – 20 MINUTES PLUS 30 MINUTES FOR 3
            SIMMERINGS

75g (2¾ oz) (1 cup) leek, the white and yellow part only
225g (8 oz) (1½ cups) potato, peeled and diced small
25g (1 oz) (1¾ tablespoons) dairy-free margarine
sea salt and freshly ground black pepper
455ml (16 fl oz) (2 cups less 1 tablespoon) boiling water
20g (¾ oz) stinging nettle leaves, the new spring growth
3 tablespoons unsweetened soya milk

Slice the leeks lengthways and, if necessary, rinse well to remove any soil, shaking well to remove excess water. Slice thinly. Add the prepared leeks and diced potatoes to the melted margarine in a medium saucepan. Season well. Stir to coat evenly then cover and simmer for

9–10 minutes on a very low heat, stirring occasionally to prevent sticking. Add the water, bring to the boil and continue to simmer for a further 13–15 minutes until tender.

Rinse the nettle leaves, cut roughly and add to the soup. Simmer for a further 3–4 minutes. Liquidize the soup then stir in the milk. Season with a little extra pepper to serve.

Fish

Crab with Asparagus

Crab, asparagus, artichoke and whole grain rice contain valuable antioxidants to boost the immune system; to detoxify, regulate and regenerate immune cells. The rice can be cooked well in advance and used cold to finish the dish if preferred.

SERVES 2 AS A MAIN COURSE, 4 AS A STARTER
PREPARATION TIME – 45 MINUTES

140g (5 oz) (⅔ cup) whole grain brown rice
340ml (12 fl oz) (1⅓ cups plus 1 tablespoon) water
1 rounded tablespoon pine nut kernels, lightly toasted
100g (3½ oz) pack pre-trimmed medium asparagus tips
2 rounded tablespoons freshly cut parsley/flat-leaf parsley
1 dressed crab, fresh or frozen and thawed crabmeat about 130g (4½ oz)
390g (14 oz) tin artichoke hearts, rinsed and drained well

dressing:

finely grated rind ½ lime and 1¼ teaspoons juice
3 teaspoons extra virgin olive oil
2 teaspoons white wine vinegar
2 teaspoons balsamic vinegar
freshly ground black pepper

Rinse the rice in a sieve under cold running water and drain well. Add the rice to the lightly salted boiling water in a small covered saucepan. Return to the boil, then simmer for about 20 minutes until the water has been absorbed. Leave to one side.

Mix the dressing ingredients in a small basin.

Lightly grill (broil) the pine nut kernels.

Steam the asparagus tips for about 4–6 minutes until just tender. Plunge them into cold water. When cold, drain and pat dry carefully.

Fluff up the rice with a fork, mix in the parsley then spread onto serving plates. Drizzle the dressing over the rice. Arrange the crabmeat over the rice and top with the asparagus to form a lattice pattern. Scatter over the pine nut kernels. Arrange 8 artichoke halves around the edge of each plate.

Goujons of Sole with Seafood & Avocado

Any thin white fish fillets can be used but here I use strips of sole dipped in egg and seasoned flour, and fried for just a few minutes. As an alternative, to make egg-free, cover the strips of fish with lemon juice then dust with flour.

SERVES 4 | PREPARATION TIME – 25 MINUTES

540g (1 lb 3 oz) skinned sole fillets, cut into 2.5cm (1") wide strips
1 large free-range egg, beaten
3 rounded tablespoons rice flour
sea salt and freshly ground black pepper
120g (4½ oz) (1¼ cups) frozen cooked seafood cocktail, thawed
shredded lettuce
2 large ripe avocado pears
gluten-free, dairy-free Seafood Sauce (*see page 220*)
50g (2 oz) (⅓ cup) cooked peeled prawns (shrimp)
6 cherry tomatoes, halved
lemon wedges to garnish

gluten-free, dairy-free Mayonnaise to serve (*see page 218*)

Heat the oil for deep frying.
Dip the strips of fish in beaten egg then roll in seasoned flour, shaking off the excess. Deep-fry in batches of five over a medium heat until cooked and lightly browned – about 4–6 minutes per batch. Remove with a slotted spoon and place on absorbent kitchen paper to drain thoroughly. Lightly dust the seafood in the flour and deep-fry for a minute only. Serve the fish onto warm plates and garnish with the seafood.
Arrange the lettuce onto serving plates. Cut the avocados in half, then push out the stones from underneath. Score the flesh into cubes then release by turning the skin inside out. Scatter over the lettuce, drizzle with the seafood sauce and decorate with prawns (shrimp) and tomato halves. Garnish with lemon wedges and mayonnaise to serve.

SERVING SUGGESTION: serve with thin triangles of gluten-free bread or corn thins.

Kedgeree

SERVES 4 | PREPARATION TIME – 55 MINUTES

565g (1¼ lb) traditionally smoked undyed haddock fillets/275g (10oz) each of smoked haddock and unsmoked salmon fillets
400ml (14 fl oz) (1⅔ cups) water
2 bay leaves
1 rounded tablespoon dairy-free margarine
1 medium onion, sliced finely
1 rounded teaspoon gluten-free, dairy-free mild curry powder
1 rounded teaspoon white mustard seeds, partially ground
240g (8½ oz) (1¼ cups less 1 tablespoon) basmati rice

255ml (9 fl oz) (1 cup plus 1 tablespoon) rice milk, shaken well before using

---

3 or 4 large free-range eggs

130g (4½ oz) (generous 1½ cups) leek, sliced finely (white to yellowy green part only)

85g (3 oz) (1¼ cups) chestnut mushrooms, sliced thinly and halved

---

2 rounded tablespoons freshly cut parsley

---

a good squeeze lemon juice

---

salad leaves, finely shredded

---

1 lemon cut into wedges, to garnish

In a medium saucepan, just cover the fish, skin side down, with the water. Add the bay leaves. Bring to the boil and simmer uncovered until cooked – about 5–8 minutes. Remove from the heat leaving the fish in the cooking liquor.

Meanwhile, warm the margarine in a large saucepan and soften the onion for about 4 minutes. Stir in the curry powder and mustard seeds, cook together for a further minute. Stir in the rice until well coated and translucent – about 2 minutes. Add 200ml (7 fl oz) (¾ cup) fish cooking liquor (reserving the remainder) and rice milk. Bring to the boil, stirring. Reduce the heat, cover and simmer for 12–15 minutes, until rice is tender and liquid absorbed.

While the rice is cooking, hard boil the eggs in simmering water for 6–7 minutes then drain. Cover with cold water and tap the shells with the back of a spoon to prevent discolouration around the yolks. Cool under cold running water.

Soften the leeks in a little margarine – for about 5 minutes. Add the mushrooms and cook together for a further 2 minutes.

Remove the fish skin and any bones, flake into large pieces and fold into the rice. Stir in the leeks, mushrooms, parsley and lemon juice. Remove the egg shells. Cut the eggs into quarters and fold in carefully. Add a further 2 tablespoons of the reserved cooking liquor to moisten the rice. Serve immediately with salad leaves and lemon wedges.

Mackerel with Sweet Mustard Sauce

The sweet mustard sauce is good served with unsmoked or smoked mackerel, salmon or kippers. Also try it spread on Thai rice crackers with thin slivers of smoked salmon for buffets. Mackerel contain high levels of purine and might precipitate an attack of gout in susceptible people. Other foods that can precipitate gout are sweetbreads, anchovies, sardines, brains, meat extracts, herrings, scallops and game meats.

SERVES 4 | PREPARATION TIME – 15 MINUTES

100g (3½ oz) (6½ tablespoons) dairy-free margarine
2 large egg yolks
½ tablespoon white wine vinegar
¾ tablespoon gluten-free Dijon mustard
2 tablespoons freshly cut dill
½ teaspoon maple syrup
4 large mackerel fillets
shredded lettuce to garnish

Melt the margarine in a small saucepan until hot.

Place the egg yolks in a basin over simmering water. Beat well adding the wine vinegar. Beat continuously while adding the hot margarine, a few drops at a time, until half has been incorporated. Remove the basin from the saucepan and continue beating while adding the remainder in a slow trickle. Stir in the mustard, dill and maple syrup.

Preheat the grill (broiler) to high. Grill (broil) the mackerel each side for a few minutes until cooked. Serve with the sauce and the shredded lettuce to garnish.

Rainbow Trout with Honey, Lime & Ginger Sauce

A gentle oriental blend of flavours accompany plain grilled rainbow trout to make it an out-of-the-ordinary experience. The rainbow trout would also be ideal for a barbecue, cooked in foil with the sauce made in advance.

SERVES 4 | PREPARATION TIME – 25 MINUTES

4 rounded tablespoons thin honey
2 heaped teaspoons thinly sliced and diced fresh root ginger
finely grated rind and juice ½ lime (juice reserved)
1 teaspoon gluten-free Dijon mustard
1½ teaspoons gluten-free soy sauce
4 whole rainbow trout, cleaned and dried
1 gluten-free fish stock (bouillon) cube
2½ tablespoons fish cooking liquor (or water to make up)
1 tablespoon potato flour (farina)

Preheat the grill (broiler) to high.

Place the honey, ginger, lime rind, mustard and soy sauce in a small basin. Stir to blend together.

Lightly oil and season the fish then spoon a teaspoon of the sauce along each cavity. Grill (broil) for 4–6 minutes each side or until cooked.

Place the remaining sauce in a small saucepan, stir in the lime juice, fish stock (bouillon) cube, fish cooking liquor (or water to make up) and potato flour (farina). Stir until smooth then bring to the boil stirring and simmer for 1 minute, adding a little more liquid if required. Serve the sauce in a pool beside the trout.

SERVING SUGGESTION: serve with new potatoes and Stir-fried Carrots, Courgettes (zucchini) and Peas (*see page 105*) sprinkled with a little lime juice and garnished with coriander (cilantro). Alternatively serve with mixed green salad leaves and watercress. Sweet Potato Cakes/Sweet Potato and Swede Cakes (*see page 106*) also make a good accompaniment.

Salmon Parcels

Cooking the salmon in foil keeps it really moist and succulent, together with its mixed rice and dried fruit stuffing. Unpolished rice is a great source of protein and energy, fibre and B vitamins. Wild rice is actually a seed unrelated to common rice but equally nutritious. Salmon contains omega-3 fatty acids – good food for a healthy heart.

35g (1½ oz) (2½ tablespoons) whole grain brown rice

10g (½ oz) (¾ tablespoon) whole grain wild rice

1 pinch sea salt

140ml (5 fl oz) (½ cup plus 1 tablespoon) water

100g (3½ oz) (½ cup) ripe vine tomatoes, peeled and chopped small

½ medium onion, sliced finely and diced

barely ½ teaspoon ground allspice

1 teaspoon olive oil

2 pinches dried oregano

3 pieces sun-dried tomatoes, cut finely

3 unsulphured dried apricots, cut finely

3 dates, cut finely

4 salmon steaks

freshly ground black pepper

aluminium foil

The darker-coloured unsulphured apricots are free from the

*preservative sulphur dioxide. Susceptible people (e.g.
asthmatics) may experience an allergic reaction to sulphured
apricots.*

Place the two varieties of rice in a sieve and rinse in cold running
water. Bring the lightly salted water to the boil in a small saucepan
then simmer the rice for about 20 minutes until the water is absorbed.
Leave to one side.

Preheat the oven to 190°C (375°F) (gas mark 5).

Simmer the tomatoes, onion, allspice and oil in a small covered
saucepan until soft, stirring occasionally. Liquidize. Turn the cooked
rice into a basin together with the tomato mixture, oregano, sun-dried
tomatoes, apricots and dates. Season and mix well.

Brush the salmon steaks with oil and place each one in the centre
of a large, oiled square of foil. Divide the stuffing between the steaks to
fill the cavities. Drizzle a little more oil over the salmon and stuffing.
Season the fish with pepper. Bring opposite sides of the foil together
leaving space around the fish, fold the edges over twice, then fold the
other ends twice each to form a loose parcel. Place on a baking tray
and cook in the oven for 20 minutes. Serve. Pour the cooking juices
over the salmon.

SERVING SUGGESTION: serve with watercress or a salad of your choice.

Smoked Fish Pie

The colourful rich-flavoured pie comes with plenty of tasty
sauce and golden-browned potato topping. If you prefer to
reduce your intake of smoked fish however, you could use unsmoked haddock but still add the smoked salmon for an
enhanced flavour.

SERVES 4 | PREPARATION TIME – 50 MINUTES PLUS 30 MINUTES FOR
         COOKING

565g (1¼ lb) (3¾ cups) potatoes, peeled and cut

400g (14 oz) traditionally smoked undyed skinless
  haddock

500ml (17½ fl oz) (2 cups) rice milk
20cm (8") piece celery, sliced lengthways and halved
4 black peppercorns
2 bay leaves
180g (6½ oz) (2 cups) leeks (from 2 large leeks, sliced thinly, using the white and light green part only)
1 rounded tablespoon potato flour (farina)
100g (3½ oz) (⅔ cup) thin slices smoked salmon, cut
100g (3½ oz) (⅔ cup) cooked and peeled large prawns (shrimp)
freshly ground black pepper
1 tablespoon dairy-free margarine
2 teaspoons soya cream

Use an unopened carton of rice milk if possible as this is less likely to separate during poaching. However if using an already opened carton, the milk comes together again when thickening the sauce.

Add the potatoes to lightly salted boiling water, return to the boil then simmer until tender. Drain thoroughly until as dry as possible.

Preheat the oven to 180°C (350°F) (gas mark 4).

Poach the haddock in a large saucepan with the rice milk, celery, peppercorns and bay leaves, bringing just to the boil and simmering gently uncovered until tender – about 5–8 minutes. Set aside to cool.

Meanwhile warm a tablespoon of dairy-free margarine in a large non-stick frying pan (skillet). Add the leeks and cook over a low heat for 6–7 minutes without colouring.

Lift the fish from the cooking liquid and separate into large pieces discarding any bones. Mix the potato flour (farina) with the warm poaching liquid, bring to the boil, stirring, simmer for 1 minute. Remove from the heat. Discard the celery, peppercorns and bay leaves. Add the smoked salmon, haddock pieces, prawns (shrimp) and three-quarters of the leeks.

Turn the mixture into a greased 1.7 litre (3 pint) ovenproof dish. Season the potato with pepper, mash and stir in the reserved leeks.

Add the margarine and soya cream to make a creamy topping. Cover the fish mixture with the potato topping and fork the surface roughly. Cook in the oven for about 25–30 minutes until the potato has browned.

Summer Smoked Salmon Omelette

The three varieties of nasturtiums I grow produce flowers ranging from lemon yellow to orange and red with varying shades of foliage. These make a pleasant peppery omelette, capturing the colours and textures of high summer. Have all the ingredients ready beforehand so that the omelette is just cooked and appetizing.

SERVES 1 | PREPARATION TIME – 15 MINUTES

3 large free-range eggs

2 red and 2 green peppercorns, crushed

1 pinch sea salt (*optional*)

½ tablespoon dairy-free margarine

25g (1 oz) thin slices smoked salmon, cut small

½ tablespoon freshly cut chives

3 nasturtium flowers, cut

salad:

young dandelion leaves

little gem lettuce leaves

3 young nasturtium leaves, cut

Lightly beat the eggs and seasoning in a basin.

Heat the margarine in a 20cm (8") non-stick omelette/frying pan (skillet) until bubbling. Pour in the eggs. Cook over a medium heat, drawing in the edges with a non-stick spatula to allow the uncooked egg to run underneath. Whilst moist, quickly add the salmon, chives and half of the prepared nasturtium flowers. Flip one half of the omelette over the other and slide onto a warm plate. Serve immediately with the salad and remaining nasturtium flowers scattered over.

To make a two-egg omelette, use a 15cm (6") pan adjusting the other ingredients accordingly.

Swordfish Steaks with Mediterranean Garnish

SERVES 2 | PREPARATION TIME – 25 MINUTES

200g (7 oz) Jersey mids/small new potatoes, scraped/peeled*
2 swordfish steaks, weight about 350–375g (12–13 oz)
sea salt and freshly ground black pepper
mixed salad leaves
35g (1¼ oz) (scant ⅓ cup) carrot, peeled and grated
35g (1¼ oz) (scant ⅓ cup) celeriac, peeled and grated

*Organic new potatoes can be boiled in their skins.

garnish:

3 thin slices green pepper, diced small
3 small spring onions (scallions), sliced thinly, using the white and light green part only
6 small pitted green olives, rinsed, sliced thinly and diced
1 rounded tablespoon capers in 2 teaspoons of white wine vinegar
2 teaspoons olive oil
sea salt and freshly ground black pepper

Mix together the garnish ingredients in a dish and leave to one side.
Cook the potatoes in simmering, lightly salted water, until tender.
Preheat the grill (broiler) to high. Brush the fish liberally with olive oil and season. Place under the grill (broiler) for about 3–4 minutes

each side until cooked. While the fish is cooking, arrange the salad leaves, grated carrot and celeriac onto serving plates.

Serve the potatoes. Garnish the fish with the Mediterranean garnish. Any remaining garnish liquid can be sprinkled over the salad.

Tiger Prawn Curry

The subtle blend of spices combine well to make this a pleasant, mild curry.

SERVES 4 | PREPARATION TIME – 50 MINUTES (OR LESS IF USING A FOOD PROCESSOR)

225–340g (8–12 oz) (generous 1–1⅔ cups) basmati rice (or whole grain brown rice)
4 medium vine tomatoes, halved
1 tablespoon groundnut/sunflower oil
1 large onion, finely sliced and diced
2 cloves garlic, crushed
2 medium sticks celery, finely sliced lengthways and diced
1 large yellow pepper, deseeded and finely sliced and diced
1½ teaspoons each whole fenugreek, coriander (cilantro) and cumin seeds, partially ground
1½ teaspoons each garam marsala and turmeric powder
1 rounded *and* 1 level tablespoon tomato purée (paste)
5cm (2") cube creamed coconut dissolved in 200ml (7 fl oz) (¾ cup) boiling water
finely grated rind 1 lime
350g (12½ oz) (2 cups) ready-peeled raw tiger prawns (shrimp)*
sea salt and freshly ground black pepper
2 rounded tablespoons plain soya yoghurt
3–4 teaspoons lime juice
4 tablespoons freshly cut coriander (cilantro) leaves

If the prawns (shrimp) are not ready peeled and deveined, remove the dark intestinal vein which runs down the back.

Cook the rice according to instructions and leave covered until required.

Meanwhile, preheat the grill (broiler) to the highest setting. Place the tomatoes skin side up and cook until the skins blister and split. When cool enough to handle, remove the skins and chop roughly. Leave to one side.

Warm the oil in a large non-stick frying pan (skillet). Add the onion, garlic, celery, yellow pepper and whole spices. Stir-fry together over a low heat for about 8 minutes. Add the powdered spices, tomatoes, tomato purée (paste), creamed coconut (dissolved) and lime rind. Stir to combine the ingredients. Simmer for a further 8 minutes.

Add the tiger prawns (shrimp). Season and stir until they are cooked – about 2 minutes, but don't cook for too long or they will become rubbery. Remove from the heat. Mix the yoghurt and lime juice to taste. Stir briskly until smooth then stir into the curry. Add half of the coriander (cilantro) leaves. Serve the curry on a bed of rice and garnish with the remaining coriander (cilantro) leaves.

SERVING SUGGESTION: accompany with steamed vegetables or a mixed green salad of shredded little gem lettuce, chicory (endive) and celery.

White Fish in Creamy Lemon Sauce

This makes a lovely 'comforting' meal with a delicate creamy, lemon sauce. The combination of lemon and hint of chives always complement each other well.

SERVES 4 | PREPARATION TIME – 1 HOUR

800g (1¾ lb) (5⅓ cups) old potatoes, peeled and cut into even-sized pieces

312ml (11 fl oz) (1¼ cups) water

625g (1 lb 6 oz) skinned pollack/coley fillets

4 black peppercorns

1 good pinch sea salt

½ stick celery, quartered

1 small carrot, quartered

2 bay leaves

240ml (8½ fl oz) (1 cup) rice milk, shaken well before using

2 tablespoons gluten-free cornflour (cornstarch)/potato flour (farina)

2 large egg yolks

1½ tablespoons lemon juice

sea salt and pinch white pepper (*optional*)

½ tablespoon freshly cut chives

40g (1½ oz) (2½ tablespoons) dairy-free margarine

1½ tablespoons soya cream

Add the potatoes to lightly salted boiling water, return to the boil, cover and simmer until cooked. Drain well and mash until soft. Leave to one side, covered, until required.

Bring the water to the boil in a large saucepan. Cut the fish into about 8 pieces and add to water together with peppercorns, salt, celery, carrot and bay leaves. Return to the boil, cover and simmer until just cooked – about 7–9 minutes.

Strain 270ml (9½ fl oz) (1 cup plus 2 tablespoons) of the fish stock (bouillon) into a small saucepan. Add the rice milk and blend in the flour. Bring to the boil and simmer for 1 minute, stirring. Remove from the heat. Add the egg yolks one at a time, stirring vigorously. Return to a very low heat, stirring continuously until the sauce thickens slightly more and just comes to boiling point. Remove from the heat, stir in the lemon juice and adjust the seasoning if necessary.

Preheat the grill (broiler) to a high setting. Drain the fish well, remove any bones and discard the peppercorns, stock vegetables and bay leaves. Carefully place the portions in a greased lasagne dish (or similar ovenproof dish) – minimum capacity 1.7 litres (3 pints). Cover with the sauce. Scatter with finely cut chives.

Stir the margarine and cream into the mashed potatoes, season with black pepper and mix together well. Spoon into a food forcing bag fitted with a large 'star' nozzle. Pipe swirls to cover the sauce. Dot with a little margarine. Place under the preheated grill (broiler) until the potatoes are lightly golden.

SERVING SUGGESTION: serve with garden peas or steamed broccoli, alternatively watercress and green salad leaves, garnished with chives.

Meat

Beef Casserole

Shin of beef is an inexpensive cut of beef with exceptionally good flavour. The casserole is easy to prepare and pop in the oven with some jacket potatoes, then forget about for the next 1¾ to 2 hours. Just right for that cold winter's evening.

SERVES 4 | PREPARATION TIME – 35 MINUTES PLUS 2 HOURS FOR COOKING

1 large onion, quartered and sliced thickly
2–2½ tablespoons sunflower oil
650g (1 lb 7oz) shin of beef
1½ rounded tablespoons rice flour
sea salt and freshly ground black pepper
455ml (16 fl oz) (2 cups) hot beef stock (bouillon)/water plus 1 gluten-free beef stock (bouillon) cube
4½ tablespoons red wine
1 teaspoon gluten-free Worcestershire sauce
1 bay leaf
150g (5½ oz) (1⅓ cups) carrots, peeled and cut into chunks
150g (5½ oz) (1⅓ cups) parsnips, peeled and cut into chunks
2 large potatoes (for jacket potatoes)

Preheat the oven to 170°C (325°F) (gas mark 3).

Fry the onion in half a tablespoon of the oil over a low heat until lightly coloured – about 8–10 minutes. Leave to one side.

Remove any fat and obvious fibrous tissue from the meat and cut into 2.5cm (1") chunks. Toss in the seasoned flour, shaking off the excess. Stir-fry small batches in a large non-stick frying pan (skillet), each with a little of the remaining oil. Fry over a moderate to high heat to seal in the juices on all sides. Return the meat and onions to the pan. Add the excess seasoned flour and stir.

Add the beef stock (bouillon), wine, Worcestershire sauce and bay leaf. Bring to the boil stirring, simmer for 1 minute. Add the carrot and parsnip chunks. Return to the boil then turn into a 1.7 litre (3 pint) ovenproof dish with a close-fitting lid, or foil in between the dish and lid. Cook in the oven with the potatoes for 1¾–2 hours. Serve with the jacket potatoes, cut and spread with a little dairy-free margarine and additional vegetables.

Beef Stroganoff

SERVES 4 | PREPARATION TIME – 1 HOUR

285g (10 oz) (1⅓ cups plus 1 tablespoon) basmati rice/American easy-cook long grain rice

765ml (27 fl oz) (3 cups plus 2 tablespoons) water

625g (1 lb 6 oz) thinly sliced blade/rump steak*

1 rounded tablespoon dairy-free margarine

1 large onion, sliced thinly

225g (8 oz) (2¾ cups) closed-cap mushrooms, sliced thinly

1 rounded *and* 1 level teaspoon gluten-free Dijon mustard

1 rounded *and* 2 level tablespoons rice flour

¼ teaspoon sea salt and freshly ground black pepper

1 rounded tablespoon tomato purée (paste)

210ml (7½ fl oz) (¾ cup plus 1 tablespoon) boiling water plus ¾ gluten-free beef stock (bouillon) cube

3 tablespoons soya cream

4 rounded tablespoons plain soya yoghurt

½ tablespoon lemon juice

freshly cut parsley to garnish

Order the steak in advance from your butcher, already cut into strips to save time.

Wash the rice in a sieve under cold running water. Drain well. Lightly salt the water and bring to the boil in a medium saucepan. Add the rice. Return to the boil then simmer until cooked – about 14–15 minutes. Leave to one side, covered.

Trim away any gristle from the meat. Cut into 4cm x ½ cm (1½" x ¼") strips cutting across the grain of the meat. Leave to one side until required.

Warm the margarine in a large non-stick frying pan (skillet). Fry the onion for 4 minutes then add the mushrooms and cook together for a further 4 minutes, stirring occasionally. Remove to a plate.

Mix the mustard with the strips of meat. Roll small batches of meat in the seasoned flour, shaking off the excess. Stir-fry each batch in more hot margarine over a high heat for about 2 minutes to seal in the juices. When all the meat is sealed, return the onions, mushrooms and meat to the pan. Cook together for a further 2 minutes over a low heat, stirring occasionally. Add the excess flour, tomato purée (paste) and water plus stock (bouillon) cube. Stir well and bring to the boil then simmer covered for about 8 minutes until the meat is tender, stirring once or twice during that time. Remove from the heat.

Mix the cream and yoghurt in a small basin. Stir in the lemon juice until smooth. Mix a tablespoon of the stroganoff into the cream mixture then stir it all back into the stroganoff.

Fluff up the rice with a fork and serve onto plates with the stroganoff in the centre. Garnish with parsley.

Cajun Spiced Sausages

Gluten-free (coeliac) sausagemeat is available from good butchers made to Coeliac Society specifications. Check that it is also dairy free. Cajun spiced sausages can be made with fresh sausagemeat, cooked and eaten immediately, or may be frozen, cooked or uncooked. Ideal for the barbecue.

MAKES 12 | PREPARATION TIME – 15 MINUTES PLUS 10 MINUTES FOR
COOKING

½ teaspoon celery seeds
½ teaspoon dried thyme
1½ teaspoons dried oregano
1 teaspoon ground allspice
½ teaspoon cayenne pepper
3 teaspoons paprika
freshly ground black pepper
1 medium clove garlic, crushed to a pulp
455g (1 lb) (2 cups) gluten-free, dairy-free raw pork sausagemeat

Partially grind the celery seeds and herbs with a pestle and mortar then mix with the Cajun spices and seasoning on a plate. Add the garlic and stir.

Preheat the grill (broiler) to high.

Shape the sausagemeat into 12 sausages and lightly oil. At first, roll sparingly in the Cajun spices and herbs then use the remainder to coat evenly.

Cook under the grill (broiler) for about 8–10 minutes, turning occasionally until cooked.

SERVING SUGGESTION: good with baked beans on gluten-free toast or as a main meal with potatoes and vegetables.

Chicken Broth with Leeks, Lemon Grass and Tarragon

A satisfying one-pot meal where the vegetables are added at intervals while the chicken is cooking. It helps considerably if all the ingredients are assembled prior to making. The broth may also be served with new potatoes, when in season, or gluten-free pasta.

SERVES 4 | PREPARATION TIME – 65 MINUTES

8 chicken drumsticks, skinned
850ml (30 fl oz) (3⅔ cups) cold water
2 bay leaves
175g (6½ oz) (2 cups) leeks (a large leek, white to yellowy green part only)
1 tablespoon dairy-free margarine
sea salt and freshly ground black pepper
2 sticks celery, sliced thickly
8 whole baby onions/small shallots, peeled
4 small cloves garlic, peeled
1 medium carrot, cut into thick sticks
1 fresh lemon grass, tough outer leaves removed, cut into 4 lengthways and bruised
2 rounded teaspoons brown rice miso
455g–565g (1–1¼ lb) (3⅔–3¾ cups) potatoes, peeled and cut
155g (5½ oz) (¾ cup) butter beans (lima beans)* (or small tin, drained)
2 rounded tablespoons freshly cut tarragon
240g (8½ oz) (3⅓ cups) broccoli florets (with only 2.5cm (1") stalk left on)
2 tablespoons potato flour (farina)

To use dried butter (lima) beans, soak in cold water overnight. Drain and rinse well. Cover with fresh water and bring to the boil. Boil rapidly for 10 minutes, then simmer for a further 35–40 minutes until tender. Cool in the liquid. Drain and use as required or freeze for later use (thawed) in soups, casseroles, etc.

Place the prepared drumsticks in a large saucepan and cover with the water. Bring to the boil and skim off any scum. Add the bay leaves, cover and simmer for 45–50 minutes until tender – adding the other ingredients at intervals during the cooking time (*see following paragraphs*).

Slice the leeks in half lengthways and rinse well to remove any soil. Shake well. Slice thickly. Melt the margarine in a large non-stick frying pan (skillet), add the leeks, season and sweat over a very low heat for about 5 minutes, turning from time to time. Add to the chicken.

Add the celery, onions, garlic and carrot to the frying pan (skillet) with a little more margarine, and toss together for a few minutes to slightly colour. About 15 minutes into the cooking time, turn the vegetables into the saucepan with the simmering chicken, together with the lemon grass. Stir in the miso.

Add the potatoes to lightly salted boiling water and simmer until cooked.

Around 10 minutes before the end of the chicken cooking time, stir in the butter beans (lima beans) and tarragon. Place the broccoli stalks into the sauce leaving the florets to steam above. Cover and cook for about 8 minutes so that the chicken is tender and broccoli just cooked. Carefully remove the broccoli to serving plates. Mix the potato flour (farina) into a little of the cooled sauce then stir into the chicken broth to thicken. Bring to the boil and simmer for 1 minute. Adjust seasoning if necessary. Remove the bay leaves and lemon grass. Serve the broth with the broccoli and potatoes. Sprinkle with a little more tarragon to garnish.

Chicken Curry with Banana

This recipe is a combination of mild chicken curry and sautéed banana.

SERVES 4 | PREPARATION TIME – 50 MINUTES

225–340g (8–12 oz) (1–1⅔ cups) basmati rice (or whole grain rice)

4 large skinless chicken breasts (about 680g (1½ lb))

3 green cardamom pods

1 rounded teaspoon coriander (cilantro) seeds

1 rounded teaspoon fenugreek seeds

1 tablespoon groundnut oil

1 large onion, sliced thinly and diced

2 cloves garlic crushed

1 heaped teaspoon finely cut fresh root ginger

1½ rounded teaspoons turmeric

1 rounded teaspoon garam masala

2 rounded teaspoons gluten-free, dairy-free medium curry powder

½ teaspoon chilli powder

2.5cm (1") cube creamed coconut dissolved in 225 ml (8 fl oz) (¾ cup plus 2 tablespoons) hot water

1 heaped tablespoon tomato purée (paste)

½ tablespoon tomato ketchup

1 pinch sea salt

2 tablespoons freshly cut coriander (cilantro) leaves

2 large ripe bananas, cut lengthways, then into 8 pieces each

4 rounded tablespoons plain soya yoghurt

As a variation, sauté one large banana and a ripe sliced mango to mix with the curry.

Cook the basmati rice according to instructions. Remove from the heat and leave covered until required.

Meanwhile, cut the chicken into 2.5cm (1") cubes.

Add the cardamom pods, coriander (cilantro) and fenugreek seeds to a large dry non-stick frying pan (skillet) or wok. Place over a moderate heat to darken a little then crush with a pestle and mortar. Return to the pan with half of the oil, onion, garlic and ginger. Stir-fry together over a low heat for about 4 minutes.

Add the remaining oil and chicken. Stir-fry over a high heat until the chicken is sealed on all sides. Reduce the heat and add the turmeric, garam masala, curry powder, chilli powder, coconut and water, tomato purée (paste), tomato ketchup, salt and coriander (cilantro) leaves. Simmer together for 8–10 minutes, stirring occasionally. When cooked remove from the heat.

Sauté the banana pieces in a little dairy-free margarine (or butter, if tolerated as part of a low-lactose diet), for about a minute each side. Stir the yoghurt into the curry then carefully mix in the bananas to coat with the sauce.

SERVING SUGGESTION: the curry can also be served with raisin and almond pilau rice (*see Lamb with Apricots, Chickpeas & Pilau Rice on page 74*). Accompany with a side salad and gluten-free, dairy-free poppadums.

Duck Stir-fry with Plum & Orange Sauce

In this unusual stir-fry dish the duck is grilled (broiled) while the vegetables are stir-fried, conveniently reducing the cooking time – and time spent in the kitchen! If you can, use marjorie plums when available in late summer and early autumn, otherwise Victoria plums make a good, slightly sweeter version. Stir-frying vegetables is a healthy option as they retain their 'bite' and vital nutrients.

SERVES 4 | PREPARATION TIME – 45 MINUTES

4 duck breasts, weight about 565–700g (1¼–1½ lb)
sunflower/groundnut oil
sea salt and freshly ground black pepper
1 medium onion, sliced finely
1 clove garlic, crushed
200g (7 oz) mangetout (snowpeas), cut diagonally twice
250g (8½ oz) (2 cups) carrots, peeled, sliced into 4cm (1½") pieces, then into matchsticks
400g (14 oz) beansprouts
a few drops sesame oil

sauce:

310g (11 oz) marjorie plums, stoned (pitted) and cut roughly
3 clementines, peeled and parted into segments
1 teaspoon clementine rind, pith removed and finely cut
3 tablespoons gluten-free blackbean sauce
1 tablespoon dry sherry
1½ tablespoons water
2 pinches gluten-free Chinese five-spice powder
sea salt and freshly ground black pepper

Preheat the grill (broiler) to high.

With a very sharp knife, score the duck skin. Brush the meat with oil and season. Cook the duck skin side up under the grill (broiler) until just cooked. Leave to rest.

While the duck is cooking, warm a little oil in a large non-stick frying pan (skillet). Soften the onion and garlic over a low heat without colouring – about 8–10 minutes. Remove to a plate.

Simmer the sauce ingredients in a covered saucepan, stirring occasionally until tender – about 8–10 minutes.

Stir-fry the mangetout and carrots in a tablespoon of hot oil over a high heat, turning frequently for a few minutes – keeping them crunchy. Add the onion and stir to heat through. Remove to a plate.

Briefly stir-fry the beansprouts in a little oil. Sprinkle with a few drop of sesame seed oil. Place a bed of beansprouts onto serving plates, followed by the vegetables. Reserve 4 tablespoons of the sauce then pour the remainder over the vegetables. Thinly slice the duck diagonally and arrange over the sauce. Trickle the remaining sauce over the duck.

Gammon & Mushrooms with Sage Apple Jelly

This is a really quick meal if you have a ready-made jar of Sage Apple Jelly (*see page 223*). Some gammon is rather salty and could be soaked for an hour or so before cooking. Shitake mushrooms are rich in calcium, phosphorus and vitamin D which helps the body absorb calcium from the diet. When making four servings it is best to cook in two large ovenproof dishes.

SERVES 2 | PREPARATION TIME – 10 MINUTES PLUS 25 MINUTES FOR COOKING

1 large thin slice gammon weighing about 350g (12½ oz)
½ tablespoon sunflower oil
5–6 medium shitake mushrooms, sliced thinly
4 rounded tablespoons sage apple jelly
freshly ground black pepper
2 teaspoons arrowroot powder

As a variation, a 1cm (½") slice of cooking apple can be used instead of mushrooms.

Preheat the oven to 180°C (350°F) (gas mark 4).
    Trim the fat from the gammon. Over a high heat, fry in oil briefly on each side to seal in the juices. Turn into a large ovenproof dish. Scatter the mushrooms over the meat. Spoon over the sage apple jelly. Season with pepper. Cover with a close-fitting lid or foil in between the dish and lid. Cook in the oven for 20–24 minutes until cooked.
    Turn the sauce and mushrooms into a small saucepan. Thicken with the arrowroot powder mixed with a little of the cooled sauce. Bring to the boil, stirring. Simmer for 1 minute then serve.

Gammon with Figs

SERVES 2 | PREPARATION TIME – 17 MINUTES PLUS 20 MINUTES FOR
    COOKING

1–2 thin slices gammon, total weight about 350–370g (12–13 oz)
sunflower oil
55ml (2 fl oz) (3 tablespoons) water
100ml (3½ fl oz) (⅓ cup plus 1 tablespoon) freshly pressed pineapple juice
½ gluten-free chicken/vegetable stock (bouillon) cube
½ tablespoon arrowroot powder
1 pinch ground cinnamon
freshly ground black pepper
3 small/2 large Turkish black figs

Preheat the oven to 180°C (350°F) (gas mark 4).

Trim the fat from the gammon. Fry briefly in a little hot oil to seal on both sides. Transfer to an ovenproof dish.

In a small saucepan, mix the water, juice, stock (bouillon) cube, arrowroot powder and cinnamon. Stir and bring to the boil, stirring until thickened and cook for 1 minute. Season with pepper and pour over the gammon. Cut the figs in half and place cut side down in the sauce. Cover with a close-fitting lid or foil in between the dish and lid. Cook in the oven for about 20 minutes then serve.

SERVING SUGGESTION: slice and blanch some courgettes (zucchini) in boiling water for 1 minute and drain. Place on absorbent kitchen paper and pat dry. Heat a little dairy-free margarine (or a tiny amount of butter, if tolerated as part of a low-lactose diet) in a saucepan. Add the courgettes (zucchini), season and stir-fry over a moderate heat until lightly browned. Serve together with new potatoes.

Ham & Chicken Pie

This is a firm family favourite. The sugar snap peas and baby corn retain their crunch which is a nice contrast to the rest of the dish. There's also plenty of tasty gravy so you won't need to make extra.

SERVES 4 | PREPARATION TIME – 1–1¼ HOURS PLUS 30 MINUTES FOR COOKING

225g (8 oz) skinless chicken breast, cut into 2.5cm (1") strips, oiled
1½ tablespoons sunflower oil
1 small onion, sliced thinly
1 large leek (the light part), sliced thinly, using about 110g (4 oz) (1⅓ cups), reserving the remainder for the stock
1 stick celery, sliced lengthways and chopped
½ small fennel bulb (with plenty of fresh green feathery leaves), reserving the outer part of the bulb and stalk for the stock, or if unavailable ½ teaspoon fennel seeds, partially ground
1 small clove garlic
8 fresh whole baby corn
75g (3 oz) (⅔ cup) fresh sugar snap peas/dwarf green beans, cut
225g (8 oz) home boiled ham, cut into 2.5cm (1") cubes
½ gluten-free chicken/vegetable stock (bouillon) cube for home-made stock
1 lightly rounded tablespoon gluten-free cornflour (cornstarch)/potato flour (farina)
sea salt and freshly ground black pepper
unsweetened soya milk

stock:
   710ml (25 fl oz) (3 cups) boiling water

½ stick celery, quartered

the reserved leek cut lengthways rinsed and quartered and
outer part of fennel bulb/stalk, sliced, if used

½ carrot, quartered

2 bay leaves

sea salt and 2 black peppercorns

OR

485ml (17 fl oz) (2 cups) hot water

1 gluten-free chicken/vegetable stock (bouillon) cube

pastry:

125g (4½ oz) (generous ¾ cup) rice flour

20g (¾ oz) (2 tablespoons) potato flour (farina)

20g (¾ oz) (3¾ tablespoons) soya flour

10g (½ oz) (1½ tablespoons) millet flakes

¼ teaspoon gluten-free baking powder

¼ teaspoon xanthum gum

80g (2¾ oz) (5 tablespoons) dairy-free margarine, straight
from the fridge

2¼–2½ tablespoons cold water

Sieve the flours into a mixing bowl then add the millet flakes, baking
powder and xanthum gum. Leave to one side until the pie filling is
finished.

Add the stock ingredients (if using) and seasoning to the boiling
water in a large saucepan and simmer for 15 minutes. Leave to one
side.

Preheat the grill (broiler) to high and cook the strips of chicken.
When cooked, cut into 2.5cm (1") cubes.

Warm the oil in a large non-stick frying pan (skillet). Add the
onion, leek, celery, fennel (reserving the leaves)/fennel seeds and garlic.
Soften over a low heat for 7–8 minutes.

Preheat the oven to 180°C (350°F) (gas mark 4).

Add the baby corn, peas/beans, snipped fennel leaves, ham and chicken. Discard the stock ingredients except for the bay leaves. Measure 485ml (17 fl oz) (2 cups) of the stock (bouillon) then crumble in the stock (bouillon) cube. Mix in the cornflour (cornstarch)/potato flour (farina), stirring well. Season, bring to the boil and cook, stirring, for 1 minute. Adjust seasoning if necessary.

Add the margarine to the dry pastry ingredients and rub lightly with fingertips until the texture of fine breadcrumbs. Add the water, then cut and stir with a knife until the consistency of damp to wettish pastry. Bring together into a dough. Flour the work surface and rolling pin. Roll out the pastry to 8mm (⅜"). Place the top of a 1.7 litre (3 pint) ovenproof dish upside down on the pastry, then cut around the edge. Turn the meat and vegetables into the dish. Cut the pastry in half. Lift with two thin metal fish slices into place over the pie. Lightly score a lattice pattern into the pastry. Brush with soya milk and cook in the oven for 30–35 minutes. Serve, removing the bay leaves.

Lamb with Apricots, Chickpeas & Pilau Rice

This meal needs a little forethought but is delicious. If you wish to reap the nutritional benefits from sprouted chickpeas (garbanzo beans) they will need to be soaked and rinsed 3–4 days before making the meal. The apricots need to be soaked for about 6 hours in the clementine juice with its rind and candied peel. The extra thought is well worth the effort.

SERVES 4 | PREPARATION TIME – 30 MINUTES PLUS 1 HOUR FOR
COOKING (6 HOURS TO SOAK APRICOTS)

75g (3 oz) (½ cup) soaked and sprouted chickpeas
(garbanzo beans)*/equivalent weight of tinned chickpeas

100g (3½ oz) (½ cup) unsulphured dried apricots

140ml (5 fl oz) (½ cup plus 1 tablespoon) clementine juice,
squeezed from 4–5 clementines

rind ½ clementine, pith removed and cut finely

½ tablespoon finely sliced whole orange candied peel
(*optional*)

| 1½ tablespoons sunflower oil |
| 1 red onion, sliced thickly |
| 1 large red pepper, deseeded and sliced thickly |
| 1 clove garlic, crushed |
| 455g (1 lb) lamb fillet/boneless shoulder steaks, 1cm (½") thick |
| 1 rounded tablespoon rice flour |
| 4 good pinches ground cinnamon |
| sea salt and freshly ground black pepper |
| 285ml (10 fl oz) (1¼ cups) vegetable stock (bouillon)/hot water plus ½ gluten-free beef stock (bouillon) cube |
| 2 bay leaves |
| 1 tablespoon gluten-free Worcestershire sauce |
| 2 thin slices fresh root ginger, sliced finely |

pilau rice:

| 225g (8 oz) (1 cup plus 1 tablespoon) American easy-cook long grain rice/basmati rice |
| 340ml (12 fl oz) (1⅓ cups plus 1 tablespoon) hot water |
| 1 teaspoon unrefined dark muscovado sugar/½ teaspoon black strap molasses |
| ½ teaspoon ground cinnamon |
| sea salt and freshly ground black pepper |
| 2 tablespoons dairy-free margarine |
| 2 tablespoons flaked almonds |
| 50g (2 oz) (⅓ cup) raisins |

*If using dried chickpeas (garbanzo beans), follow the instructions at the end of the recipe for sprouting them prior to making the dish.

Soak the apricots in clementine juice together with rind and mixed peel, for about 6 hours prior to making the meal.

Preheat the oven to 180°C (350°F) (gas mark 4).

Warm a third of the oil in a large non-stick frying pan (skillet). Add the onion, pepper and garlic. Cook over a low heat for 5 minutes. Turn into a 1.7 litre (3 pint) ovenproof casserole dish. Cut the lamb into large pieces, trimming away excess fat and toss the pieces in the cinnamon-spiced seasoned flour. Turn half the meat into the frying pan (skillet) with half the remaining oil to lightly brown and seal on all sides, cooking over a moderate heat. Seal the remaining meat in oil. Return the meat and vegetables to the frying pan (skillet), add the remaining flour, stock (bouillon), apricot mixture (including marinade), bay leaves, Worcestershire sauce and ginger. Bring to the boil and simmer, stirring to thicken for 1 minute. Return to the casserole, with foil between the dish and lid. Cook in the oven for 1 hour. While the casserole is cooking, make the pilau rice.

Remove the bay leaves from the cooked casserole. Stir in the chickpeas (garbanzo beans) to warm through. Serve immediately with pilau rice.

For the pilau rice, soak the rice for 30 minutes in cold water then rinse and drain well. Add the water to a large saucepan, stir in the sugar/black strap molasses to dissolve. Add the cinnamon, seasoning, drained rice and half the margarine. Stir to melt the margarine then bring to the boil, cover and simmer for 10 minutes. Meanwhile melt the remaining margarine and fry the almonds to lightly brown. Add the raisins and stir together. Stir into the cooked rice. Serve.

To use sprouted chickpeas (garbanzo beans):

Soak 75g (3 oz) (scant ½ cup) dried chickpeas (garbanzo beans) overnight in cold to tepid water (i.e. 3–4 days before you wish to use them). Rinse, then leave in a dark, warm place to germinate, rinsing twice daily until the sprouts are about 2–2.5cm (¾–1") long. Weigh 75g (3 oz) (½ to generous ½ cup) sprouting chickpeas (garbanzo beans) (discarding any unsprouted ones) for the casserole, using the remainder for salads or mixing with other sprouting seeds and beans.

Lambs' Kidneys & Fresh Noodles in Red Wine Sauce

Kidneys contain high levels of purine and might precipitate an attack of gout in susceptible people. Other foods that can precipitate gout are sweetbreads, anchovies, sardines, brains, meat extracts, herrings, scallops and game meats.

SERVES 2 | PREPARATION TIME – 50 MINUTES

1 large red onion, sliced thinly
1 tablespoon balsamic vinegar
170ml (6 fl oz) (⅔ cup) red wine
6 lambs' kidneys halved, cored and cut into pieces
1 rounded tablespoon rice flour
sea salt and freshly ground black pepper
½ tablespoon olive oil
140ml (5 fl oz) (½ cup) hot water plus ½ gluten-free beef stock (bouillon) cube
1 bouquet garni
freshly cut mustard to garnish

The meal can also be made with 5 lambs' kidneys and 1 rasher of short back bacon if preferred.

buckwheat noodles:

50g (1¾ oz) (generous ⅓ cup) buckwheat flour, sieved
25g (1 oz) (2¾ tablespoons) rice flour, sieved
sea salt and freshly ground black pepper
1 large free-range egg

Alternatively, serve with other pasta or whole grain brown rice instead of home-made noodles.

Place the onion in a small saucepan with the vinegar and wine. Bring to the boil then simmer, covered, for 12 minutes.

Meanwhile, toss the kidney pieces in seasoned flour and add to a large non-stick frying pan (skillet) with the warmed oil. Stir-fry over a moderate heat until browned on all sides. Turn into the onions, add the water, stock (bouillon) cube, bouquet garni and any remaining flour. Bring to the boil and simmer, until tender – about 12–15 minutes, stirring once or twice. Remove bouquet garni.

While the kidney mixture is cooking, make the noodles and bring a half-filled large saucepan of lightly salted water to the boil. Mix the noodle flours and seasoning in a mixing bowl. Make a well in the centre and drop in the egg. Stir with a wooden spoon until all the flour has gradually been drawn into the mixture. Bring together to form a pliable dough. Knead for 1 minute on a floured surface. Roll out into a long thin strip, turning frequently, adding more flour if necessary. Cut into 5mm (¼") strips then into 7.5cm (3") length ribbons. Add to the boiling water, return to the boil, then boil uncovered for about 4–5 minutes. Drain well. Turn into the kidney mixture, stir then serve. Garnish with mustard leaves.

Lamb with Redcurrant Sauce & Red Grapes

A comforting lamb casserole with a beautifully blended red wine and redcurrant sauce, just 'freshened' with red grapes to finish. While the batches of meat are being sealed in hot fat, the prepared potatoes can be boiling so both can be placed in the oven about the same time.

SERVES 4 | PREPARATION TIME – 40 MINUTES PLUS 45 MINUTES FOR
          COOKING

790g (1¾ lb) lamb fillet/boneless shoulder steaks
2 tablespoons rice flour
sea salt and freshly ground black pepper
1½ tablespoons sunflower oil
115ml (4 fl oz) (½ cup) red wine

140ml (5 fl oz) (½ cup) hot water plus ½ gluten-free
  beef/vegetable stock (bouillon) cube

4 rounded tablespoons redcurrant sauce

½ tablespoon gluten-free Worcestershire sauce

½ tablespoon red wine vinegar

125g (4½ oz) (1 cup) seedless red grapes

*Cumberland sauce may be used as an alternative to
redcurrant sauce.*

roast potatoes:
  790g (1¾ lb) potatoes

  ¾ tablespoon olive oil

  sea salt and freshly ground black pepper

  ½ teaspoon dried rosemary

*For a variation try a combination of roasted red onion
segments and potatoes.*

Preheat the oven to 180°C (350°F) (gas mark 4).
    Peel and cut the potatoes roughly into 3cm (1¼") cubes.
    Place the oil in a shallow ovenproof dish or lid and heat in the
oven.
    Trim excess fat from the meat and cut into large pieces. Leave to
one side.
    Bring a large saucepan half-filled with water to the boil. Boil the
prepared potatoes for about 2 minutes, drain and pat dry. Toss them
in the hot oil, season and sprinkle with the rosemary. Return the dish
to the oven on a medium to high shelf and cook for about 45–50
minutes, turning halfway through the cooking time.
    Toss the prepared meat in the seasoned flour, shaking off the
excess. Warm a third of the oil in a large non-stick frying pan (skillet).
Fry a third of the meat briskly over a high heat to seal in the juices
and brown slightly. Repeat with the remaining meat and oil. Remove
the frying pan (skillet) from the heat. Add the wine and stir to loosen
any sediment from the base. Add the hot water and stock (bouillon)

cube, sauces and wine vinegar. Stir to incorporate any remaining flour. Bring to the boil, stirring, return the meat to the pan and simmer together for 1 minute. Turn into a 1.7 litre (3 pint) ovenproof casserole dish. Cover with a close-fitting lid, or foil between dish and lid.

Cook in the oven for 35 minutes then add the grapes and cook for a further 10 minutes. When the meat is cooked, place absorbent kitchen paper over the gravy to absorb any excess fat. Serve with the roast potatoes and vegetables to accompany.

Layered Mince with Soufflé Topping

In this tasty layered dish, each layer has its own unique flavour. When eaten as a whole, the flavours blend very well. The soufflé topping is a bit of a cheat, but it works – using parsnips instead of cheese!

SERVES 4 | PREPARATION TIME – 40 MINUTES PLUS 40 MINUTES FOR COOKING

350g (12½ oz) (2¾ cups) potatoes, peeled and cut
120g (4½ oz) (¾ cup) parsnips, peeled and cut
350g (12½ oz) (1⅔ cups) minced (ground) beef steak
1 large onion, sliced thinly and diced
400g (14 oz) tin plum tomatoes, chopped, reserving the juice
a good ½ tablespoon finely cut fresh sage
sea salt and freshly ground black pepper
1 tablespoon dairy-free margarine
1¾ tablespoons gluten-free cornflour (cornstarch)/potato flour (farina)
285ml (10 fl oz) (1¼ cups less 1 tablespoon) unsweetened soya milk
1 large free-range egg, separated
½ teaspoon freshly grated nutmeg

*For a vegetarian equivalent, substitute the meat with
textured soya protein chunks.*

Add the potatoes and parsnips to lightly salted boiling water in
separate saucepans. Simmer until the potatoes are just cooked and
parsnips tender. Drain the vegetables and set aside.

Meanwhile, stir-fry the mince in large non-stick frying pan (skillet)
over a high heat, until browned. Pour away excess fat. Reduce the heat
to low. Add the onion and cook together for 4–5 minutes, turning
frequently. Stir in the tomatoes with 3 tablespoons of the juice and
sage. Season and continue to simmer for about 8 minutes more,
stirring from time to time.

Preheat the oven to 180°C (350°F) (gas mark 4).

Melt the margarine in a small saucepan, add the flour and a little of
the milk. Stir until smooth then add the remaining milk and bring to
the boil, stirring. Simmer for 1 minute. Remove from the heat. Mash
the parsnips well and add to the sauce, stirring thoroughly. Mix in the
egg yolk and nutmeg. Season well.

Spoon half the mince into a 1.7 litre (3 pint) ovenproof
casserole/soufflé dish. Slice half of the potatoes over the mince and
pour over half the sauce. Repeat the mince and potato layer.

Whisk the egg white until stiff then fold into the remaining sauce
with a metal spoon. Cover the potatoes with the sauce. Cook in the oven
for about 35–40 minutes until the top is lightly browned and puffy.

SERVING SUGGESTION: serve with a selection of steamed vegetables or
mixed salad.

Liver, French Style

In common with other meats, liver provides protein which is a
vital part of all body cells and necessary for their growth and
repair. Liver is rich in vitamin A, required for healthy hair, skin,
bones, teeth and eyes. However, it is high in cholesterol and
most doctors advise people with high cholesterol to avoid it.
Liver is often recommended for anaemia sufferers as iron from
meat is easily absorbed. Liver, eaten in moderation, helps to

prevent birth defects that may be caused by an inadequate intake of folic acid. It contains high levels of purine and might precipitate an attack of gout in susceptible people. Other foods that can precipitate gout are sweetbreads, anchovies, sardines, brains, meat extracts, herrings, scallops and game meats.

SERVES 2 | PREPARATION TIME – 30 MINUTES

½ small onion, sliced thinly
½ tablespoon olive oil
2 ripe vine tomatoes, halved
1 rounded tablespoon potato flour (farina)
sea salt and freshly ground black pepper
225g (8 oz) lambs' liver, sliced thinly
1 tablespoon dairy-free margarine
2 small cloves garlic, crushed
3 tablespoons freshly cut parsley
2 tablespoons white wine vinegar/cider vinegar
3 tablespoons vegetable water plus ½ gluten-free chicken/vegetable stock (bouillon) cube

In a large non-stick frying pan (skillet), soften the onion slices in oil over a low heat allowing them to colour slightly.

Preheat the grill (broiler) to high and cook the tomatoes skin side up.

On a plate, mix the flour and seasoning, then turn the liver in the seasoned flour to coat evenly. Shake off the excess flour and reserve. When the onion slices are cooked, push them to one side and place the liver in the pan with a little more oil. Cook over a low to medium heat for about 1 minute each side. Transfer the liver and onions to a warm plate.

Melt the margarine in the pan. Remove from the heat while adding the garlic, parsley, vinegar, vegetable water, stock (bouillon) cube and reserved flour. Stir well. Return to the heat and bring to the boil, stirring constantly until thick. Cook for 1 minute. Serve immediately with the tomatoes. Pour the sauce over the liver and onions.

SERVING SUGGESTION: serve with seasoned mashed potatoes and haricot beans, or try serving with mashed potato topped with boiled pulped garlic cloves.

Pork Chops with Juniper, Port & Thyme Sauce

The flavourful sauce transforms plain pork chops into something more inspired. It's an extremely quick meal, ready to serve as soon as the chops are cooked.

SERVES 4 | PREPARATION TIME – 30 MINUTES

4 pork chops
285g (10 oz) (2 cups) each parsnips and carrots, peeled and sliced
1 tablespoon sunflower oil
150g (5 oz) (scant 2 cups) chestnut mushrooms, sliced and halved
20 juniper berries, well bruised
1 tablespoon port
2 good pinches dried thyme/1 teaspoon fresh thyme leaves
285ml (10 fl oz) (1¼ cups) parsnip and carrot water plus 1 gluten-free chicken/vegetable stock (bouillon) cube
sea salt and freshly ground black pepper
1 tablespoon arrowroot powder

Preheat the grill (broiler) to high. Lightly oil and season the pork chops, grill (broil) each side until cooked – about 20 minutes.

Add the parsnips and carrots to lightly salted boiling water and simmer until tender. Drain, reserving the water.

While the vegetables are cooking, warm the oil in a large non-stick frying pan (skillet), add the mushrooms and cook for about 2 minutes turning them over from time to time. Add the juniper berries and port and sizzle together for 1 minute. Add the thyme. Pour in all but

2 tablespoons of the reserved measured vegetable water, stock (bouillon) cube and seasoning. Mix the arrowroot powder into the 2 tablespoons of cooled vegetable water and add to the pan. Bring to the boil stirring, turn to low and cook for 1 minute. Serve with the parsnips and carrots. Pour the juniper sauce over the chops.

SERVING SUGGESTION: serve with new/mashed potatoes or mixed whole grain red Camargue and wild rice.

Pork Paprika Casserole

For this recipe, try to obtain red Hungarian paprika if you can, it has a far superior flavour.

SERVES 4 | PREPARATION TIME – 35 MINUTES PLUS 80 MINUTES FOR COOKING

4 medium vine tomatoes, halved
700g (1½ lb) diced leg/shoulder pork
1–2 tablespoons sunflower oil
1 large onion, sliced thickly
1 large clove garlic, crushed
½ teaspoon caraway seeds, partially ground
1 rounded tablespoon paprika
¾ tablespoon potato flour (farina)
1 tablespoon tomato purée (paste)
1 medium red pepper, cored, deseeded and sliced thickly
270ml (9½ fl oz) (1 cup plus 2 tablespoons) beef stock (bouillon)/hot water plus 1 gluten-free beef/vegetable stock (bouillon) cube
2 pinches sea salt

sour cream:

3 rounded tablespoons plain soya yoghurt
½ tablespoon lemon juice

Preheat the grill (broiler) to high. Grill (broil) the tomatoes, skin side up, until the skins are blistered. When cool enough, peel away the skins.

Preheat the oven to 170°C (325°F) (gas mark 3).

Stir-fry small batches of pork at a time, each with a little of the oil. Turn frequently over a high heat to seal in the juices. Remove to a plate.

Turn the heat to low. Add the onion and garlic, adding a little more oil. Cook for about 3 minutes. Add the prepared tomatoes and caraway seeds, cooking for a further 2 minutes. Remove from the heat. Stir in the paprika and flour, then the tomato purée (paste), red pepper and stock (bouillon). Season with salt. Return the pork to the pan and combine well. Bring to the boil, stirring then cook for 1 minute.

Turn into a 1.7 litre (3 pint) ovenproof casserole dish, cover with a close-fitting lid, or foil between the dish and lid. Cook in the oven for 70–80 minutes.

For the sour cream, mix the lemon juice into the yoghurt then stir briskly until smooth. Stir 2 tablespoons of the paprika sauce into the sour cream then stir it all into the casserole and serve.

SERVING SUGGESTION: serve with jacket potatoes/rice and vegetables.

Spaghetti Carbonara

Many flavours combine for a tasty but cheeseless 'carbonara'.

SERVES 2 | PREPARATION TIME – 45 MINUTES

2 pinches celery seeds
3 pinches dried rosemary
1 pinch freshly grated nutmeg
sea salt and freshly ground black pepper
1½ large free-range eggs
2 tablespoons soya cream
5 drops natural vanilla extract
155g (5½ oz) gluten-free corn and rice spaghetti

| ½ tablespoon olive oil |
| 1 small onion, sliced finely and diced |
| 1 clove garlic, crushed |
| 220g (7½ oz) de-rinded lean smoked/unsmoked middle bacon, cut into pieces – 5 or 6 rashers |
| 4 tablespoons white wine |
| 1 tablespoon dairy-free margarine |
| 1 tablespoon freshly cut parsley |

Grind the celery seeds, rosemary, nutmeg and seasoning with a pestle and mortar. Add a quarter teaspoon of the herbs and seasonings to a small basin together with the eggs, cream and vanilla extract. Beat well.

Bring plenty of lightly salted water to the boil in a large saucepan. Add the spaghetti, stir to separate and simmer for about 8–10 minutes until just tender. Drain and rinse with boiling water. Drain again.

While the spaghetti is simmering, warm the oil in a large non-stick frying pan (skillet). Soften the onion and garlic over a low heat for 2 minutes without burning. Add the bacon pieces and remaining herbs and seasonings. Stir together over a high heat until the bacon is just cooked. Add the wine, bring to the boil and boil rapidly, stirring until wine has evaporated – about 3–5 minutes, and the bacon just showing a hint of crispness.

Add the bacon mixture to the drained spaghetti together with the margarine and toss together. Add the egg mixture, return to a very low heat and stir continuously for about 30–40 seconds to cook through the egg without scrambling, to form a slightly thicker sauce. Serve immediately. Garnish with parsley.

SERVING SUGGESTION: crush a little garlic and spread onto a thin slice of gluten-free crusty white bread. Drizzle with a good quality extra virgin olive oil, season and toast under the grill (broiler). Serve with a fresh crisp, mixed side salad.

Grated pecorino sheep's cheese (romano) can be sprinkled over the carbonara, if tolerated as part of a low-lactose diet.

Turkey & Ham Risotto

It's a good idea to have all your ingredients ready before making the risotto because it's difficult to leave the risotto while you're constantly stirring!

To cook a joint of gammon/ham in advance of making the meal – place the gammon/ham in cold water and bring to the boil, drain then bring to the boil again in fresh water (this removes excess salt). Add a bay leaf, a piece of carrot and celery to the water and simmer for 25–30 minutes per 455g (1 lb) plus 30 minutes. Leave to cool in the cooking liquor then remove, wrap and refrigerate. Reserve enough cooking liquor for the meal and refrigerate if not using immediately.

SERVES 4 | PREPARATION TIME – 70 MINUTES

sunflower oil
200g (7 oz) fresh diced turkey breast
½ medium yellow pepper, deseeded, sliced thinly and diced
½ medium red pepper, deseeded, sliced thinly and diced
½ medium green pepper, deseeded, sliced thinly and diced
5 rounded tablespoons non-dairy alternative to full-fat soft cheese
3 tablespoons soya cream
1 tablespoon dairy-free margarine
1 medium onion, sliced thinly and diced
1 stick celery, sliced lengthways and thinly diced
1 large clove garlic, crushed
2 rashers lean smoked middle bacon, rind and fat removed, cut into pieces
250g (9 oz) (1 cup plus 1½ tablespoons) Arborio/Carnaroli risotto rice
170ml (6 fl oz) (⅔ cup) white wine
540ml (19 fl oz) (2¼ cups) gammon/ham cooking

liquor/hot vegetable stock (bouillon) plus 1 gluten-free chicken/vegetable stock (bouillon) cube

salt and freshly ground black pepper

200g (7 oz) home boiled gammon/roast ham, cut into 2cm (¾") dice

1 tablespoon each freshly cut sage and lemon thyme

freshly cut mustard and cress to garnish

If lemon thyme is not available, thyme may be used.

Warm a little oil in a large non-stick frying pan (skillet). Stir-fry the turkey over a fairly high heat, turning frequently to seal in the juices. Turn to low and continue to cook until tender. Remove to a plate. Add the prepared peppers to the pan but do not cook until the risotto is finished.

Blend the soft cheese and cream together in a small saucepan until smooth. Leave to one side.

Melt the margarine in a large saucepan. Soften the onion, celery and garlic over a low heat for 2 minutes. Add the bacon and stir until opaque. Add the rice, stirring until translucent and well coated. Pour in the wine, and over a medium heat continue stirring until just absorbed by the rice. Add a third of the cooking liquor/stock (bouillon) and stock (bouillon) cube, stirring continuously over a lowish to medium heat until absorbed. Continue stirring in a third of the stock (bouillon) at a time until absorbed but not dry. This should take about 20 minutes and the grain should be just cooked. Remove from the heat. Season. Add the cooked turkey, gammon/ham, sage and lemon thyme. Stir until well mixed.

Stir-fry the diced peppers briefly in oil over a high heat. Warm the blended soft cheese and cream then stir into the risotto. Add the peppers and mix evenly. Serve immediately. Garnish with plenty of mustard and cress.

SERVING SUGGESTION: serve with a side salad or lightly cooked green beans.

Vegetarian & Vegetables

Black-eyed Bean & Lentil Stew with Dumplings

Root vegetables and beans provide plenty of complex, carbohydrates, soluble fibre, protein, iron, and potassium for a low-fat, balanced and satisfying meal. Extra portions of the stew can be cooled and frozen for an easy meal another time. If you have any previously cooked and frozen Sweet Potato and Swede Cakes (*see page 106*), these make a quick alternative to making dumplings. Just thicken the stew at the end of cooking and reheat the thawed potato cakes.

SERVES 4 | PREPARATION TIME – 50 MINUTES PLUS 15 MINUTES FOR FINAL SIMMERING

50g (1¾ oz) (3 tablespoons) puy lentils
425ml (15 fl oz) (1¾ cups) cold water
1 medium onion, sliced and diced
1½ sticks celery, sliced lengthways and diced
140g (5 oz) (scant 1 cup) carrots, peeled, sliced and diced
100g (3½ oz) (generous ⅔ cup) turnip, peeled, sliced and diced
100g (3½ oz) (generous ⅔ cup) swede, peeled, sliced and diced
1 pinch whole aniseeds, partially ground

300g (10½ oz) tin black-eyed beans, rinsed and drained

sea salt and freshly ground black pepper

2 tablespoons gluten-free yellow bean sauce/plum sauce

Brown or green lentils can be used as an alternative to puy lentils.

dumplings:

25g (1 oz) (2¾ tablespoons) stoneground/brown rice flour

25g (1 oz) (3 tablespoons) gram flour

10g (½ oz) (1 tablespoon) potato flour (farina)

1 teaspoon gluten-free baking powder

sea salt and freshly ground black pepper

20g (¾ oz) gluten-free shredded vegetable suet

1 tablespoon finely cut flat-leaf parsley/coriander (cilantro) leaves

2½ tablespoons water

Rinse the lentils well, in a sieve, under cold running water. Place in a small saucepan with the water, bring to the boil and boil rapidly, uncovered, for 10 minutes. Reduce the heat, cover and simmer gently for 30 minutes. Drain any remaining liquid. Rinse, drain well and leave to one side.

Meanwhile, bring 685ml (24 fl oz) (2¾ cups plus 1½ tablespoons) water to the boil in a large saucepan. Add the prepared onion, celery, carrot, turnip, swede and aniseeds. Cover, return to the boil and simmer for 10 minutes until vegetables are tender. Remove from the heat and leave to one side until required.

For the dumplings, sieve and mix the flours into a mixing bowl together with the baking powder and seasoning. Stir in the suet, parsley/coriander (cilantro) and bring the mixture together with the water. Shape into 8 dumplings.

Add the lentils and beans to the vegetables together with the seasoning. Stir and bring back to the boil. Place the dumplings on the surface of the stew. Return to the boil, cover and simmer gently for 15 minutes.

Carefully remove the dumplings. Stir in yellow bean/plum sauce. Serve. Garnish with a little freshly cut parsley/coriander (cilantro).

Celery, Leek & Fennel Quiche

This quiche can also be made for non-vegetarians with the addition of some lightly fried bacon scattered over the pastry base.

SERVES 3–4 AS A MAIN MEAL, 4 AS A SNACK
PREPARATION TIME – 45 MINUTES PLUS 40 MINUTES FOR COOKING

1 medium inner stick celery, sliced thinly
½ medium fennel bulb, trimmed, triangular core removed, sliced thinly and chopped, reserving the feathery leaves
½ tablespoon dairy-free margarine/sunflower oil
50g (1¾ oz) (⅔ cup) leek (light to yellow part only), sliced thinly
¼ teaspoon each celery and fennel seeds, ground
¾ teaspoon gluten-free Dijon mustard
a little cheddar-style soya cheese (*optional*)
3 large free-range eggs
210ml (7½ fl oz) (¾ cup plus 1 tablespoon) unsweetened soya milk
sea salt and freshly ground black/white pepper
5cm (2") piece courgette (zucchini)

pastry:

125g (4½ oz) (generous ¾ cup) rice flour
20g (¾ oz) (2 tablespoons) potato flour (farina)
20g (¾ oz) (3¾ tablespoons) soya flour
10g (½ oz) (1½ tablespoons) millet flakes
¼ teaspoon gluten-free baking powder
¼ teaspoon xanthum gum

80g (2¾ oz) (5 tablespoons) dairy-free margarine, straight from the fridge
2¼–2½ tablespoons cold water

Sieve the flours into a mixing bowl. Add the millet flakes, baking powder and xanthum gum. Mix together, then rub in the margarine lightly with the fingertips until it resembles fine breadcrumbs. Add the water then cut and stir into the mixture with a knife until it is the consistency of soft, damp to wettish pastry. Bring together into a dough with the hands. Flour the work surface and rolling pin with rice flour then turn the dough onto the surface. Roll out on a floured surface and line the base and sides of a greased 18cm (7") non-stick sponge/flan tin.

Preheat the oven to 180°C (350°F) (gas mark 4).

Add the celery and fennel to lightly salted boiling water and simmer until just cooked. Drain, reserving the cooking liquid. Pat dry with absorbent kitchen paper towel.

Melt the margarine/sunflower oil in a large non-stick frying pan (skillet). Add the leek with celery seeds, fennel seeds and a pinch of salt. Soften for about 6–7 minutes over a low heat without colouring. Turn into the pastry base, cover with celery and fennel and dot with mustard. Crumble over a little soya cheese.

Beat the eggs in a basin. Stir in the soya milk and seasoning. Pour over the vegetables.

With a vegetable peeler, slice thin strips of courgette (zucchini). Place the strips to form an inner and outer ring over the custard, to radiate out like sun rays. Cook in the oven for 30–40 minutes until the custard has risen and coloured.

SERVING SUGGESTION: serve hot with Jersey mids/new potatoes and White Onion Sauce (*see page 225*), using 140ml (5 fl oz) (½ cup plus 1 tablespoon) reserved fennel/celery vegetable water, adding a tablespoon of fennel leaves when the sauce is cooked. Alternatively, serve with salad.

A little vegetarian mature cheddar/pecorino sheep's cheese (romano) can be grated over the vegetable layer if tolerated as part of a low-lactose diet, prior to baking.

Fresh Tomato Sauce

This is an extremely versatile sauce as it can be served with chargrilled roasted Mediterranean vegetables, meatballs or a savoury tofu meal. Excess portions can be frozen then thawed at a later date for use in Lasagne with Courgette (zucchini) & Aubergine (*see page 95*).

SERVES 2 AS A BROTH, SERVES 4 USING HALF THE MIXTURE FOR TOPPING FRESH HERB SCONE PIZZA (*SEE PAGE 116*), SERVES 2–4 BLENDED FOR A THICK SMOOTH SAUCE WITH GLUTEN-FREE SPAGHETTI OR PASTA SPIRALS PREPARATION TIME – 20 MINUTES PLUS 30 MINUTES FOR SIMMERING

565g (1¼ lb) ripe vine tomatoes (or plum vine tomatoes)
¾ tablespoon olive oil
1 small onion, sliced finely and diced
1 clove garlic, crushed
1 bay leaf
1 rounded teaspoon tomato purée (paste)
salt and freshly ground black pepper
freshly cut basil/oregano to garnish

Bring a large saucepan of water to the boil. Drop each tomato into the boiling water for about 45 seconds to split/loosen the skins. Remove from the saucepan. Peel when cool enough to handle, then halve, slice and dice.

Warm the oil in a small saucepan. Add the onion and garlic. Soften over a very low heat for about 4 minutes, stirring occasionally. Do not allow to colour. Add the tomatoes, bay leaf, tomato purée (paste) and seasoning. Bring to the boil, cover and simmer for about 15–20 minutes, stirring occasionally, until soft. Uncover and continue to simmer for a further 5–10 minutes, stirring occasionally, to thicken. Remove the bay leaf. Either serve as a thick broth or liquidize for a smooth soup/sauce. Garnish with basil/oregano.

Pecorino sheep's cheese (romano) could be grated over the top, if this is tolerated as part of a low-lactose diet.

Kidney Bean & Vegetable Risotto

This is an extremely colourful and appetizing wholefood energy meal – unrefined and full of protein and protective fibre. When making it, look for tinned kidney beans without added sugar or salt. The parsley and some garlic are added immediately before serving to preserve the precious health-giving nutrients.

SERVES 4 | PREPARATION TIME – 1 HOUR

3 tablespoons olive oil
1 large onion, sliced and diced
3 small cloves garlic, crushed
175g (6 oz) (¾ cup plus 1 tablespoon) whole grain brown rice
600ml (21 fl oz) (2½ cups) hot water plus 1 gluten-free vegetable stock (bouillon) cube
sea salt and freshly ground black pepper
1 large red pepper, cored, deseeded, sliced and diced
2 large sticks celery, sliced
250g (9 oz) (3 cups) small button/closed-cap chestnut mushrooms, sliced thinly
75g (3 oz) (generous ½ cup) unsalted cashew nuts
425g (15 oz) tin red kidney beans in water, drained and rinsed
4 heaped tablespoons freshly cut parsley
watercress and salad leaves and/or mixed sprouting seeds and beans to serve

For a variation of rice, a mixture of whole grain, red Camargue and wild rice can be used.

Warm half the oil in a large saucepan. Soften the onion, stirring occasionally over a low heat – about 5 minutes. Stir in one of the cloves of garlic and cook for a further 2 minutes. Add the rice, stirring until well coated with the oil. Add the water and stock (bouillon) cube, season then bring to the boil, stirring from time to time. Simmer, covered, for 35–45 minutes until stock has been absorbed (adding the other ingredients at intervals whilst cooking, as below).

When the risotto has been simmering for 20 minutes warm the remaining oil in a large non-stick frying pan (skillet). Add the red pepper and celery, stir-fry for 5 minutes. Mix in the mushrooms and another clove of garlic and stir-fry for a further 4–5 minutes.

Lightly toast the nuts and reserve.

When the stock has just been absorbed by the rice, remove from the heat and add the vegetables. Add the well-drained kidney beans and nuts. Stir to combine and return to a very low heat, stirring, to warm through without burning. Remove from the heat, stir in the parsley and remaining clove of garlic. Serve immediately with watercress and salad leaves and/or mixed sprouting seeds and beans.

Lasagne with Courgette & Aubergine

This lasagne can be made with Fresh Tomato Sauce (*see page 93*) for an excellent flavour but tinned tomatoes provide a convenient alternative.

Serves 4 | Preparation time – 55 minutes plus 30 minutes for cooking

1 tablespoon olive oil
1 small onion, thinly sliced and diced
1 large clove garlic, crushed
170g (6 oz) (2⅓–2½ cups) aubergines (eggplants), 1cm (½") sliced and diced
370g (13 oz) (2¾ cups) courgettes (zucchini), 1cm (½") sliced and diced
1½ sticks celery, 1cm (½") sliced
400g (14 oz) tin chopped tomatoes
4 tablespoons carrot juice
½ teaspoon dried rosemary

sea salt and freshly ground black pepper
400ml (14 fl oz) (1⅔ cups) unsweetened soya milk
2 whole cloves
1 bay leaf
1 pinch freshly grated nutmeg
100g (3½ oz) gluten-free lasagne sheets
1 tablespoon dairy-free margarine
1 good rounded tablespoon gluten-free cornflour (cornstarch)
110g (4 oz) (generous ¾ cup) mature cheddar-style soya cheese, crumbled
¾ teaspoon dried rosemary

Warm half the oil in a large non-stick frying pan (skillet). Add the onion and garlic and cook together for about 3 minutes. Add the aubergines (eggplants), courgettes (zucchini) and celery to the pan together with the remaining oil. Stir-fry together over a moderate heat for about 4 minutes. Reduce the heat to low and add the chopped tomatoes with their juices, carrot juice, rosemary and seasoning. Turn into a saucepan, cover and simmer together, stirring occasionally, for a further 15 minutes.

Preheat the oven to 200°C (400°F) (gas mark 6).

While the vegetables are simmering, add the milk, cloves, bay leaf and nutmeg to a small saucepan. Slowly bring to boiling point. Remove from the heat and leave to infuse for a few minutes.

Meanwhile, half fill a large saucepan with lightly salted water and bring to the boil. Add the pasta. Return to the boil and pre-cook for a minute. Drain, rinse with cold water, drain again and separate the sheets.

Melt the margarine in the milk, add the cornflour (cornstarch) then return to the boil, stirring. Reduce the heat and cook for 1 minute. Season to taste and remove the cloves and bay leaf.

Layer half the vegetables in their sauce in the base of a greased lasagne or similar ovenproof dish – minimum capacity 1.7 litre (3 pint). Arrange half the lasagne sheets over the vegetables. Spoon 5 tablespoons of the white sauce over the lasagne sheets. Repeat the vegetable and pasta layers. Finely crumble the soya cheese over the pasta and then pour over the sauce. Sprinkle with rosemary. Cook in the oven for 25–30 minutes.

SERVING SUGGESTION: serve with an Italian-style salad.

Lentil Curry Sauce

The sauce is delicious served with Quinoa Spiced Nut Cutlets, (*see page 104*), making it a complete protein meal – especially useful for vegetarians. It could equally be served over halved boiled eggs, cooked vegetables or plain grilled (broiled) meats if not vegetarian. The recipe makes a mild – medium nourishing curry sauce. Like other legumes, protein-rich lentils are high in iron, calcium, magnesium, phosphorus, potassium and B vitamins. The soluble fibre content helps to reduce blood cholesterol levels.

SERVES 4–5 | PREPARATION TIME – 15 MINUTES PLUS 30 MINUTES FOR COOKING

1 tablespoon groundnut oil
1 large onion, sliced and diced
2 cloves garlic, crushed
1cm (½") piece fresh root ginger, peeled and chopped finely
½ teaspoon chilli powder
1 teaspoon ground coriander (cilantro)
1 teaspoon ground cumin
½ teaspoon ground fennel
1 teaspoon paprika
425ml (15 fl oz) (1¾ cups) hot water plus ½ gluten-free vegetable stock (bouillon) cube
90g (3¼ oz) (6 tablespoons) split red lentils
200g (7 oz) (½ large tin) chopped tomatoes

| 2.5cm (1") cube creamed coconut |
| 1 rounded tablespoon plain soya yoghurt |

Warm the oil in a small saucepan. Add the onion and fry over a low heat for 3 minutes, stirring occasionally without colouring. Stir in the garlic, ginger, chilli powder, spices and paprika. Cook together stirring for a further 1 minute. Add the water and stock (bouillon) cube, lentils, tomatoes and their juices, then bring to the boil. Reduce to a low heat. Simmer, covered, for 25–30 minutes stirring occasionally until lentils are tender. Stir in the creamed coconut until dissolved. Liquidize then stir in the yoghurt. Serve.

Goats' milk yoghurt (if tolerated as part of a low-lactose diet) can be used as an alternative to soya yoghurt.

Macaroni Cheese

This is not a lactose-free recipe (i.e. not dairy free), but a low-lactose version using mature cheddar cheese (if tolerated as part of a low-lactose diet) and soya milk. For another delicious low-lactose variation using goats' cheese and milk, see the end of the recipe.

SERVES 2 | PREPARATION TIME – 13 MINUTES

| 110g (4 oz) (1 cup) gluten-free corn and buckwheat macaroni |
| 425ml (15 fl oz) (1¾ cups) unsweetened soya milk |
| 25 ml (1 fl oz) (1½ tablespoons) water |
| 1 tablespoon dairy-free margarine |
| 1 rounded *and* 1 almost rounded tablespoon gluten-free cornflour (cornstarch) |
| 1 rounded teaspoon gluten-free whole grain mustard |
| sea salt and freshly ground black pepper |
| 130g (4½ oz) (1 cup) vegetarian mature cheddar cheese, grated |

2 grilled tomatoes to garnish

2 slices Crusty White Bread (*see page 115*)/other gluten-free bread

Bring plenty of lightly salted water to the boil in a large saucepan. Add the macaroni, return to the boil and simmer until cooked, according to instructions.

Meanwhile, heat the milk, water and margarine to just melt the margarine, then mix in the cornflour (cornstarch), stirring constantly to boiling point. Turn to low and simmer for 1 minute. Remove from the heat. Stir in the mustard, seasoning and cheese to melt.

Grill (broil) the tomatoes.

Toast the bread, spread with margarine and cut into triangles.

Add the cooked, drained pasta to the cheese sauce and mix well. Pile onto plates and decorate with the toast triangles and tomatoes.

Goats' milk/cheese version

All Goats' Milk Processors Federation (GMPF) cheeses are suitable for vegetarians as the rennet used does not come from animal sources.

110g (4 oz) (1 cup) gluten-free corn and buckwheat macaroni

455ml (16 fl oz) (2 cups less 1 tablespoon) pasteurised goats' milk

1 tablespoon dairy-free margarine

1 rounded *and* 1 almost rounded tablespoon gluten-free cornflour (cornstarch)

1 almost rounded teaspoon gluten-free whole grain mustard

sea salt and freshly ground black pepper

110g (4 oz) (¾ cup) goats' cheddar cheese grated

2 grilled tomatoes to garnish

2 slices Crusty White Bread (*see page 115*)/other gluten-free bread

Make as the recipe given above.

Moussaka with Aubergine & Porcini Mushrooms

I have used small TVP (textured vegetable protein) for this dish, which vaguely resembles minced (ground) beef when cooked. TVP – a soya product – is also available in larger chunks, in natural or flavoured form.

SERVES 2–3 AS A MAIN MEAL OR 4 AS A SNACK WITH SALAD
PREPARATION TIME – 55 MINUTES PLUS 45 MINUTES FOR COOKING

1 aubergine (eggplant), weighing 350g (12 oz), cut into 8mm (⅜") slices
210ml (7½ fl oz) (¾ cup plus 1 tablespoon) warm water plus ¾ gluten-free vegetable stock (bouillon) cube
1 heaped tablespoon tomato purée (paste)
10g (½ oz) (generous ⅓ cup) dried porcini mushrooms, cut into small pieces
50g (1¾ oz) (⅔ cup) natural unflavoured small TVP mince
1 rounded teaspoon mixed dried herbs
¾ teaspoon ground cinnamon
sea salt and freshly ground black pepper
½ tablespoon olive oil
1 large onion, sliced and diced
1 large clove garlic, crushed

sauce:

50g (1¾ oz) (3 tablespoons) dairy-free margarine
485ml (17 fl oz) (2 cups) unsweetened soya milk, reserving 3 tablespoons
30g (1 oz) (1 heaped tablespoon) gluten-free cornflour (cornstarch)
50g (1¾ oz) (2½ tablespoons) mature cheddar-style soya cheese, crumbled
1 large free-range egg, beaten

½ teaspoon freshly grated nutmeg

sea salt and freshly ground black pepper

Sprinkle the aubergine (eggplant) slices with salt in a colander and leave for 30–40 minutes to remove excess moisture. Rinse well and pat dry.

Meanwhile mix the water, stock (bouillon) cube and tomato purée (paste) in a basin. Add the mushrooms and stir. Add the mince, herbs, cinnamon, seasoning and stir together.

Preheat the oven to 180°C (350°F) (gas mark 4).

Warm the oil in a large non-stick frying pan (skillet). Fry the onion and garlic over a low heat for a few minutes until onions are slightly coloured. Add the mince mixture, mix well and warm through.

Place half of the aubergines in a layer in the base of a greased 1.7 litre (3 pint) ovenproof dish. Cover with the mince and then the remaining aubergines.

For the sauce, melt the margarine in a medium saucepan, add most of the milk and heat. Mix the cornflour (cornstarch) with the reserved milk then add to the saucepan. Bring to the boil, stirring, then simmer for 1 minute. Remove from the heat. Mix in the cheese then beat in the egg briskly until smooth. Add the nutmeg and seasoning. Pour over the aubergines. Cook in the oven for 40–45 minutes until golden.

Goats' cheddar cheese can be used instead of soya cheese, if tolerated as part of a low-lactose diet.

Onion Bhajias with Dipping Sauce

Bhajias are appetizing little morsels and versatile too. Serve them as a starter or snack, or with plain grilled (broiled) meats or vegetarian meals. They freeze well when cooked – thaw and reheat gently under the grill (broiler) when required.

MAKES 17 SMALL BHAJIAS

PREPARATION TIME – 25 MINUTES PLUS 6 MINUTES PER BATCH FOR COOKING

170g (6 oz) (1¾ cups) onions, peeled, quartered and sliced finely

1 teaspoon each ground cumin and ground coriander (cilantro)

¼ teaspoon each ground fennel and turmeric

¼ teaspoon sea salt and freshly ground black pepper

2 rounded tablespoons freshly cut coriander (cilantro) leaves*

85g (3 oz) (¾ cup plus 1½ tablespoons) gram flour, sieved

4 tablespoons water

2 rounded tablespoons plain soya yoghurt

1 teaspoon lemon juice

vegetable/sunflower oil for deep frying

slices lime to garnish

dipping sauce:

2 heaped tablespoons plain soya yoghurt

¼ teaspoon turmeric

1 clove garlic, crushed

1 rounded tablespoon freshly cut coriander (cilantro) leaves*

sea salt and freshly ground black pepper

few drops lime juice (*optional*)

Or use a combination of coriander (cilantro) and mint leaves, for the bhajias and dipping sauce.

Add the onion, cumin, coriander (cilantro), fennel, turmeric, seasoning and coriander (cilantro) leaves to a small basin. Stir together to separate the onion slices. Add the flour, water, yoghurt and lemon juice then stir thoroughly.

Heat the oil for deep-frying. Slide level tablespoons of the mixture into the hot oil, cooking in batches of 4. Cook over a low to medium heat for about 6 minutes, turning once. When golden, remove with a slotted spoon and drain thoroughly on absorbent kitchen paper. Keep warm until all the bhajias are cooked.

Mix together the ingredients for the dipping sauce.
Serve the bhajias with the dipping sauce and lime slices to garnish.

SERVING SUGGESTION: serve with a simple green salad of diced cucumber, shredded lettuce and freshly podded peas, garnished with fresh coriander (cilantro) leaves and a few drops of lime juice.

Quick Pepper & Tofu Stir-fry

Briefly stir-frying the peppers and adding the orange juice at the end of cooking preserves precious vitamin C.

SERVES 2 | PREPARATION TIME – 35 MINUTES

150g (5½ oz) firm tofu
2¼–2½ tablespoons sunflower/groundnut oil
1 medium onion, sliced thinly
1 large green pepper, deseeded, sliced thickly and cut diagonally
½ large orange pepper, deseeded, sliced thickly and cut diagonally
2 rounded tablespoons unsalted cashew nuts
1 tablespoon orange juice
a few drops sesame oil (*optional*)

marinade:

2 tablespoons gluten-free soy sauce
2 teaspoons gluten-free sweet chilli sauce
1 teaspoon black strap molasses
1 clove garlic, crushed

Drain the liquid from the tofu and place on absorbent kitchen paper. Cut into 1cm (½") cubes and leave on the paper to drain.

Blend the marinade ingredients together in a small dish. Add the tofu and coat thoroughly. Leave for 20 minutes to marinate.

Meanwhile, warm half the oil in a wok or frying pan (skillet) and stir-fry the onion over a low to moderate heat, until lightly browned – about 5 minutes. Leave to one side.
Stir-fry the peppers in half the remaining oil until lightly cooked – but still retaining their bite. Leave to one side.
Add the tofu and nuts to the pan, reserving the marinade. Stir-fry in the remaining oil over a moderate heat – about 3 minutes. Return onion and peppers to the pan. Add the marinade and warm through over a low heat. Remove from the heat and stir in the orange juice. Serve. Sprinkle with sesame oil, if using.

SERVING SUGGESTION: serve with stir-fried beansprouts or home-grown 'leggy' fenugreek/mung bean sprouts.

Quinoa Spiced Nut Cutlets

These cutlets are good served with Lentil Curry Sauce (*see page 97*), poppadums (gluten-free, dairy-free) and a crisp salad. Quinoa, the ancient grain of the high Andes, has a significantly higher content of protein than other grains, vegetables or soya, so it is especially valuable for vegetarians and vegans. There are excellent levels of calcium, iron, B vitamins and vitamin E. They freeze well, uncooked or cooked.

SERVES 2 AS A MAIN MEAL, 4 AS A SNACK, 8 AS A STARTER
PREPARATION TIME – 35 MINUTES PLUS 6 MINUTES PER BATCH FOR FRYING

| 140ml (5 fl oz) (½ cup plus 1 tablespoon) water |
| 25g (1 oz) (3½ tablespoons) quinoa flakes |
| 50g (2 oz) (⅓ cup) whole hazelnuts |
| 25g (1 oz) 10 whole brazil nuts |
| 25g (1 oz) 24 whole almonds |
| 1 large onion |
| 1 stick celery |

1 clove garlic, flattened and peeled
½ tablespoon groundnut oil
1 teaspoon ground coriander (cilantro)
1 teaspoon ground cumin
½ gluten-free vegetable stock (bouillon) cube
sea salt and freshly ground black pepper
1 rounded tablespoon stoneground/brown rice flour

Bring the water to the boil in a small saucepan. Add quinoa, cover and simmer until water is absorbed – about 4–5 minutes. Leave covered until required.

Preheat the grill (broiler) to high. Using a food processor, briefly chop the nuts, then lightly toast them. Leave to one side.

Finely process the onion, celery and garlic. Warm the oil in a large non-stick frying pan (skillet) then fry the onion mixture over a low heat for 4–5 minutes stirring occasionally. Add the spices and crumbled half stock (bouillon) cube, stir and cook for 1 further minute. Return to the food processor together with the nuts, and seasoning. Process well. Turn into a large basin.

Fluff up the quinoa with a fork and add to the mixture. Stir in the flour and mix well. Shape into 8 balls. Flatten into 1–1.5cm (½–⅝") cutlets. Fry in a little more oil over a low to moderate heat for 3–4 minutes each side until golden brown. Serve.

Quinoa Herb Nut Cutlets:

Replace coriander (cilantro) and cumin with 1 rounded teaspoon each dried basil and oregano, use olive oil instead of groundnut oil. Serve with Fresh Tomato Sauce (*see page 93*).

Stir-fried Carrots, Courgettes & Peas, with Lime & Coriander

This is a really fresh, simple vegetable stir-fry and will make a good accompaniment to Chicken Curry with Banana (*see page 66*) or Rainbow Trout with Honey, Lime & Ginger (*see page 51*).

Serves 2 | Preparation time – 12 minutes

75g (3 oz) (¾ cup) carrots, sliced at 2.5cm (1") intervals, cut into julienne (thin matchsticks)
75g (3 oz) (¾ cup) courgette (zucchini), sliced at 2.5cm (1") intervals, cut into julienne
a little sunflower/groundnut oil
about 35g (1½ oz) (3 rounded tablespoons) freshly podded peas
sea salt and freshly ground pepper
a squeeze of lime juice
freshly cut coriander (cilantro) leaves to garnish

Stir-fry the carrots and courgettes (zucchini) over a high heat in a little oil for about 2–3 minutes turning frequently. Add the peas for a minute just before serving. Lightly season if necessary. Serve. Squeeze over a few drops of lime juice and garnish with a few coriander (cilantro) leaves.

Sweet Potato Cakes

These potato cakes make a pleasant change from plain boiled potatoes and go well with fish, meat or vegetarian dishes. They freeze well when they are cooked. See the variations below for Sweet Potato & Parsnip Cakes and Sweet Potato & Swede Cakes. All the potato cakes are good with poached eggs or egg, bacon, sausage and beans. Sweet potatoes are a healthy source of antioxidants, being rich in vitamin A (from beta-carotene) and vitamins C and E.

Serves 4 | Preparation time – 30 minutes plus 8 minutes per batch for frying

250g (9 oz) (scant 2 cups) sweet potatoes, peeled and chopped into even-sized pieces
250g (9 oz) (scant 2 cups) potatoes, peeled and chopped into even-sized pieces

| 1 teaspoon dairy-free margarine |
| sea salt and freshly ground black pepper |
| 4 tablespoons rice flour |
| extra rice flour and freshly ground black pepper for dusting |

Add the potatoes to boiling water (in separate saucepans). Return to the boil, simmer until tender then drain really well. Mash both potatoes together with the margarine and seasoning. Work in the flour. Shape into 12 balls when cool enough to handle. Roll them in the seasoned flour and flatten slightly into patties.

Warm a little margarine or sunflower oil in a large non-stick frying pan (skillet). Fry the potato cakes over a medium heat for about 4 minutes each side – adding more margarine/oil if necessary when turning, until golden brown on both sides.

Sweet Potato and Parsnip Cakes: make as above and for a slightly spicy alternative, add ½ teaspoon gluten-free, dairy-free curry powder to the mashed vegetables with the flour – they are good with curries.

Sweet Potato and Swede Cakes: make as above and add ½ teaspoon ground cinnamon to the mashed vegetables with the flour – they are good with Moussaka with Aubergine & Porcini Mushrooms (*see page 100*) or Rainbow Trout with Honey, Lime & Ginger Sauce (*see page 51*).

The combined vegetable water from the sweet potatoes, parsnip and swede is quite delicious – especially good to drink if organic vegetables are chosen. Or use for vegetable stock (bouillon).

Tagliatelle with Crimini Mushrooms & Tapenade

An almost instant pasta dish with home-made blitzed tapenade. The bottled whole, sweet piquanté peppers are really worth looking for as they perfectly balance warm, spicy and sweet flavours in this Mediterranean tagliatelle. They can be found in good supermarkets. If the piquanté peppers are unobtainable, substitute with fresh mild red chilli or failing that ¼–½ teaspoon crumbled dried chilli when stir-frying the mushrooms and garlic.

SERVES 4 | PREPARATION TIME – 30 MINUTES

455–485g (16–17 oz) gluten-free dried tagliatelle (or any other ribbon pasta such as fettuccini)

3–3½ tablespoons extra virgin olive oil

500g (17½ oz) (5¾ cups) crimini mushrooms*, sliced

1 clove garlic, crushed

9–10 bottled whole sweet piquanté peppers (red, roundish and warmly hot), sliced finely

Crimini mushrooms are a chestnut button variety.

tapenade:

70g (2½ oz) (¾ cup) stoned (pitted) black olives

3 tablespoons extra virgin olive oil

scant ½ tablespoon lemon juice

5cm (2") sprig fresh rosemary, leaves removed

2 very large fresh basil leaves

sea salt and freshly ground black pepper

Place the tapenade ingredients in a food processor and process until a small bitty consistency is reached.

Add the pasta to plenty of lightly salted boiling water, stir then simmer for 10–12 minutes until just cooked.

While the pasta is cooking, warm 1¼ tablespoons of the oil in a large non-stick frying pan (skillet). Add the mushrooms and garlic. Stir-fry together over a high heat for about 4–5 minutes until the mushroom juices have evaporated. Reduce the heat, add the sweet peppers briefly to warm through, also half of the tapenade.

Drain the pasta, return to the saucepan, then mix in the remaining oil. Stir in the mushrooms, sweet peppers and tapenade. Pile onto plates and sprinkle with the remaining tapenade to taste.

Shavings of vegetarian pecorino sheep's cheese (romano) can be used as a garnish if tolerated as part of a low-lactose diet.

Tempeh Vegetarian Kebabs

Tempeh is a traditional Indonesian soya bean food, used here marinated with vegetables for the barbecue. Be sure to buy tempeh which is not in a gluten-containing marinade – block form should be naturally gluten free.

SERVES 4 AS A LIGHT MEAL, 8 AS A STARTER
PREPARATION TIME – 25 MINUTES PLUS 1½–2 HOURS TO MARINATE PLUS 10 MINUTES FOR COOKING

150g (5½ oz) tempeh, drained, cut into 8 pieces
2 corn on the cob, each cut into 4 pieces
1 courgette (zucchini), cut into 8 x 2.5cm (1") pieces
1 small aubergine (eggplant), cut into 8 x 2.5cm (1") thick chunks
8 cloves garlic, peeled
8 cherry tomatoes
1 red onion, cut into 8 pieces
8 medium–large crimini/chestnut mushrooms
sea salt and freshly ground black pepper

For a variation, when in season, use baby vegetables for the kebabs.

marinade:

1½ tablespoons lime juice
1½ tablespoons rice wine/dry sherry

1½ tablespoons gluten-free soy sauce
2½ tablespoons olive oil
2 teaspoons liquid honey
2 cloves garlic, crushed
2 spring onions (scallions), chopped finely

Mix the marinade ingredients in a dish. Add the prepared tempeh and vegetables. Leave to marinate for 1½–2 hours, stirring occasionally.

Thread a selection of tempeh and vegetables onto skewers and place on the barbecue (or under the grill/broiler), reserving a little of the marinade. Season. Cook for about 10 minutes, turning frequently and basting with the marinade at intervals until cooked.

SERVING SUGGESTION: serve with raw/briefly stir-fried beansprouts and mixed salad leaves.

If considering cheese for the barbecue, Halloumi sheep's cheese keeps its shape well whilst cooking, if tolerated as part of a low-lactose diet. Note that some Halloumi contains cows' milk.

Tofu & Chinese Vegetable Stir-fry

Tofu is invaluable to vegetarians as it is the only non-meat source of complete protein and contains all the vital amino acids we need. It is rich in iron, calcium, magnesium and B vitamins.

SERVES 2 | PREPARATION TIME – 55 MINUTES

150g (5½ oz) firm tofu
2 lightly rounded tablespoons ground almonds/quinoa flakes
2 teaspoons each sesame oil and sunflower oil
1 clove garlic, crushed

2 rounded teaspoons finely cut fresh root ginger

4 pinches whole aniseeds, partially ground

1 medium onion, sliced and cut diagonally

1 medium green pepper, sliced, deseeded (pithy ribs removed) and cut diagonally

2 tinned pineapple rings in natural juice, sliced, reserving 4 tablespoons juice

150g (5½ oz) (2 cups) oyster mushrooms, cut roughly diagonally

8 baby sweetcorn cobs

¾ tablespoon Chinese rice wine/dry sherry

¾ tablespoon gluten-free soy sauce

¾ tablespoon rice vinegar

½ tablespoon Chinese wild-flower honey

2 pinches gluten-free Chinese five-spice powder

2 teaspoons gluten-free cornflour (cornstarch)

100g (3½ oz) bok choi, sliced *

5–6 large Chinese leaves, sliced finely

If bok choi is not available, use baby leaf green cabbage.

Drain the excess liquid from the tofu and place on absorbent kitchen paper. Cut into 1cm (½") cubes. Lightly press the tofu into the almonds/quinoa until well covered. Warm the combined oils in a wok or small non-stick frying pan (skillet) and fry the tofu until golden on all sides – about 7–10 minutes. Remove from the pan to a warm plate.

Add a little sunflower oil to the wok or large non-stick frying pan (skillet). Stir-fry the garlic, ginger, aniseed, onion and green pepper without burning for 2–3 minutes. Add the pineapple, reserved juice, mushrooms, baby corn, wine/sherry, soy sauce, vinegar, honey, five-spice powder and cornflour (cornstarch). Stir and bring to the boil then simmer for 2 minutes, stirring occasionally. Add the bok choi and Chinese leaves. Stir-fry together over a moderate heat for 2

minutes or so, until the greens are semi-wilted but still retain some
of their bite. Serve onto plates and scatter the tofu over the stir-fry.

Two-Cheese Soufflé

This is not a lactose-free recipe (i.e. not dairy-free), but a low-
lactose version using goats' milk and goats' and sheep's cheeses
(if tolerated as part of a low-lactose diet). All Goats' Milk
Processors Federation (GMPF) cheeses are suitable for
vegetarians as the rennet used does not come from animal
sources.

SERVES 2 AS A LIGHT MEAL, 3 AS A SNACK
PREPARATION TIME – 30 MINUTES PLUS 30 MINUTES FOR COOKING

340ml (12 fl oz) (1⅓ cups plus 1 tablespoon) pasteurised goats' milk
25g (1 oz) (1¾ tablespoons) dairy-free margarine
25g (1 oz) (2¾ tablespoons) rice flour
1 teaspoon gluten-free Dijon mustard
1 pinch paprika
sea salt and freshly ground black pepper
70g (2½ oz) (scant ⅔–⅔ cup) goats' cheddar cheese, grated
20g (¾ oz) (3 tablespoons) pecorino sheep's cheese (romano), grated
4 large free-range eggs, separated
watercress to serve

Preheat the oven to 200°C (400°F) (gas mark 6).

Heat the milk, margarine and flour in a medium saucepan stirring
constantly to boiling point. Simmer and stir for 1 minute as it thickens.
Remove from the heat. Add the mustard, paprika and seasoning. Mix
in the cheeses then the beaten egg yolks.

Whisk the egg whites to the 'soft peak' stage. (When lifting out the
beaters a soft peak is left behind. Over-beating to the 'stiff' stage will

result in the air bubbles bursting and losing lightness and volume.) Fold 1 tablespoon into the sauce with a metal spoon to soften it then fold in the remainder lightly to mix evenly. Pour into a greased 1.5 litre (2¾ pint) ovenproof soufflé dish. Cook in the oven for about 30 minutes until well risen/golden. The inside should be still soft and saucy – not too dry when tried with a metal skewer. Serve immediately with watercress.

Bread, Pastry, Pizza, Savoury Biscuits & Scones

Banana Bread

The recipe makes a nourishing, soft breakfast bread. Sliced thickly and toasted, it has an appetizing scent of teacakes toasting!

MAKES 900g (2lb) LOAF
PREPARATION TIME - 30 MINUTES PLUS 30 MINUTES FOR BAKING

1 tablespoon golden linseeds (flax)
130g (4½ oz) banana (from 1 large banana)
250g (8¾ oz) (1¾ cups) rice flour, sieved
25g (1 oz) (3¾ tablespoons) gram flour, sieved
75g (2¾ oz) (4½ tablespoons) dairy-free margarine
75g (2¾ oz) (⅓ cup plus ½ tablespoon) unrefined golden caster (superfine) sugar
1 large free-range egg
2 teaspoons bicarbonate of soda (baking soda)
¼ teaspoon ground cinnamon
¼ teaspoon gluten-free ground mixed (pie) spice
5–5½ tablespoons hot water
50g (1¾ oz) (⅓ cup) raisins

Preheat the oven to 180°C (350°F) (gas mark 4).

Grease a 900g (2lb) non-stick loaf tin. Line the base and sides with greaseproof paper (wax paper) and grease again.

Slightly grind the linseeds (flax) with a pestle and mortar. Mash the banana on a plate until smooth. Measure the flours onto another plate.

Beat the margarine and sugar in a mixing bowl until light and creamy. Beat in the egg with 2 heaped tablespoons of the measured flour. Mix in the mashed banana. Fold in the remaining flours, bicarbonate of soda (baking soda), spices and linseeds. Stir in the water to make a soft, spongy dropping consistency. Lightly fold in the raisins. Turn immediately into the prepared tin and roughly level the surface. Cook in the oven for about 30 minutes until golden brown. When tested with a skewer it should come out clean to almost clean. Leave in the tin for 10 minutes before turning out onto a wire rack to cool. When cold, peel away the lining paper. To store, wrap in a polythene bag. Eat while fresh, within about 4 days, or slice thickly and freeze.

Crusty White Bread

This quick, simple and versatile bread is suitable for sweet and savoury uses. It works just as well for toast and marmalade as it does for poached eggs on toast.

MAKES 900g (2 lb) LOAF

PREPARATION TIME – 20 MINUTES PLUS 35 MINUTES FOR BAKING

150g (5¼ oz) (1 cup plus 1 tablespoon) stoneground/brown rice flour
150g (5¼ oz) (1 cup plus 1 tablespoon) potato flour (farina)
150g (5¼ oz) (scant 1½ cups) tapioca flour
2 teaspoons xanthum gum
1 teaspoon bicarbonate of soda (baking soda)
2 teaspoons gluten-free cream of tartar
¼ teaspoon sea salt
30g (1 oz) (2 tablespoons) dairy-free margarine

1 large free-range egg, beaten

312ml (11 fl oz) (1¼ cups) rice milk, shaken well before
  using

*A little soya/rice bran can be sprinkled on the surface of the
loaf prior to cooking, if desired.*

Preheat the oven to 180°C (350°F) (gas mark 4).
Grease a 900g (2 lb) non-stick loaf tin.
Sieve and mix the flours in a large mixing bowl. Stir in the gum,
bicarbonate of soda (baking soda), cream of tartar and salt. Lightly
rub in the margarine. Mix the egg and milk in a basin and add to the
dry ingredients. Beat with a fork to produce a sticky dough. Turn
immediately into the prepared tin. Level the surface and cook in the
oven for about 35 minutes. The loaf should have slightly shrunk away
from the edge of the tin and lightly browned. Turn onto a wire rack to
cool. When cold, wrap in a polythene bag. It is best eaten within 4–5
days or slice and freeze.

Fresh Herb Scone Pizza

The pizza and topping recipe can be made quickly using half of
a frozen batch of Fresh Tomato Sauce (*see page 93*).

SERVES 2–4 | PREPARATION TIME – 25 MINUTES PLUS 15 MINUTES FOR
  COOKING

110g (4 oz) (¾ cup) rice flour

50g (1¾ oz) (generous ⅓ cup) potato flour (farina)

50g (1¾ oz) (generous ⅓ cup) gluten-free maize flour

½ teaspoon gluten-free baking powder

1 pinch sea salt and freshly ground black pepper

75g (2¾ oz) (4½ tablespoons) dairy-free margarine

1 tablespoon freshly cut parsley/mixed herbs

4 tablespoons unsweetened soya milk

mixed salad leaves, olive oil and white wine vinegar

topping:

½ quantity previously frozen fresh tomato sauce, thawed, semi-blended and heated

6 pieces gluten-free, dairy-free chorizo/salami, skinned and quartered

3 red and 3 yellow cherry tomatoes, halved

6 each green and black pitted olives

a sprinkling of dried Italian herbs

As an alternative, chorizo/salami can be replaced by Parma ham (prosciutto), Spanish Serrano ham, pancetta or bacon.

Preheat the oven to 220°C (425°F) (gas mark 7).

Sieve and mix the flours and baking powder into a mixing bowl. Season. Lightly rub in the margarine. Stir in the parsley/mixed herbs. Mix the milk into the dry ingredients. Bring together to form a soft dough.

Grease a non-stick baking tray then place the dough in the centre. Flatten out to form a 23cm (9") circle of even thickness. Tidy the edges by lightly pushing back into a circle with the fingers.

Spread the tomato sauce almost to the edge. Place the chorizo/salami into the sauce. Arrange the remaining topping ingredients. Sprinkle with herbs. Cook in the oven for 13–15 minutes until cooked. Cut into wedges and lift onto plates with a thin fish slice. Accompany with salad leaves drizzled with a little olive oil and white wine vinegar.

Plain Pastry

Plain pastry is suitable for sweet and savoury baking. The quantity below will line an 18–20cm (7–8") sponge/flan tin or cover a pie/casserole for 4 people. It is enough to make about 12–14 small jam tarts or 8–9 mince pies. It is not necessary to add the xanthum gum if making small tarts but it does help ease of handling large pastry bases into their tins.

PREPARATION TIME – 10 MINUTES

125g (4½ oz) (generous ¾ cup) rice flour
20g (¾ oz) (2 tablespoons) potato flour (farina)
20g (¾ oz) (3¾ tablespoons) soya flour
10g (½ oz) (1½ tablespoons) millet flakes
¼ teaspoon gluten-free baking powder
¼ teaspoon xanthum gum (*optional*)
80g (2¾ oz) (5 tablespoons) dairy-free margarine, straight from the fridge
2¼–2½ tablespoons cold water

Preheat the oven to 180°C (350°F) (gas mark 4).

Sieve the flours into a mixing bowl. Add the millet flakes, baking powder and xanthum gum, if using. Mix together, then rub in the margarine lightly with the fingertips until it resembles fine breadcrumbs. Add the water then cut and stir into the mixture with a knife until it is the consistency of soft, damp to wettish pastry. Bring together into a dough with the hands. Flour the work surface and rolling pin with rice flour then turn the dough onto the surface. Roll out with care adding more flour if necessary. Use fluted cutters to make small jam tart bases, etc. For lining larger flan tins, use the tin as a template for the base. Cut the pastry base in half and use a thin metal fish slice to lift each half into the greased tin. Line the sides of the tin with strips of pastry. Cook in the oven.

See the following recipes for instructions and cooking times: *Ham & Chicken Pie; Celery, Leek & Fennel Quiche; Jam/Lemon Curd/Golden Curd Tarts; Mince Pies; Lemon Meringue/Strawberry & Lime Meringue Pie and Bakewell Tart.*

Savoury Herb Scones

If you run out of gluten-free bread or would like a change from it, savoury scones are extremely quick to make. They're excellent with salads, soups and cooked meats. They can also be lightly toasted to accompany poached eggs or heated tinned fish, for a snack.

Makes 5–6 | Preparation time – 20 minutes plus 15 minutes for
baking

110g (4 oz) (¾ cup) rice flour
50g (1¾ oz) (½ cup) gram flour
50g (1¾ oz) (generous ⅓ cup) potato flour (farina)
2 teaspoons gluten-free baking powder
1 pinch each sea salt and white pepper
85g (3 oz) (5½ tablespoons) dairy-free margarine
½ teaspoon each dried basil and marjoram
1 tablespoon unsweetened soya milk
¾ teaspoon gluten-free Dijon mustard (*or Dijon mustard with white wine*)
1¼ rounded tablespoons plain soya yoghurt
unsweetened soya milk

*For a different mixture of dried herbs, try parsley, sage and
thyme or gluten-free mixed herbs.*

Preheat the oven to 190°C (375°F) (gas mark 5).

Sieve the flours and baking powder. Season. Lightly rub in the
margarine. Stir in the herbs. Mix the milk and mustard and add to
the dry ingredients together with the yoghurt to form a soft wettish
dough. Roll out on a floured surface to a thickness of 2.5cm (1"). Cut
with a 6cm (2⅜") plain or fluted cutter. Brush tops with soya milk
and place on a greased baking tray. Cook in the oven for 12–14
minutes. Cool on a wire rack.

*Sheep's milk yoghurt can be used as an alternative to soya, if
tolerated as part of a low-lactose diet.*

Sesame Biscuits

These savoury biscuits are similar to oatcakes. They taste good
when spread with a non-dairy alternative to full-fat soft cheese,
firm soya cheese, goats' cheese (if tolerated as part of a low-

lactose diet), or Tahini & Honey Spread (*see page 209*). They may also be spread and served with cold cooked meats, salads or buffets.

MAKES 15 | PREPARATION TIME – 20 MINUTES PLUS 15 MINUTES FOR BAKING

| 35g (1¼ oz) (3½ tablespoons) buckwheat flour |
| 50g (1¾ oz) (generous ⅓ cup) stoneground/brown rice flour |
| 50g (1¾ oz) (generous ⅓ cup) potato flour (farina) |
| 1 pinch sea salt |
| ¼ teaspoon bicarbonate of soda (baking soda) |
| ½ teaspoon gluten-free cream of tartar |
| 60g (2¼ oz) (3¾ tablespoons) dairy-free margarine |
| 1 slightly rounded tablespoon sesame seeds |
| 1 tablespoon cold water |

For a variation, try adding ½ tablespoon celery seeds instead of sesame seeds.

Preheat the oven to 180°C (350°F) (gas mark 4).

Sieve the flours together in a mixing bowl and season. Add bicarbonate of soda (baking soda) and cream of tartar. Rub in the margarine with fingertips. Mix in the sesame seeds. Add the water and bring mixture together into a soft but not wet dough, adding a further teaspoon of water if necessary.

Sift the work surface with rice flour and roll out to about 5mm (¼"). Cut into shapes using a 5.5cm (2¼") plain cutter (or similar). Lift with a thin palette knife onto a greased non-stick baking tray and cook for 14–15 minutes. Leave on the tray to cool for a few minutes, then remove to a wire rack until cold. Store in an airtight container.

Sweet Biscuits

Almond Biscuits

MAKES 17–20 | PREPARATION TIME – 20 MINUTES PLUS 15 MINUTES FOR BAKING

160g (5¾ oz) (1 cup plus 1½ tablespoons) rice flour

10g (½ oz) (1 tablespoon) potato flour (farina)

1 pinch sea salt

75g (2¾ oz) (⅓ cup plus ½ tablespoon) unrefined golden caster (superfine) sugar

50g (1¾ oz) (½ cup plus 1 tablespoon) ground almonds

125g (4½ oz) (½ cup) dairy-free margarine

½ teaspoon natural almond extract

flaked almonds *(optional)*

The sugar content could be reduced to 60g (2 ½ oz) (¼ cup plus 1 tablespoon).

Preheat the oven to 170–180°C (325–350°F) (gas mark 3–4).

Sieve the flours and salt, stir in the sugar and ground almonds until well mixed. Rub in the margarine, add the almond extract and work into a smooth paste.

Flour the work surface and rolling pin with rice flour and roll out to 8mm (⅜") thick. Cut into shapes using a 6cm (2 ⅜") plain cutter or other decorative cutter. Lift carefully with a thin palette knife onto greased non-stick baking trays. Lightly press a flaked almond into the centre of each biscuit. Cook in the oven for 12–15 minutes until lightly coloured. Cool for a few minutes then transfer to a wire rack with a spatula. When cold, store in an airtight container.

Chocolate Peppermint Biscuits

MAKES 10–11 SANDWICHED BISCUITS
PREPARATION TIME – 25 MINUTES PLUS 15 MINUTES FOR BAKING

biscuits:

130g (4½ oz) (1 cup less 1 tablespoon) rice flour, sieved

55g (2 oz) (½ cup) unrefined golden icing (confectioners') sugar, sieved

15g (½ oz) (2½ tablespoons) gluten-free, dairy-free cocoa powder, sieved

35g (1¼ oz) (2½ tablespoons) ground rice

1 pinch sea salt

90g (3¼ oz) (6 tablespoons) dairy-free margarine

chocolate peppermint spread:

10g (½ oz) (1½ tablespoons) gluten-free, dairy-free cocoa powder, sieved

25g (1 oz) (3½ tablespoons) unrefined golden icing (confectioners') sugar, sieved

10g (½ oz) (¾ tablespoon) dairy-free margarine

30g (1 oz) (2 tablespoons) Kendal mint cake, crushed with a rolling pin

1 teaspoon soya cream

Preheat the oven to 180°C (350°F) (gas mark 4).

Place the biscuit ingredients in a mixing bowl, stir then beat with an electric mixer to bring together. Shape into a paste ball.

Flour the work surface and paste ball with rice flour and roll out to a thickness of about 5–6mm (¼"). Cut into shapes with decorative cutters e.g. 6cm (2⅜") heart shape. With a thin palette knife, lift carefully onto well-greased non-stick baking trays. Cook in the oven for about 12 minutes. Leave on the tray for 2 minutes then remove to a wire rack to cool.

Stir the chocolate peppermint spread ingredients until combined into a smooth spread. Use to sandwich the biscuits together when cold. Eat while fresh and crisp, within 2 days of baking.

Mocha Biscuits and Mocha Spread:

Make as for the chocolate biscuits above, adding 1 rounded teaspoon coffee granules to the mixture before stirring and beating. Sandwich the biscuits together with the mocha spread using 10g (½ oz) (1½ tablespoons) gluten-free, dairy-free cocoa powder, 30g (1 oz) (4 tablespoons) unrefined golden icing (confectioners') sugar, almost ¾ tablespoon soya cream, and 1 rounded teaspoon coffee granules stirred together to form a spread, adding a dusting more icing (confectioners') sugar/soya cream if required.

Crisp Ginger Biscuits

Gram flour produces particularly well-flavoured ginger biscuits which spread and crinkle. Rice flour may be used too, producing compact biscuits with an unbroken surface. Either biscuit mixture is suitable for making gingerbread men using currants for eyes, nose, mouth and buttons.

MAKES 17–18 | PREPARATION TIME – 15 MINUTES PLUS 10 MINUTES FOR BAKING

100g (3½ oz) (6½ tablespoons) dairy-free margarine
100g (3½ oz) (½ cup) unrefined light muscovado sugar
150g (5¼ oz) (scant 1½ cups) gram flour
1½ teaspoons bicarbonate of soda (baking soda)
3 rounded teaspoons ground ginger

The biscuits may be rolled out on fibre-rich rice/soya bran.

Preheat the oven to 180°C (350°F) (gas mark 4).

Beat the margarine and sugar until light and creamy. Sieve in the remaining ingredients then stir until the mixture comes together. Bring into a soft paste ball with the fingers.

Flour the work surface, paste and rolling pin with gram flour. Lightly roll out to a thickness of 6mm (¼") using more flour to prevent sticking as necessary. Cut with 6cm (2⅜") plain cutter. Lift with a thin palette knife onto a lightly greased non-stick baking tray. Cook in the oven for 9–10 minutes. Leave on the tray until firm, then transfer to a wire rack with a spatula.

Crisp Ginger Biscuits with Rice Flour:

Use 160g (5¾ oz) (1 cup plus 1½ tablespoons) rice flour with other ingredients as above, using plenty of flour on the work surface, dough and rolling pin to prevent sticking. Lift with a thin palette knife onto a greased baking tray. Cook for 12–13 minutes. Makes 18.

Lemon Shortbread

SERVES 4 | PREPARATION TIME – 10 MINUTES PLUS 15 MINUTES FOR
        BAKING

55g (2 oz) (¼ cup) dairy-free margarine
65g (2¼ oz) (5 tablespoons) ground rice
65g (2¼ oz) (½ cup plus 1 tablespoon) gluten-free cornflour (cornstarch)
20g (¾ oz) (3 tablespoons) ground almonds
40g (1½ oz) (2¾ tablespoons) unrefined golden caster (superfine) sugar
finely grated rind ½ large lemon
2½ teaspoons lemon juice

Preheat the oven to 180°C (350°F) (gas mark 4).

Mix all the ingredients together in a mixing bowl and then beat with an electric mixer until the mixture comes together into a heavy crumble. [*At this stage it may be used as an alternative fruit crumble topping.*]

Bring the mixture together into a dough with the fingers. Place on a greased non-stick baking tray. Press into a 17cm (6½") circle of even thickness. Tidy the edge and crimp lightly between fingers and thumb to form a decorative finish. Score the surface into quarters and prick with a fork. Cook in the oven for 15–16 minutes until lightly coloured. Cool slightly then cut along the score marks and remove to a wire rack to cool. Store in an airtight container when cold.

Oat, Chocolate & Pecan Cookies

An unusual blend of flavours makes these little cookies irresistible. As they contain oats, they may not be suitable for coeliacs with a high level of sensitivity and should be discussed with your GP or dietician.

MAKES 12 | PREPARATION TIME – 15 MINUTES PLUS 15 MINUTES FOR BAKING

75g (2¾ oz) (½ cup plus ½ tablespoon) rice flour
10g (½ oz) (1½ tablespoons) gluten-free, dairy-free cocoa powder
75g (2¾ oz) (4½ tablespoons) dairy-free margarine
1 rounded tablespoon thickset honey
50g (1¾ oz) (¼ cup) unrefined light muscovado sugar
40g (1½ oz) (generous ⅓ cup) porridge oats
40g (1½ oz) (generous ¼ cup) pecan nuts, roughly chopped

The biscuits can also be made without the cocoa, replacing it with soya/rice bran for extra fibre or varied by adding 25g (1 oz) (2 tablespoons) raisins with the sugar and oats.

Preheat the oven to 180°C (350°F) (gas mark 4).

Sieve the flour and cocoa into a mixing bowl, then fork mix in the margarine and honey, until the flour and cocoa is incorporated. Fork in the sugar and oats. Shape into 12 balls, a little smaller than ping-pong balls, then flatten into the nuts to a thickness of about 8mm (⅜"). Re-shape into discs. Lift onto greased non-stick baking trays with a thin metal fish slice and cook in the oven for 12–15 minutes. Leave on the baking tray for a few minutes. Remove to a wire rack with a spatula to cool. Store in an airtight container.

Rice Biscuits

These are versatile biscuits that can be varied by adding 25g (1 oz) (2 tablespoons) glacé ginger/mixed glacé peel or made into Shrewsbury Biscuits (*see below*). Either of the biscuit mixtures would make ideal animal shape biscuits for children.

MAKES 17–20 | PREPARATION TIME – 15 MINUTES PLUS 15 MINUTES FOR BAKING

175g (6¼ oz) (1⅓ cups) rice flour
1 pinch sea salt
75g (2¾ oz) (⅓ cup plus ½ tablespoon) unrefined golden caster (superfine) sugar
50g (1¾ oz) (3¾ tablespoons) ground rice
125g (4½ oz) (½ cup) dairy-free margarine
½ teaspoon natural lemon extract (or grated rind of ½ lemon)

The sugar content could be reduced to 60g (2¼ oz) (¼ cup plus 1 tablespoon).

Preheat the oven to 170–180°C (325–350°F) (gas mark 3–4).

Sieve the flour and salt into a mixing bowl. Stir in the sugar and ground rice to mix. Rub in the margarine. Add the lemon extract and work into a smooth paste.

Flour the work surface and rolling pin with rice flour and roll out to 8mm (⅜") thick. Cut into shapes using a 6cm (2⅜") plain cutter or other decorative cutter. Lift carefully with a thin palette knife onto a greased non-stick baking tray. Cook in the oven for 12–15 minutes until hardly coloured. Cool for a minute or so then remove to a wire rack with a spatula. When cold, store in an airtight container.

Shrewsbury Biscuits:

Make as above, adding 25g (1 oz) (2 rounded tablespoons) currants to the mixture after the lemon extract. Work into a smooth paste and roll out. Cut into shapes with a decorative cutter, lift onto a greased non-stick baking tray and spike surface of the biscuits with a fork. Sprinkle with a little extra caster (superfine) sugar if desired. Cook at 170°C (325°F) (gas mark 3), for about 12–14 minutes to prevent the currants from burning.

Small Cakes

Blueberry & Pineapple Muffins

MAKES 10 | PREPARATION TIME – 25 MINUTES PLUS 25 MINUTES FOR BAKING

185g (6½ oz) (1⅓ cups plus 1 tablespoon) rice flour, sieved

40g (1½ oz) (4 tablespoons) fine–medium cornmeal, sieved

2 rounded teaspoons gluten-free baking powder

½ teaspoon bicarbonate of soda (baking soda)

100g (3½ oz) (6½ tablespoons) dairy-free margarine

2 large free-range eggs

100g (3½ oz) (½ cup) unrefined golden caster (superfine) sugar

2 tablespoons fresh orange juice and finely grated rind ½ large orange (reserved)

2 rounded tablespoons soya yoghurt

90g (3¼ oz) (½ cup) fresh pineapple (cored and trimmed weight), shredded finely and cut small

115g (4 oz) (¾ cup) fresh blueberries

muffin cases

Preheat the oven to 180°C (350°F) (gas mark 4).

Mix the flour, cornmeal, baking powder and bicarbonate of soda (baking soda) in a mixing bowl. Add the margarine, eggs, sugar and juice. Beat well. Stir in the orange rind, yoghurt and pineapple. Fold in the blueberries carefully. Place paper cases into a muffin tin then fill about three quarters full with the mixture. Cook in the oven for 20–24 minutes until golden and firmly spongy to the touch. Leave resting in the tin for 5 minutes then remove to a wire rack. Serve warm or cold. Eat while fresh, within 1–2 days.

Bran & Raisin Scones

The scones are lovely when spread with a dairy-free margarine and served warm. For plain bran scones, omit the raisins and spread with a light acacia honey/rosehip/redcurrant jelly, or a creamy non-dairy alternative to full-fat soft cheese.

MAKES 5–6 | PREPARATION TIME – 15 MINUTES PLUS 15 MINUTES FOR BAKING

110g (4 oz) (¾ cup) rice flour
50g (1¾ oz) (½ cup) gram flour
25g (1 oz) (2¾ tablespoons) potato flour (farina)
2 teaspoons gluten-free baking powder
1 pinch sea salt
75g (2¾ oz) (4½ tablespoons) dairy-free margarine
40g (1½ oz) (2¾ tablespoons) unrefined golden caster (superfine) sugar
25g (1 oz) (3½ tablespoons) cooked rice/soya bran
25g (1 oz) (2 tablespoons) raisins
3 tablespoons sweetened soya milk

Preheat the oven to 190°C (375°F) (gas mark 5).

Sieve the flours, baking powder and salt into a mixing bowl. Rub in the margarine lightly with the fingertips until it resembles fine breadcrumbs. Stir in the sugar, bran and raisins. Add the milk, stir, then bring the mixture together with the fingers to make quite a soft dough.

Roll out on a floured surface to a thickness of 2.5cm (1"). Cut into shapes with a 6cm (2 ⅜") scone cutter. Brush the tops with soya milk and place on a greased non-stick baking tray. Cook in the oven for 12–14 minutes. Leave on the tray for a few minutes then cool on a wire rack. Serve warm or cold, sliced and spread with a dairy-free margarine. They are best eaten on the day of baking but may be frozen when cold.

Chocolate Brownies

Most mixed chopped nuts bought in shops contain a high proportion of peanuts. I prefer to process equal amounts of whole almonds and hazelnuts. Almonds are particularly rich in calcium and high in protein. Both almonds and hazelnuts are rich in vitamin E.

MAKES 8–9 | PREPARATION TIME – 15 MINUTES PLUS 25 MINUTES FOR BAKING

100g (3½ oz) gluten-free, dairy-free plain chocolate, broken

60g (2¼ oz) (3¾ tablespoons) dairy-free margarine

2 large free-range eggs

150g (5¼ oz) (¾ cup) unrefined golden caster (superfine) sugar

75g (2¾ oz) (½ cup plus ½ tablespoon) rice flour, sieved

1 teaspoon gluten-free baking powder

1 pinch sea salt

½ teaspoon natural vanilla extract

75g (2¾ oz) (½ cup) mixed chopped nuts

Preheat the oven to 180°C (350°F) (gas mark 4).

Melt the chocolate and margarine in a large basin placed over a saucepan of simmering water, stirring until blended and smooth.

Remove from the heat. Beat in the eggs and sugar well with an electric mixer. Lightly fold in the flour, baking powder and salt with a metal spoon. Stir in the vanilla extract and nuts lightly. Pour into a well-greased 19cm (7½") non-stick square tray-bake tin or 20cm (8") non-stick round sponge tin. Cook for 24–25 minutes until slightly shrinking away from the side of the tin. Leave in the tin for a few minutes. Run a plastic spatula around the edge and turn out onto a wire rack to cool. When cold cut into squares or wedges.

SERVING SUGGESTION: serve with soya cream or, for a special treat, with Chocolate/Mocha Sauce (*see page 212*).

Coconut Marzipan Macaroons

Soft-centred macaroons are lovely if eaten whilst the marzipan centres are warm and gooey, but equally good eaten cold. The macaroons can also be made using marzipan only or conserve (jelly) only. The unused egg yolks could be used for making Mayonnaise (*see page 218*) or for White Fish in Creamy Lemon Sauce (*see page 58*).

MAKES 10 | PREPARATION TIME – 25 MINUTES PLUS 15 MINUTES FOR BAKING

140g (5 oz) (⅔ cup) unrefined golden caster (superfine) sugar
110g (4 oz) (1¼ cups) ground almonds
20g (¾ oz) (3 tablespoons) desiccated (shredded) coconut
2 large egg whites
½ teaspoon natural almond extract
1 tablespoon flaked almonds (*optional*)
apricot conserve (jelly)
25g (1 oz) marzipan
paper cases

The sugar content may be reduced to 130g (4½ oz) (½ cup plus 2 tablespoons). The cooked surface of the macaroons will be rougher but still soft inside.

Preheat the oven to 170°C (325°F) (gas mark 3).

Mix together the sugar, almonds and coconut in a mixing bowl.

In a separate basin, whisk the egg whites until stiff. Fold into the mixture carefully with a metal spoon until evenly combined. Stir in the almond extract and flaked almonds.

Place paper cases on a baking tray. Spoon a large teaspoon of mixture into each paper case (to cover the base). Place a little conserve on top, followed by a small flattened disc of marzipan about 2.5cm (1") diameter. Finally, place another teaspoon of cake mixture over

the marzipan. Cook in the oven for 14–15 minutes until lightly
coloured. Leave on the tray to cool for a few minutes then remove to
a wire rack.

Plain Macaroons:
Use 140g (5 oz) (1½ cups) ground almonds and leave out the coconut.
Cook as above.

Date Crumblies

As the date crumblies are naturally sweet and moist, this
provides an ideal opportunity to gradually reduce the sugar
content. The taste buds become used to less sweetness until the
sugar can be omitted altogether. Then for an added zest, grate
half an orange rind onto the crumble base. The crumble
mixture could be used for an alternative fruit crumble topping.

MAKES 9 | PREPARATION TIME – 50 MINUTES PLUS 30 MINUTES FOR
BAKING

160g (5¾ oz) (generous 1 cup) dried stoned (pitted) dates,
chopped

255g (9 oz) (2 cups) cooking apples, peeled, cored and
chopped

2 tablespoons water

120g (4¼ oz) (1 cup plus 1½ tablespoons) gram flour

120g (4¼ oz) (½ cup) ground rice

110g (4 oz) (7 tablespoons) dairy-free margarine

40g (1½ oz) (2¾ tablespoons) unrefined light muscovado
sugar (*optional*)

Preheat the oven to 180°C (350°F) (gas mark 4).
   Put the dates, apples and water in a medium saucepan. Cover and
soften over a very low heat, stirring occasionally, until all the water
has been absorbed and fruit is soft – about 5–7 minutes. Mash roughly
together to mix. Leave to one side, uncovered.

Sieve the flour into a mixing bowl and stir in the ground rice. Rub in the margarine to form a heavy crumble mixture. Stir in the sugar, if it is being used. Press half the mixture firmly into the base of a greased 19cm (7½") non-stick square tray-bake tin with the back of a metal spoon. Spread the date pulp evenly over the crumble base. Cover evenly with the remaining crumble and lightly press down. Cook in the oven for 30 minutes. Cool in the tin, loosen around the tin with a plastic spatula. Cut into 9 squares and turn out carefully.

Jam Tarts

Jam tarts seem quite ordinary, so why not use a medley of home-made curds and jams, or unusual conserves to make them more special.

MAKES 12–14 | PREPARATION TIME – 23 MINUTES PLUS 15 MINUTES FOR BAKING

pastry:

125g (4½ oz) (generous ¾ cup) rice flour
20g (¾ oz) (2 tablespoons) potato flour (farina)
20g (¾ oz) (3¾ tablespoons) soya flour
10g (½ oz) (1½ tablespoons) millet flakes
¼ teaspoon gluten-free baking powder
80g (2¾ oz) (5 tablespoons) dairy-free margarine, straight from the fridge
2¼–2½ tablespoons cold water
curd/jam/conserve/jelly

Preheat the oven to 180°C (350°F) (gas mark 4).

Sieve the flours into a mixing bowl. Add the millet flakes and baking powder. Mix together, then rub in the margarine lightly with the fingertips until it resembles fine breadcrumbs. Add the water then cut and stir into the mixture with a knife until it is the consistency of soft, damp to wettish pastry. Bring together into a dough with the hands. Flour the work surface and rolling pin with rice flour then turn the dough onto the surface. Roll out on a well-floured surface. Cut the bases using a 7.5cm (3") fluted cutter. With a thin palette knife or fish slice carefully lift the bases into shallow well-greased non-stick patty tins, easing them in from the edges. Spoon 2 teaspoons of curd/jam/conserve/jelly into the tarts. Cook in the oven for 15–16 minutes. Leave to cool in the tins for about 5 minutes before carefully removing with a plastic spatula to a wire rack.

Macaroons

Traditional macaroons are quite time consuming to make in pastry bases. However, if paper cases are used, this makes the process much quicker and easier.

MAKES 12 | PREPARATION TIME – 10 MINUTES PLUS 15 MINUTES FOR BAKING

175g (6¼ oz) (¾ cup plus 2 tablespoons) unrefined golden caster (superfine) sugar
175g (6¼ oz) (generous 1¾ cups) ground almonds
2 large free-range eggs
½ teaspoon natural almond extract
flaked almonds to decorate
paper cases

As a variation, place ½ teaspoon apricot conserve (jelly) between the spoonfuls of mixture in the paper cases.

Preheat the oven to 180°C (350°F) (gas mark 4).

Mix together the sugar and almonds in a mixing bowl. Break in the eggs and beat well. Stir in the almond extract.

Place paper cases on a baking tray. Spoon 2 large teaspoons of mixture into each case. Scatter with flaked almonds. Cook in the oven for 13–15 minutes until lightly browned. Place on a wire rack to cool.

Chocolate Macaroons:

Mix together the sugar and almonds in a mixing bowl. Break in the eggs and beat well. Add 10g (½ oz) (1½ tablespoons) sieved gluten-free, dairy-free cocoa powder and beat briefly. Stir in ½ teaspoon vanilla extract. Proceed as above.

Mango Flapjacks

For this recipe, look for Fair Trade or organic naturally sun-dried mangoes which are free from added sugar and additives. Oats are a high-protein cereal, rich in iron and soluble fibre but they need to be discussed with your GP or dietician if coeliac. Mangoes are bursting with the antioxidant beta-carotene, vitamin C and are potassium rich. The fruit can be omitted for plain flapjacks or for a variation (*see Sultana Flapjacks at the end of the recipe*).

MAKES 8–12 | PREPARATION TIME – 25 MINUTES PLUS 40 MINUTES FOR BAKING

60g (2¼ oz) (generous ¾ cup) naturally sun-dried mango slices
175g (6¼ oz) (¾ cup plus 1 tablespoon) dairy-free margarine
100g (3½ oz) (½ cup) unrefined light muscovado sugar
½ large free-range egg
1 rounded tablespoon acacia honey
275g (9¾ oz) (2⅔ cups) porridge oats
1 teaspoon freshly grated nutmeg

Preheat the oven to 170°C (325°F) (gas mark 3) *or* to 150°C (300°F) (gas mark 2).

Put the mango slices into a little hot water to soften while making the flapjacks.

Beat the margarine and sugar to mix, then beat in the egg. Stir in the honey. Add the oats and nutmeg then mix thoroughly. Press half the mixture into the base of a greased 19cm (7½") non-stick square tray-bake tin. Drain the mango slices and pat with absorbent kitchen paper. Cut into small pieces and arrange over the oat base. Cover with the remaining mixture. Press down lightly. Cook for about 30 minutes at 170°C (325°F) (gas mark 3) *or* for about 40 minutes at 150°C (300°F) (gas mark 2) until golden. Cool in the tin. Cut into squares. Store in an airtight container.

Sultana Flapjacks:
Replace the mango with 50g (1¾ oz) (⅓ cup) sultanas (golden raisins) arranged over the oat base. Cover with the remaining mixture and press lightly into the tin. Cook as above.

Mince Pies

If you wish to enjoy festive mince pies but not pile on too many calories, try the sugar-reduced, fat-reduced Mincemeat recipe (*see page 208*) for making them.

MAKES 8–9 | PREPARATION TIME – 20 MINUTES PLUS 15 MINUTES FOR BAKING

125g (4½ oz) (generous ¾ cup) rice flour
20g (¾ oz) (2 tablespoons) potato flour (farina)
20g (¾ oz) (3¾ tablespoons) soya flour
10g (½ oz) (1½ tablespoons) millet flakes
¼ teaspoon gluten-free baking powder
80g (2¾ oz) (5 tablespoons) dairy-free margarine, straight from the fridge
2¼–2½ tablespoons cold water to mix
gluten-free, dairy-free mincemeat
soya milk

For 'festive cheer' stir a little brandy/rum into the mincemeat prior to filling the pastry cases.

Preheat the oven to 180°C (350°F) (gas mark 4).
    Sieve the flours into a mixing bowl. Add the millet flakes and

baking powder. Rub in the margarine lightly with the fingertips until it resembles fine breadcrumbs. Cut and stir the water into the mixture with a knife until it is the consistency of soft, damp to wettish pastry. Bring together into a dough with the hands.

Roll out the pastry on a well-floured surface. Use a 7.5cm (3") fluted cutter for the bases and a 6cm (2⅜") for the tops. Using a thin palette knife or fish slice carefully lift the bases into shallow well-greased non-stick patty tins easing them in from the edges. Nearly fill with mincemeat, moisten the pastry edges and lightly press on the tops. Make two cuts in each top with a knife. Brush with soya milk. Cook for 12–15 minutes. Leave in the tins for a few minutes, loosen with a spatula and carefully lift out onto a wire rack to cool.

Sultana Scones

MAKES 6 | PREPARATION TIME – 20 MINUTES PLUS 15 MINUTES FOR BAKING

110g (4 oz) (¾ cup) rice flour
50g (1¾ oz) (½ cup) gram flour
50g (1¾ oz) (generous ⅓ cup) potato flour (farina)
2 teaspoons gluten-free baking powder
1 pinch sea salt
85g (3 oz) (5½ tablespoons) dairy-free margarine
25g (1 oz) (2 tablespoons) unrefined golden caster (superfine) sugar
40g (1½ oz) (¼ cup) sultanas (golden raisins)
2¼–2½ rounded tablespoons plain soya yoghurt
soya milk

Preheat the oven to 190°C (375°F) (gas mark 5).

Sieve the flours, baking powder and salt into a mixing bowl. Rub in the margarine lightly with fingertips until it resembles fine breadcrumbs. Stir in the sugar and sultanas (golden raisins).

Add the yoghurt, stir, then bring the mixture together with the fingers to make quite a soft dough. Roll out on a floured surface to a thickness of 2.5cm (1"). Cut with a 6cm (2⅜") scone cutter. Brush tops with soya milk and place on a greased non-stick baking tray. Cook in the oven for 13–15 minutes. Leave on the tray for 2 minutes then remove to a wire rack with a fish slice to cool.

Sheep's milk yoghurt, if well tolerated as part of a low-lactose diet can be used as an alternative to soya yoghurt.

Large Cakes

Apple, Almond & Cinnamon Sponge

PREPARATION TIME – 30 MINUTES PLUS 30 MINUTES FOR BAKING

110g (4 oz) (7 tablespoons) dairy-free margarine
100g (3½ oz) (½ cup) unrefined golden caster (superfine) sugar
75g (2¾ oz) (½ cup plus ½ tablespoon) rice flour, sieved
25g (1 oz) (3¾ tablespoons) gram flour, sieved
2 rounded teaspoons gluten-free baking powder
2 large free-range eggs
1 teaspoon natural vanilla extract

topping:

½ tablespoon unrefined golden caster (superfine) sugar
2 teaspoons ground cinnamon
100g (3½ oz) (5 rounded tablespoons) cooking apple, peeled, sliced and diced small
50g (1¾ oz) (½ cup) flaked almonds
½ tablespoon pine nut kernels

Preheat the oven to 180°C (350°F) (gas mark 4).

Beat the margarine and sugar in a mixing bowl until light in colour and texture. Combine the flours and baking powder on a plate. Beat in the eggs one at a time with 2 heaped tablespoons of the flour. Fold in the remaining flour. Stir in the vanilla extract. Turn into a well-greased deep 20cm (8") non-stick round cake tin. Lightly level the surface.

For the topping, mix the sugar and cinnamon, then toss the apples, almonds and pine nut kernels into the spiced sugar. Scatter evenly over the surface of the cake. Very slightly pat into the surface. Cook in the oven for 25–30 minutes until the cake has slightly shrunk away from the tin. Cool for a few minutes in the tin. Loosen around the tin with a plastic spatula and carefully turn out onto a wire rack.

SERVING SUGGESTION: sprinkle the cake with a slight dusting of icing (confectioners') sugar.

Apple Layered Victoria Sponge

This cake makes a healthier tea-time option as it is sandwiched together with freshly made apple purée.

PREPARATION TIME – 30 MINUTES PLUS 35 MINUTES FOR BAKING

sponge:

110g (4 oz) (7 tablespoons) dairy-free margarine

100g (3½ oz) (½ cup) unrefined golden caster (superfine) sugar

110g (4 oz) (¾ cup) rice flour, sieved

1 teaspoon gluten-free baking powder

2 large free-range eggs

½ teaspoon natural vanilla extract

topping:

75g (2¾ oz) (3½ rounded tablespoons) cooking apple, peeled, sliced and finely diced

2 teaspoons unrefined light soft brown sugar

1½ teaspoons ground cinnamon

apple layer:

250g (8¾ oz) (1⅔ cups) cooking apple, peeled, cored, sliced and diced

a good squeeze of lemon juice

Preheat the oven to 180°C (350°F) (gas mark 4).

Place the sponge ingredients in a mixing bowl except for the vanilla extract. Beat really well until light, thick and creamy. Stir in the vanilla extract. Turn the mixture into a well-greased 18cm (7") non-stick sponge tin and lightly level the surface.

Mix together the topping ingredients and scatter evenly over the mixture. Cook in the oven for 30–35 minutes. Leave in the tin for a few minutes. Turn out onto a wire rack to cool.

For the apple layer, drop the apples as they are prepared into a small saucepan half filled with cold water and the lemon juice to prevent discolouration. Drain away all but one tablespoon of the water. Bring to the boil, cover and simmer, stirring occasionally until soft and pulpy – about 6 minutes. Leave to cool. When cold, drain away any liquid from the apples, slice the cake and sandwich together with the purée.

Apricot Shortcake

The apricot shortcake is suitable for serving warm as a pudding with Custard (*see page 213*) or cream, or as a 'cut and come again' cake. When fresh ripe apricots are in season, 1 or 2 can be finely diced and placed over the apricot conserve (jelly) prior to cooking.

SERVES 6 | PREPARATION TIME – 25 MINUTES PLUS 30 MINUTES FOR BAKING

150g (5¼ oz) (⅔ cup) dairy-free margarine

60g (2¼ oz) (¼ cup plus 1 tablespoon) unrefined golden caster (superfine) sugar

1 large free-range egg

1 teaspoon natural almond extract

50g (1¾ oz) (3¾ tablespoons) ground rice

50g (1¾ oz) (⅓ cup) fine–medium cornmeal

170g (6 oz) (1¼ cups) rice flour

finely grated rind 1 medium orange (*or lemon rind as an alternative*)

3 rounded tablespoons apricot conserve (jelly)*
4½ natural coloured glacé cherries

Use apricot conserve (jelly) sweetened with fruit juice rather than sugar.

Preheat the oven to 170°C (325°F) (gas mark 3).

Beat the margarine and sugar until light and creamy. Add the egg and beat well. Add the almond extract, ground rice and cornmeal and beat again. Sift in the flour and stir into the mixture with the rind.

Spread half the mixture into the base of a greased 18cm (7") non-stick sponge/flan tin. Spread the conserve over the mixture, almost to the edge. Spoon the remaining cake mixture into a food forcing bag fitted with a large 'star' nozzle. Pipe 8 circles around the edge of the tin and one in the centre. Place half a glacé cherry in the centre of each piped circle. Cook in the oven for 25–28 minutes until lightly browned.

Small Apricot Shortcakes:

Make as above. Place paper cases on baking trays. Pipe the mixture into the cases to almost fill. Make a hole in each and insert ½ teaspoon of conserve. Place half a cherry in the centre of each swirl. Cook at 170°C (325°F) (gas mark 3) for 15 minutes. Makes 15–16.

Bakewell Cake

This recipe makes a special tea-time cake. It is wonderful, sliced and just eaten as it is. But if preferred, it can be spread with a good quality loganberry or raspberry conserve.

PREPARATION TIME – 20 MINUTES PLUS 35 MINUTES FOR BAKING

170g (6 oz) (¾ cup) dairy-free margarine
155g (5½ oz) (¾ cup) unrefined golden caster (superfine) sugar
2 large free-range eggs
75g (2¾ oz) (scant 1 cup) ground almonds
100g (3½ oz) (½ cup less 1 tablespoon) ground rice

50g (1¾ oz) (generous ⅓ cup) rice flour, sieved
¾ teaspoon natural almond extract
a few flaked almonds
loganberry/raspberry conserve (jelly) (*optional*)

Preheat the oven to 170°C (325°F) (gas mark 3).

Beat the margarine and sugar until light in colour and texture. Add the eggs, almonds, ground rice and rice flour. Beat well. Stir in the almond extract.

Turn into a well-greased deep 18cm (7") non-stick round cake tin. Lightly level the surface. Sprinkle with the flaked almonds. Cook in the oven for 27–32 minutes until lightly browned and just starting to shrink away from the edge of the tin. Leave in the tin for about 10 minutes then turn out onto a wire rack to cool. When cold, sandwich the cake with conserve if preferred.

Banana & Chocolate Cake

This large, moist cake deepens in flavour with keeping, and the riper the bananas the fuller the flavour.

PREPARATION TIME – 35 MINUTES PLUS 50 MINUTES FOR BAKING

175g (6¼ oz) (¾ cup plus 1 tablespoon) dairy-free margarine
160g (5¾ oz) (¾ cup plus 1 tablespoon) unrefined golden caster (superfine) sugar
240g (8½ oz) (1 cup) mashed ripe peeled bananas
¾ teaspoon natural vanilla extract
70g (2½ oz) gluten-free, dairy-free plain chocolate, chopped into small pieces (reserved)
150g (5¼ oz) (1 cup plus 1 tablespoon) rice flour
140g (5 oz) (1⅓ cups) gram flour
3 rounded teaspoons gluten-free baking powder
1 teaspoon bicarbonate of soda (baking soda)

1 pinch sea salt

3 large free-range eggs

Gluten-free, dairy-free carob drops can be used as an alternative to plain chocolate.

topping:

1 rounded *and* 1 level tablespoon rice flour

1 tablespoon unrefined demerara sugar

1 tablespoon dairy-free margarine

Grease a deep 20cm (8") non-stick round cake tin. Base line with greaseproof paper (wax paper) and grease again.

Melt the margarine and dissolve the sugar gently in a saucepan, stirring, then leave to one side.

Mash the bananas on a plate with the vanilla extract until smooth. Preheat the oven to 150°C (300°F) (gas mark 2).

Sieve the flours, baking powder, bicarbonate of soda (baking soda) and salt into a mixing bowl then combine. Stir in the melted margarine and sugar. Beat in the eggs with an electric mixer to form a smooth batter. Stir in the mashed bananas then carefully fold in the chopped chocolate, but do not over-stir. Pour into the prepared tin.

For the topping, rub the margarine into the flour and sugar. Sprinkle the topping evenly over the cake. Place the cake in the preheated oven *then immediately* turn the heat up to 170°C (325°F) (gas mark 3), and cook for about 45–50 minutes. The cake should be firm to the touch and when tested with a skewer should come out clean. Leave to cool in the tin. Turn out and remove the lining paper.

Carrot & Ginger Cake

PREPARATION TIME – 25 MINUTES PLUS 35 MINUTES FOR BAKING

110g (4 oz) (⅔ cup) peeled and finely grated carrots

190g (6¾ oz) (1⅓ cups plus 1½ tablespoons) stoneground/brown rice flour, sieved

2 rounded teaspoons gluten-free baking powder

1 good rounded teaspoon ground ginger

70g (2½ oz) (⅓ cup) unrefined golden caster (superfine) sugar

70g (2½ oz) (⅓ cup) unrefined light muscovado sugar

150g (5¼ oz) (⅔ cup) dairy-free margarine

3 large free-range eggs

50g (1¾ oz) (2 slightly rounded tablespoons) stem ginger in syrup, rinsed, dried and cut into small pieces

Preheat the oven to 180°C (350°F) (gas mark 4).

Grease and base line a deep 20cm (8") non-stick round cake tin with greaseproof paper (wax paper) and grease again.

Reserve the prepared carrots.

Beat the remaining ingredients together, except the stem ginger. Stir in the carrots evenly, then the stem ginger. Turn the mixture into the prepared tin. Cook in the oven for about 35 minutes. The cake should be just firm to the touch and slightly shrunk away from the edge of the tin. Leave in the tin for 10 minutes then turn out onto a wire rack. When cold, peel away the lining paper. Best eaten whilst fresh and within 3–4 days.

Christmas/Celebration Cake

This is an excellent moist celebration cake and I can assure you that the whole family will enjoy it – possibly even more than the gluten-containing variety. If you wish to cover it with almond paste and royal icing, the ingredients are listed at the end of the recipe. I have also given there an alternative idea for a small individual celebration cake which could be made for Christmas, Easter or a special anniversary (or gift). Its uses one third of the ingredients listed here. Making a cake at the beginning of December, allows time to 'feed' it over the next ten days, add marzipan two weeks before Christmas and to ice it five to seven days before Christmas Day itself.

400g (14¼ oz) (scant 3 cups) currants
225g (8 oz) (1⅔ cups) raisins
175g (6¼ oz) (1⅓ cups) sultanas (golden raisins)
50g (1¾ oz) (⅓ cup) whole candied peel cut/mixed chopped candied peel or other unsulphured fruit
75g (2¾ oz) (scant ½ cup) natural coloured glacé cherries rinsed, dried and cut into thirds
170g (6 oz) (1¼ cups) rice flour
70g (2½ oz) (1 cup) soya flour
1 tablespoon gluten-free baking powder
2 pinches sea salt
¾ teaspoon freshly grated nutmeg
¾ teaspoon gluten-free mixed (pie) spice
½ teaspoon ground cinnamon
225g (8 oz) (1 cup) dairy-free margarine
175g (6¼ oz) (scant 1 cup) unrefined light soft brown sugar
50g (1¾ oz) (¼ cup) unrefined light muscovado sugar
4 large free-range eggs
25g (1 oz) (⅓ cup) ground almonds
1 teaspoon black strap molasses
25g (1 oz) (1½ tablespoons) grated dessert apple
finely grated rind 1 medium unwaxed lemon*
finely grated rind ½ large unwaxed orange*
1 tablespoon orange juice
2 tablespoons brandy

If waxed, scrub under hot water to remove the wax.

Grease and double line a deep 20cm (8") non-stick round solid-base cake tin with greaseproof paper (wax paper) and grease again.

Weigh the fruit, peel and cherries into a large basin. Sieve the flours, baking powder, salt and spices onto a large plate.

Preheat the oven to 150°C (300°F) (gas mark 2).

In a large mixing bowl, beat the margarine and sugars until creamy and light in colour and texture – about 2 minutes. Beat in the eggs one at a time with 2 heaped tablespoons of the mixed flours and spices, to prevent curdling. Fold in the remaining flour and almonds with a metal spoon. Lightly fold in the measured fruit, black strap molasses, apple, lemon and orange rinds. Stir in the orange juice and brandy. Spoon immediately into the prepared tin and level the surface.

Stand the cake on a baking tray lined with 2 layers of brown paper. Fold a double band of brown paper around the cake tin and secure in place. Place a double sheet of greaseproof paper (wax paper) over the cake tin to protect the cake whilst cooking, with a hole cut in the centre about 2.5cm (1") diameter.

Bake in the oven (on a lower shelf) for about 1 hour 50 minutes to 2 hours and 20 minutes until evenly brown – *but try not to open the oven before 1 hour 50 minutes*. When tested with a skewer in the centre of the cake, it should come out clean. The cake should feel 'firmly spongy' to the touch. Leave to cool in the tin for 30 minutes. Turn out onto a wire rack. When cold, peel off the lining paper, wrap it in greaseproof paper (wax paper) and store in an airtight container.

Next day, spike the surface of the cake with holes using a thin skewer and 'feed' with half a tablespoon of brandy. 'Feed' again once or twice more over the next 5–10 days, if you wish.

Marzipan

PREPARATION TIME 10–15 MINUTES

For a 20cm (8") round cake (top and sides), you will need a minimum of 500g (1 lb 2 oz) natural coloured almond paste (though 565g/1¼ lb allows for a more comfortable coverage), a little warm sieved apricot conserve (jelly) and a dusting of icing (confectioners') sugar.

Brush the cake lightly with conserve. Dust the work surface with sifted icing (confectioners') sugar. Roll out the almond paste to cover the top and sides of the cake, using the cake tin as a template for the top. Cover with a clean cloth to allow the almond paste to dry for a few hours. Loosely wrap in greaseproof paper (wax paper) and store in an airtight container. Allow five to seven days before icing the cake.

Royal Icing

PREPARATION TIME 20 MINUTES PLUS 10 MINUTES FOR ICING

I have intentionally made a minimum amount of royal icing to reduce the sugar content. This will be ample to produce a thin layer (top and sides), for a marzipan-covered 20cm (8") round cake, with a small allowance for extra piping or 'snow' effect if desired. Raw egg white may pose a risk of salmonella and listeria, especially during illness or pregnancy and for vulnerable groups such as the elderly and mothers breastfeeding their babies.

1 large egg white
225g (8 oz) (1½ cups) white/unrefined golden icing (confectioners') sugar*, sieved
1 teaspoon lemon juice
½ teaspoon glycerine

Unrefined golden icing (confectioners') sugar can be used, but it does not give quite the same visual effect or texture.

Briefly whisk the egg white in a grease-free bowl until slightly frothy. Stir in the icing (confectioners') sugar a tablespoon at a time with a wooden spoon until half has been incorporated. Add the lemon juice and stir. Continue adding the sugar a tablespoon at a time, whisking well with an electric whisk after each addition (to ensure a light textured icing). When all the sugar has been incorporated and the whisk is lifted out of the mixture it should leave soft peaks behind. Stir in the glycerine to prevent the mixture becoming too hard.

To ice the cake, use a spatula or metal palette knife to spread about half (a fraction more for a snow effect, or a fraction less than half if extra is required for piping) over the surface and the remainder around the sides. Leave to dry and harden.

Decorate with a deep festive satin ribbon and bow plus Christmas trimmings.

Small Celebration Cake

PREPARATION TIME – 50 MINUTES PLUS 1 HOUR 40 MINUTES FOR BAKING

130g (4½ oz) (generous ¾ cup) currants

70g (2½ oz) (½ cup) raisins

55g (2 oz) (⅓ cup) sultanas (golden raisins)

15g (½ oz) (1 rounded tablespoon) whole candied peel cut/mixed chopped candied peel

25g (1 oz) 10 natural coloured glacé cherries rinsed, dried and cut into thirds

50g (1¾ oz) (generous ⅓ cup) rice flour

25g (1 oz) (4½ tablespoons) soya flour

1 teaspoon gluten-free baking powder

1 small pinch sea salt

¼ teaspoon freshly grated nutmeg

¼ teaspoon gluten-free mixed (pie) spice

2 pinches ground cinnamon

75g (2¾ oz) (4½ tablespoons) dairy-free margarine

55g (2 oz) (¼ cup) unrefined light soft brown sugar

20g (¾ oz) (1½ tablespoons) unrefined light muscovado sugar

1½ large free-range eggs

10g (½ oz) (1½ tablespoons) ground almonds

¼–½ teaspoon black strap molasses

10g (½ oz) (¾ tablespoon) grated dessert apple

grated rind ½ small lemon

grated rind ½ small/¼ large orange

2 teaspoons orange juice

2 teaspoons brandy

Grease and double line a deep 13.5cm (5¼") non-stick round cake tin with greaseproof paper (wax paper) and grease again.

Make as for Christmas/Celebration cake. Cook at 150°C (300°F) (gas mark 2), for about 1 hour 35–40 minutes.

The cake can be fed with the occasional teaspoon of brandy over the next week or so, if you wish.

Marzipan:
Top only 150g (5¼ oz), top and sides 330–350g (11¾ oz–12¼ oz) – allowing for a generous 5mm (¼") layer of almond paste, a little warm sieved apricot conserve (jelly) and a dusting of icing (confectioners') sugar. Follow the instructions to marzipan the Christmas/Celebration Cake.

Royal Icing:*
½ large egg white, 110–120g (4–4¼ oz) (¾ cup plus 2 tablespoons–1 cup) white/unrefined golden icing (confectioners') sugar, sieved, ½ teaspoon lemon juice, ¼ teaspoon glycerine. Follow the instructions to ice the Christmas/Celebration Cake.

See raw egg white health risk under the main Christmas Cake recipe for royal icing.

Dark Chocolate Orange Cake

This is a dark, sophisticated cake with a spread that gives it a fudgy texture. If you're feeling more indulgent, double the quantity of Chocolate Orange Spread (*see page 204*) to ice the cake as well.

PREPARATION TIME – 15 MINUTES PLUS 35 MINUTES FOR BAKING

150g (5¼ oz) (1 cup plus 1 tablespoon) rice flour, sieved

1 rounded *and* 1 level teaspoon gluten-free baking powder, sieved

50g (1¾ oz) (½ cup plus 1½ tablespoons) gluten-free, dairy-free cocoa powder, sieved

160g (5¾ oz) (¾ cup plus 1 tablespoon) unrefined light muscovado sugar

110g (4 oz) (7 tablespoons) dairy-free margarine
2 large free-range eggs
3¾ tablespoons soya cream
3¾ tablespoons soya milk
finely grated rind ½ large orange

Preheat the oven to 180°C (350°F) (gas mark 4).

Place the ingredients, except for the orange rind, in a large mixing bowl. Beat well until the mixture is thick, creamy and lighter in colour – about 2 minutes. Stir in the orange rind. Turn into a well-greased deep 18cm (7") non-stick round cake tin. Lightly level the surface. Cook in the oven for 32–35 minutes until just firm to the touch in the centre of the cake. Cool slightly, then turn out onto a wire rack to cool. When cold, slice and sandwich together with chocolate orange spread and frost with a little sieved cocoa and unrefined icing (confectioners') sugar.

Small Chocolate Orange Cakes:
Make as above. Place paper cases on baking trays, put 1 generous rounded tablespoon of mixture in each case, top with half a natural-coloured cherry and cook in the oven for 14–15 minutes. Makes 18–19.

Honey & Sour Yoghurt Loaf

This recipe produces pleasant blended flavours of honey and cinnamon. The loaf can be sliced and eaten plain, or spread with a little dairy-free margarine.

PREPARATION TIME – 15 MINUTES PLUS 45 MINUTES FOR BAKING

75g (2¾ oz) (4½ tablespoons) dairy-free margarine
4 tablespoons acacia honey
4 tablespoons plain soya yoghurt
2 teaspoons lemon juice
100g (3½ oz) (½ cup) unrefined light soft brown sugar

1 large free-range egg

150g (5¼ oz) (1 cup plus 1 tablespoon) rice flour

75g (2¾ oz) (¾ cup) gram flour

1 teaspoon bicarbonate of soda (baking soda)

2 teaspoons ground cinnamon

1 rounded *and 1* level tablespoon mixed chopped
nuts/chopped whole almonds (*optional*)

Grease and base line a 900g (2 lb) non-stick loaf tin with greaseproof paper (wax paper) then grease again.

Preheat the oven to 150°C (300°F) (gas mark 2).

Gently melt the margarine and honey in a small saucepan.

Place the yoghurt in a mixing bowl then stir in the lemon juice until smooth. Lightly beat in the sugar and egg. Sift in the flours, bicarbonate of soda (baking soda) and cinnamon then add the nuts. Stir. Add the honey mixture and stir until well combined. Pour into the prepared tin. Scatter a few chopped nuts over the surface, if preferred. Cook in the oven for about 35–42 minutes. Leave in the tin for 15 minutes. Turn out onto a wire rack to cool. Peel away the lining paper.

SERVING SUGGESTION: slice and spread with a dairy-free margarine or try topping with finely sliced and diced ripe pear.

Lemon Syrup Cake

PREPARATION TIME – 25 MINUTES PLUS 35 MINUTES FOR BAKING

175g (6¼ oz) (¾ cup plus 1 tablespoon) dairy-free
margarine

165g (5¾ oz) (¾ cup plus 1½ tablespoons) unrefined light
muscovado sugar

175g (6¼ oz) (1⅓ cups) rice flour, sieved

2 teaspoons gluten-free baking powder

3 large free-range eggs

finely grated rind 1 medium lemon

lemon syrup:
  rind 1 medium lemon

  2½ tablespoons lemon juice

  3½ tablespoons unrefined golden caster (superfine) sugar

Grease and base line a deep 20cm (8") non-stick round cake tin with greaseproof paper (wax paper) then grease again.
    Preheat the oven to 180°C (350°F) (gas mark 4).
    Beat the margarine, sugar, flour, baking powder and eggs until smooth and the mixture lightens in colour and texture. Stir in the lemon rind. Spoon the mixture into the prepared tin and level the surface. Cook in the oven for about 30–35 minutes. Turn out onto a wire rack. Make the lemon syrup and pour over the cake while both are still warm.
    For the lemon syrup, cut the rind into thin strips with a lemon zester. Poach in a small saucepan in a little water for about 4–5 minutes. When tender, drain and turn onto absorbent kitchen paper. Heat the lemon juice and 3 tablespoons of the sugar in a saucepan and stir until dissolved. Boil for 1–1½ minutes until thinly syrupy. Lightly spike the surface of the warm cake with a skewer and spoon over the syrup. Roll the lemon strips in the remaining sugar and use to decorate the top of the cake. Remove the lining paper when cold.

Light Chocolate Almond Cake

This is a pleasant light-textured cake sandwiched together with Chocolate Almond Spread (*see page 204*). It also makes an ideal children's Easter cake – see instructions for making, at the end of the recipe. The cake can be made with carob flour instead of cocoa, but make sure this is gluten free. Alternatively, sandwich the cake with raspberry, blueberry or blackcurrant conserve (jelly), free from preservatives, flavourings and colours, sweetened only by the fruit and fruit juice.

PREPARATION TIME – 10 MINUTES PLUS 30 MINUTES FOR BAKING

175g (6¼ oz) (¾ cup plus 1 tablespoon) dairy-free margarine

170g (6 oz) (¾ cup plus 2 tablespoons) unrefined golden caster (superfine) sugar

110g (4 oz) (¾ cup) rice flour, sieved

50g (1¾ oz) (½ cup plus 1 tablespoon) ground almonds

2 teaspoons gluten-free baking powder

3 large free-range eggs

40g (1½ oz) (½ cup) gluten-free, dairy-free cocoa powder, sieved

4½ tablespoons warm water

Grease and base line two 18cm (7") non-stick sponge tins with grease-proof paper (wax paper) then grease again.

Preheat the oven to 170°C (325°F) (gas mark 3).

Place the ingredients, except for the cocoa and warm water, in a large mixing bowl. Beat well for 2 minutes until the mixture lightens in colour and texture. Blend the cocoa and warm water in a small basin until smooth. Lightly stir into the mixture until evenly blended then divide between the prepared tins. Cook in the oven for about 25–30 minutes until the cake slightly shrinks away from the edge of the tin and feels spongy to the touch. Run a plastic spatula around the tin and turn out onto a wire rack to cool. Peel away the lining paper when cold. Sandwich together with chocolate almond spread.

Children's Chocolate Easter Cake:

You will need double quantity of Chocolate Almond Spread (*see page 204*). Make the cake as above. When completely cold, spread the base of one of the cakes with half of the spread. Nestle the top surface of the other cake into the spread. Scoop a shallow depression in the surface of the cake to form the nest. Cover the surface and nest with the remaining spread. Decorate with small gluten-free, dairy-free chocolate eggs, alternatively fluffy yellow chickens. To finish, tie a deep Easter gold ribbon around the cake and secure in a bow.

Light Whisked Chocolate Sponge

PREPARATION TIME – 25 MINUTES PLUS 15 MINUTES FOR BAKING

4 large free-range eggs

150g (5¼ oz) (¾ cup) unrefined golden caster (superfine) sugar

150g (5¼ oz) (1 cup plus 1 tablespoon) rice flour

25g (1 oz) (3½ tablespoons) gluten-free, dairy-free cocoa powder

Preheat the oven to 170°C (325°F) (gas mark 3).

Grease and flour two 18cm (7") non-stick sponge tins.

Stand a mixing bowl in a larger bowl containing about 2.5cm (1") hot water (this will speed up the whisking process). Whisk the eggs and sugar until they are thick and pale – about 8–10 minutes, so that when the whisk is removed, the trails and peaks remain. Sieve half of the flour and cocoa into the mixture and lightly fold in with a metal spoon, then fold in the remainder. Pour into the prepared tins. Cook in the oven for 14–16 minutes until just firm to the touch. Run a plastic spatula around the tin to loosen then turn out onto a wire rack to cool. When cold, sandwich together with conserve, 'butter' cream made with dairy-free margarine and icing (confectioners') sugar or conserve.

Rich Fruit Cake

This fruit cake is adapted from my Mom's favourite recipe, which she made for us countless times, as we grew from children into adults. It is a really nice family fruit cake.

PREPARATION TIME – 25 MINUTES PLUS 40 MINUTES FOR BAKING

95g (3¼ oz) (¾ cup) raisins

95g (3¼ oz) (¾ cup) sultanas (golden raisins)

25g (1 oz) (2 tablespoons) mixed peel*

45g (1½ oz) 12 natural coloured glacé cherries, rinsed to remove syrup, dried and cut into thirds

110g (4 oz) (¾ cup) rice flour

25g (1 oz) (3¾ tablespoons) gram flour

25g (1 oz) (4½ tablespoons) soya flour

50g (1¾ oz) (generous ⅓ cup) potato flour (farina)

2 rounded teaspoons gluten-free baking powder

110g (4 oz) (7 tablespoons) dairy-free margarine

90g (3¼ oz) (½ cup less 1 tablespoon) unrefined golden caster (superfine) sugar

1 large free-range egg

3½ 4¼ tablespoons sweetened soya milk

Mixed peel contains the preservative sulphur dioxide which can trigger symptoms in asthmatics. Replace with unsulphured dried dates/apricots, or more dried fruit and cherries if necessary.

Grease a deep 18cm (7") non-stick round cake tin. Line the base and side with greaseproof paper (wax paper) and grease again.

Preheat the oven to 170°C (325°F) (gas mark 3).

Weigh the fruit and leave to one side.

Sieve the flours and baking powder into a large mixing bowl and stir. Rub in the margarine lightly with fingertips until breadcrumb-like. Stir in the sugar.

Beat the egg in a basin, add 3½ tablespoons of the milk and stir into the dry ingredients to make a fairly soft dropping consistency, adding a further ½–¾ tablespoon if necessary. Mix in the fruit thoroughly. Turn the mixture into the prepared tin, smooth the surface and sprinkle with a teaspoon of caster (superfine) sugar.

Cook in the oven for 25–27 minutes *then* cover the surface of the cake with greaseproof paper (wax paper), with a hole about 2.5cm (1") diameter in the centre, to prevent the fruit from burning. Continue to cook for about a further 10–13 minutes. Leave to cool for about 10 minutes before turning onto a wire rack. When cold, peel away the lining paper.

Simnel Cake

This is a traditional cake made for Easter using the richness of the fruit and spices of a Christmas cake. In addition to the ingredients for Christmas/Celebration Cake you will need 500g (1 lb 2 oz) almond paste.

PREPARATION TIME – 1½ HOURS PLUS UP TO 2½ HOURS FOR BAKING PLUS 15 MINUTES FOR MARZIPAN

Follow the recipe for Christmas Cake (*see page 144*) until you are ready to spoon the mixture into the prepared tin. Spoon half of the mixture into the tin and level the surface. Roll out a third of the almond paste on a little sieved icing (confectioners') sugar to prevent sticking. Cut a fraction smaller than the tin and lift into place over the fruit. Spoon in the remaining cake mixture and level the surface.

Stand the cake tin on a baking tray, double lined with brown paper. Fold a double band of brown paper around the cake tin and secure in place. Place a double sheet of greaseproof paper (wax paper) over the cake and tin to protect it whilst cooking, with a hole cut in the centre about 2.5cm (1") diameter.

Cook on a lower shelf in the preheated oven at 150°C (300°F) (gas mark 2), for about 1 hour 55 minutes to 2 hours 20 minutes until evenly brown – *but try not to open the oven before 1 hour 50 minutes.* It's not really possible to test the cake with a skewer as the almond paste remains soft, but it should feel 'firmly spongy' when cooked. Leave to cool in the tin for 30 minutes. Turn out onto a wire rack. When completely cold peel off the lining paper.

Brush the surface of the cake with a little sieved apricot conserve (jelly). Roll out about 215g (7½ oz) of the remaining almond paste to fit the top of the cake. Crimp the edges with fingers and thumb and with the back of a knife, make a lattice pattern in the centre. Brush the almond paste with egg white or apricot conserve. Shape the remaining paste into eleven small balls and evenly space them around the cake, a little way in from the edge. Brush these with egg white or conserve. Place the cake under a moderately hot grill (broiler) until the almond paste is lightly browned.

To complete for Easter, tie a deep satin gold ribbon around the cake and secure in a bow.

For a special children's Easter Cake, see Light Chocolate Almond Cake on page 152.

Tea Loaf

This recipe makes a nice moist tea loaf. The sugar content is kept to a minimum, relying on fruit sugar to provide the sweetness.

PREPARATION TIME – 10 MINUTES TO PREPARE FOR SOAKING OVERNIGHT
25 MINUTES PLUS 50 MINUTES FOR BAKING

240ml (8½ fl oz) (1 cup) strong Elderflower/Earl Grey tea
120g (4¼ oz) (¾ cup) raisins
120g (4¼ oz) (¾ cup) sultanas (golden raisins)
2 sun-dried pineapple rings, cut finely
75g (2¾ oz) (⅓ cup plus ½ tablespoon) unrefined golden caster (superfine) sugar
finely grated rind 1 small lemon
50g (1¾ oz) (3 tablespoons) dairy-free margarine, melted
150g (5¼ oz) (1 cup plus 1 tablespoon) rice flour, sieved
60g (2¼ oz) (scant ⅔ cup) tapioca flour, sieved
10g (½ oz) (1 tablespoon) buckwheat flour, sieved
1 teaspoon gluten-free cream of tartar
½ teaspoon bicarbonate of soda (baking soda)
1 large free-range egg, beaten
½ tablespoon thin honey
1 teaspoon crushed hemp seeds/2 teaspoons sunflower seeds, semi-crushed

Make the tea, stir well and leave to infuse for about 5 minutes. While the tea is infusing, put the raisins, sultanas (golden raisins), cut pineapple rings and sugar into a large basin. Stir the tea again, strain and pour over the fruit. Stir well to dissolve the sugar. Cover with a clean cloth and leave overnight for the fruit to 'plump up'.

Next day, preheat the oven to 170°C (325°F) (gas mark 3).

Grease and double line (base and sides) a non-stick 900g (2 lb) loaf tin with greaseproof paper (wax paper) then grease again.

Add the rind and melted margarine to the fruit/tea mixture. Sieve the flours, cream of tartar and bicarbonate of soda (baking soda) onto a plate. Add the beaten egg to the mixture then stir in the flour from the plate. Add the honey and stir again. Immediately spoon the mixture into the prepared tin. Sprinkle with the crushed hemp seeds/sunflower seeds. Cook in the oven for 45–50 minutes. When tested with a skewer it should come out clean. Leave to cool in the tin. Peel away the lining paper when cold.

To serve, cut into slices and spread with a dairy-free margarine. It is best eaten while moist, within 5–6 days, or slice and freeze.

Victoria Sandwich

This light Victoria sandwich recipe is made by the all-in-one method. If you prefer a classic Victoria sandwich texture, use the creaming method described at the end of the recipe. Whichever you choose, the result is equally good. Use Honey Vanilla Spread (*see page 206*), Lemon Curd (*see page 206*) or Golden Curd (*see page 205*) to sandwich the cake when cold. There is also an excellent range of fruit spreads available where the sweetness is provided by the fruit and fruit juices alone – no preservatives or colourings are used.

PREPARATION TIME – 13 MINUTES PLUS 25 MINUTES FOR BAKING

175g (6¼ oz) (¾ cup plus 1 tablespoon) dairy-free margarine
165g (5¾ oz) (¾ cup plus 1½ tablespoons) unrefined golden caster (superfine) sugar
175g (6¼ oz) (1⅓ cups) rice flour, sieved
2 teaspoons gluten-free baking powder
3 large free-range eggs
few drops natural vanilla extract (*optional*)

Preheat the oven to 180°C (350°F) (gas mark 4).

Place the ingredients in a mixing bowl. Beat really well until light, thick and creamy. Stir in the vanilla extract. Divide the mixture between two well-greased 18cm (7") non-stick sponge tins. Cook in the oven for about 23–25 minutes until firmly springy to the touch. Cool in the tin for a couple of minutes, loosen with a plastic spatula then turn out onto a wire rack.

CREAMING METHOD: beat the margarine and sugar until light in colour and texture. Add each egg separately with a heaped tablespoon of flour and beat well. Fold in the remaining flour and baking powder with a metal spoon. Proceed as above.

Chocolate Victoria Sandwich:

Use 155g (5½ oz) (1 cup plus 1 tablespoon) rice flour and 20g (¾ oz) (3 tablespoons) gluten-free, dairy-free cocoa powder, sieved, with other ingredients the same. Make and cook as above. When cold, sandwich with Chocolate Almond Spread (*see page 204*), replacing the almond extract with 4 drops of vanilla extract.

Puddings

Apples & Elderberries with Biscuit Crust

Look for heavy, plump, black elderberry heads when harvesting
in late summer to early autumn. Rinse them well, allowing time
for any insects to escape, then tease the berries off with a fork.
Use while fresh or freeze. A sugar-free alternative can be made
by covering the fruit with plain pastry and cooking according
to the recipe.

SERVES 4 | PREPARATION TIME – 30 MINUTES PLUS 30 MINUTES FOR
COOKING

565g (1¼ lb) cooking apples, cored and peeled

a good squeeze lemon juice

1 tablespoon water/apple juice

50g (1¾ oz) (3 slightly rounded tablespoons) elderberries,
rinsed and de-stalked

a good pinch of whole aniseeds, slightly ground

biscuit crust:

110g (4 oz) (¾ cup) rice flour

50g (1¾ oz) (¼ cup) unrefined golden caster (superfine)
sugar

55g (2 oz) (4 tablespoons) ground rice

80g (2¾ oz) (5 tablespoons) dairy-free margarine

a few drops natural lemon extract

Slice and dice the apples into large chunks, plunging them into cold
water and lemon juice to prevent discolouration. Drain the apples and
cook in a covered medium saucepan with the tablespoon of

water/apple juice. Soften slightly over a moderate heat, stirring occasionally – about 3 minutes. Mix in the elderberries and aniseeds. Remove from the heat and leave to one side, covered.

Preheat the oven to 180°C (350°F) (gas mark 4).

For the biscuit crust, sieve the flour into a mixing bowl then stir in the sugar and ground rice to mix. Rub in the margarine, add the lemon extract and work into a smooth paste. Roll out on a floured surface to 8mm (⅜") thick. Place the top of a small ovenproof dish – 1.2 litre (2 pint) or 4 x 7.5cm (3") ramekin dishes, on the mixture and cut around the edge. Turn the fruit into the dish or ramekins. Smooth the surface. Carefully lift the biscuit crust with two thin metal fish slices and place over the fruit (or cut in half first for a larger base). Cook in the oven for about 25–30 minutes (or 15–20 minutes for ramekin dishes). Serve hot with Custard (*see page 213*).

Apple, Sultana & Lime Pudding

This is a sugar-free pudding sweetened only by the sultanas (golden raisins) and lime. Alternatively, use grated rind and juice of half a small orange instead of half a lime to sweeten.

SERVES 3 | PREPARATION TIME – 10 MINUTES PLUS 25 MINUTES FOR COOKING

350g (12 oz) cooking apples
a good squeeze of lemon juice
grated rind and juice ½ lime
25g (1 oz) (2 tablespoons) sultanas (golden raisins)

Preheat the oven to 180°C (350°F) (gas mark 4).

Peel, core and slice the apples. Cut into large dice, placing them in a medium saucepan, half filled with cold water and a little lemon juice to prevent discolouration. Drain then add lime rind, juice and sultanas (golden raisins). Cover and cook for 2–3 minutes over a medium heat, stirring from time to time. Turn into a small covered ovenproof dish. Cook in the oven for 20–25 minutes, until apples are soft and fluffy. Serve with Custard (*see page 213*) or soya cream.

Sugar-free Apple, Sultana and Lime Pie:

After cooking the apples for 2–3 minutes on the hob, turn into a small
ovenproof dish and cover with plain pastry or a sugar-free crumble
topping. Cook in the oven for 15 minutes at the above temperature.

Individual Pies (but not sugar free):

Divide the fruit between 3 x 7.5cm (3") ramekin dishes, press down
lightly and cover with Rice Biscuit/Almond Biscuit crust (*see pages
126 and 121*), rolled out to 8mm (⅜"). Half the quantity of the biscuit
recipe will cover three ramekins. Cook at the above temperature for
23–28 minutes until lightly coloured.

Bakewell Tart

SERVES 4–6 | PREPARATION TIME – 30 MINUTES PLUS 30 MINUTES FOR
            BAKING

pastry:

125g (4½ oz) (generous ¾ cup) rice flour

20g (¾ oz) (2 tablespoons) potato flour (farina)

20g (¾ oz) (3¾ tablespoons) soya flour

10g (½ oz) (1½ tablespoons) millet flakes

¼ teaspoon gluten-free baking powder

¼ teaspoon xanthum gum

80g (2¾ oz) (5 tablespoons) dairy-free margarine, straight
  from the fridge

2¼–2½ tablespoons cold water

sponge:

110g (4 oz) (7 tablespoons) dairy-free margarine

95g (3¼ oz) (½ cup) unrefined golden caster (superfine)
  sugar

2 free-range eggs

85g (3 oz) (1 cup) ground almonds

60g (2¼ oz) (4½ tablespoons) ground rice

30g (1 oz) (3 tablespoons) rice flour, sieved

½ teaspoon natural almond extract

raspberry/loganberry conserve (jelly)

a few flaked almonds

Sieve the flours into a mixing bowl. Add the millet flakes, baking powder and xanthum gum. Mix together, then rub in the margarine lightly with the fingertips until it resembles fine breadcrumbs. Add the water then cut and stir into the mixture with a knife until it is the consistency of soft, damp to wettish pastry. Bring together into a dough with the hands.

Flour the work surface and rolling pin with rice flour then turn the dough onto the surface. Roll out to line a non-stick 20cm (8") sponge/flan tin, using the tin as a template for the base. Cut the pastry base in half and use a thin metal fish slice to lift each half into the greased baking tin, then align the two halves together. Line the sides of the tin with strips of pastry, reserving the remainder.

Preheat the oven to 180°C (350°F) (gas mark 4).

Beat the margarine and sugar until light in colour and texture. Beat the egg, almonds, ground rice and flour well into the mixture. Mix in the almond extract.

Spread the pastry base with conserve and spoon in the sponge mixture. Lightly level the surface. Decorate with thin strips of pastry, lifted into place with the fish slice to form a lattice pattern. Scatter with flaked almonds. Cook in the oven for about 27–30 minutes.

Banana & Pear Puddings with Ginger Crust

This unusual fruit combination goes well with a ginger biscuit crust. Use ripe fruit for sweetness and good flavour. A sugar-free version can be made by covering the fruit with Plain Pastry (*see page 117*).

MAKES 4 | PREPARATION TIME – 25 MINUTES PLUS 15 MINUTES FOR
COOKING

| 100g (3½ oz) (6½ tablespoons) dairy-free margarine |
| 90g (3¼ oz) (½ cup less 1 tablespoon) unrefined light muscovado sugar |
| 160g (5¾ oz) (1 cup plus 1½ tablespoons) rice flour |
| 1 teaspoon bicarbonate of soda (baking soda) |
| 2 lightly rounded teaspoons ground ginger |
| 200g (7 oz) peeled ripe bananas, sliced (2–3 medium bananas) |
| 200g (7 oz) peeled ripe pears, sliced (1½–2 pears) |
| finely grated rind and juice ½ small lemon |

Preheat the oven to 180°C (350°F) (gas mark 4).

Beat the margarine and sugar until light and creamy. Sieve in the flour, bicarbonate of soda (baking soda) and ginger. Stir to bring the mixture together then use the hands to form a soft dough. Flour the work surface, dough and rolling pin with rice flour. Lightly roll out the dough to a thickness of about 8mm (⅜"), using more flour to prevent sticking as necessary. Place a 7.5cm (3") ramekin over the biscuit crust to cut four tops. [Any remaining biscuit dough can be rolled out to 5mm (¼"), cut with a decorative shape and cooked at the above temperature for 9–10 minutes, to make crisp ginger biscuits.]

Mix and divide the fruit between 4 x 7.5cm (3") ramekin dishes, pressing down lightly if necessary. Grate over a little lemon rind and sprinkle with juice. Lift the tops with a spatula into place over the fruit. Lightly make a lattice pattern on the surface with a knife. Cook in the oven for 14–16 minutes.

To make in a small ovenproof dish:

Use 275g (9¾ oz) each peeled ripe bananas and pears (about 3½ medium bananas and 2 good medium-sized pears), sliced and combined with 1 tablespoon juice and rind from half a small lemon. Turn into the dish. Roll out the biscuit dough to 8mm (⅜"). Use 2 thin fish slices to lift into place over the fruit. Cook for about 25–30 minutes.

Christmas Pudding

These gluten-free and dairy-free puddings can be made four to
six weeks in advance of Christmas. An extra one could be
made, stored in a cool, dry cupboard, ready for Easter.
Although the recipe is sugar reduced it is still surprisingly sweet
to the tastebuds. If you cannot eat nuts, the ground almonds
can be replaced by an extra 40g (1½ oz) (4 tablespoons) rice
flour.

MAKES 1 PUDDING IN A 568ml (1 PINT) BASIN, 2 IN 280ml (½ PINT)
BASINS, OR 4 IN 140ml (¼ PINT) BASINS
PREPARATION TIME – 30 MINUTES PLUS SOAKING OVERNIGHT PLUS UP
TO 6 HOURS FOR BOILING

40g (1½ oz) (4 tablespoons) rice flour, sieved
40g (1½ oz) (scant ½ cup) ground almonds
50g (1¾ oz) (½ cup) gluten-free shredded vegetable suet
½ teaspoon ground cinnamon
½ teaspoon gluten-free mixed (pie) spice
½ teaspoon freshly grated nutmeg
¼ teaspoon ground ginger
50g (1¾ oz) (¼ cup) unrefined dark soft brown sugar
140g (5 oz) (1 cup) currants
70g (2½ oz) (½ cup) raisins
70g (2½ oz) (½ cup) sultanas (golden raisins)
20g (¾ oz) (2 tablespoons) whole candied peel, cut finely/mixed chopped candied peel*
20g (¾ oz) (2 tablespoons) glacé ginger
60g (2¼ oz) (3½ rounded tablespoons) cooking apple, peeled, sliced finely and diced
finely grated rind ¼ large lemon
finely grated rind ¼ large orange
1 large free-range egg, beaten

3–3½ tablespoons orange juice
1¾ tablespoons brandy/rum
1 teaspoon black strap molasses

Unsulphured apricots can be used instead of sulphured candied peel if concerned about an adverse reaction.

Place the flour, almonds, suet, spices and sugar in a mixing bowl, stirring well with each addition. Mix in the fruit, peel, ginger, apple and rinds.

Add the beaten egg, 3 tablespoons of the orange juice and all of the brandy to the dry ingredients. Stir well to make a slightly 'sloppy' dropping consistency, adding the remaining orange juice if necessary. Stir in the molasses thoroughly. Cover the mixing bowl with a clean cloth and leave overnight.

Next day, spoon the mixture into greased pudding basins, cover with greased greaseproof paper (wax paper), pleated along the centre and then pleated foil. Secure in place with string.

Boil a 568ml (1 pint) pudding for 6 hours, 280ml (½ pint) puddings for 3 hours or 140ml (¼ pint) puddings for 2 hours, with water to come halfway up the basins. Top up the water level as necessary whilst cooking.

When the puddings are cold, replace with fresh greaseproof paper (wax paper), foil and string. Store in a cool dry place.

When required, boil the puddings for 1–1¾ hours, depending on size. Serve with Brandy Sauce (*see page 211*) or Custard (*see page 213*).

Eve's Pudding

For this classic family pudding, the apples are sweetened only by soft summer fruits. A combination of half cooking apples and half Cox's (eating) apples can be used for a sweeter taste.

SERVES 6–8 | PREPARATION TIME – 20 MINUTES PLUS 40 MINUTES FOR COOKING

A good squeeze of lemon juice
700g (1½ lb) cooking apples

50g (1¾ oz) (½ cup) fresh/frozen and thawed soft summer
  fruits

---

sponge:

110g (4 oz) (7 tablespoons) dairy-free margarine

100g (3½ oz) (½ cup) unrefined golden caster (superfine)
  sugar

110g (4 oz) (¾ cup) rice flour, sieved

¾ teaspoon gluten-free baking powder

---

2 large free-range eggs

½ teaspoon natural vanilla extract

Preheat the oven to 180°C (350°F) (gas mark 4).

Half fill a large saucepan with cold water and add the lemon juice. Peel, core and slice the apples into 2.5cm (1") pieces, dropping them into the water to prevent discolouration. Drain away all but a tablespoon of the water. Bring to the boil, cover and simmer over a moderate heat. Stir from time to time until semi-soft – about 5 minutes. Leave to one side, covered to keep warm, whilst making the sponge.

Place the sponge ingredients in a mixing bowl, except the vanilla extract. Beat really well until light, thick and creamy. Stir in the vanilla extract.

Mix the soft fruit into the apples and turn into a large greased 1.7 litre (3 pint) ovenproof dish. Roughly level the fruit. Cover with the sponge mixture. Cook in the oven for about 40 minutes. Serve with Custard (*see page 213*).

French Buckwheat Pancakes with Apple & Blackcurrant Filling

Buckwheat is a member of the rhubarb family and not related to wheat. These pancakes are a little different from traditional ones but hopefully you'll develop a taste for them. For this recipe I use home-grown blackcurrants, so full of vitamin C.

The pancakes and filling are sugar free unless you prefer to sprinkle them with sugar and lemon juice to serve. They are also suitable for a savoury/vegetarian filling.

MAKES 4–5 SMALL PANCAKES
PREPARATION TIME – 20 MINUTES TO PREPARE FOR FRYING AND FILLING

pancakes:

40g (1½ oz) (4 tablespoons) buckwheat flour, sieved

10g (½ oz) (1 tablespoon) rice flour, sieved

1 pinch sea salt

½ large free-range egg

140ml (5 fl oz) (½ cup plus 1 tablespoon) sweetened soya milk

1 rounded tablespoon dairy-free margarine, melted

sunflower oil

filling:

255g (9 oz) (1¾ cups) Cox's (eating) apples, peeled, cored, sliced and diced

½ tablespoon water

100g (3½ oz) (¾ cup) blackcurrants

Add the flours and salt to a small mixing bowl, make a hollow in the centre and drop in the egg. Stir in half the milk and the melted margarine. Beat thoroughly until smooth. Stir in the remaining milk. Leave to stand while making the filling.

Add the prepared apples and water to a small saucepan. Cover and cook over a medium heat for about 2–3 minutes, stirring occasionally, until semi-soft. Add blackcurrants and continue to simmer over a low heat until soft.

Heat a little oil in a small non-stick omelette pan. Stir the batter then spoon 3 nearly level tablespoons into the pan and swirl around until the base is evenly coated. Cook on a medium to high heat until the surface is drying out and browning at the edges. Turn the pancake over, adding a little more oil if necessary and cook until coloured. Turn out onto a warm plate. Spread half the pancake with about 2 tablespoons of the fruit filling, fold over and serve.

Fruited Pancakes (but not sugar free):

Leave the batter to stand for about half an hour. Spoon 3 nearly level tablespoons of the batter into the oiled pan and immediately sprinkle with a few raisins or sultanas (golden raisins) or leave plain if preferred. Cook as above. Turn onto a warm plate – fruit-side up. To serve, sprinkle with unrefined golden caster (superfine) sugar and lemon juice.

Fresh Peaches with Macaroons

This light pudding reminds me of high summer, when all the luscious fruits are available. If you can, choose white-fleshed peaches or nectarines and serve simply with the fragrant juices. Peaches and nectarines are rich in beta-carotene, which is converted into vitamin A in the body. Vitamin A aids detoxification in the body but cooking does unfortunately destroy some of the precious nutrients.

SERVES 4 | PREPARATION TIME – 20 MINUTES PLUS 30 MINUTES FOR COOKING

4 ripe large white peaches

1 miniature bottle/double measure peach schnapps

macaroons:

45g (1½ oz) (3 tablespoons) unrefined golden caster (superfine) sugar

45g (1½ oz) (½ cup) ground almonds

½ large free-range egg

¼ teaspoon natural almond extract

Preheat the oven to 180°C (350°F) (gas mark 4).

Cut the peaches in half and remove the stones. Scrape away any roughness from the hollows. With a fork, pierce the hollows right through the skins a couple of times. Place cut-side up in a lightly greased shallow ovenproof dish so that the peaches fit close together. Pour a teaspoon of peach schnapps into each of the peach halves and the remainder into the base of the dish.

Mix the sugar and almonds in a basin. Add the egg and beat well. Stir in the almond extract. Spoon a teaspoon of the macaroon mixture into each peach half. Place in the oven for about 25–30 minutes until peaches are tender with juices just running, but not burning, and macaroons are lightly coloured. Serve hot or warm with the juices poured around the peaches.

Fruit Crumble

This pudding can be made with any fresh or frozen and thawed fruit. There is a minimal amount of sugar in the crumble, most of the sweetness coming from the fruit. Experiment using naturally sweet fruit, or use this to mix with other less sweet fruit to avoid adding sugar. If coeliac with a high level of sensitivity, the oats may be replaced by millet flakes.

SERVES 4–5 | PREPARATION TIME – 10 MINUTES FOR THE CRUMBLE
(VARIABLE TIME FOR FRUIT) PLUS 35 MINUTES FOR
COOKING

700g (1½ lb) prepared fruit*
75g (2¾ oz) (½ cup plus ½ tablespoon) rice flour
25g (1 oz) (1¾ tablespoons) ground rice
25g (1 oz) (3¾ tablespoons) gram flour
25g (1 oz) (3½ tablespoons) porridge oats
70g (2½ oz) (⅓ cup) dairy-free margarine
20g (¾ oz) (1½ tablespoons) unrefined demerara sugar
½ tablespoon sunflower seeds, roughly broken

*SUGGESTED FRUIT MIXTURES: Bramley (cooking), Cox's (eating) apples, or pears with apricots, blackcurrants, blueberries or cranberries or a mixture of fruits.

Preheat the oven to 180°C (350°F) (gas mark 4).

Sieve the flours into a mixing bowl. Add the oats. Rub in the margarine lightly until a heavy crumble consistency is reached. Stir in the sugar and sunflower seeds.

If using firm to very firm fruit, lightly stew in a saucepan with a tablespoon of water and a squeeze of lemon juice (to prevent discolouration) – for a few minutes. Place the fruit in a greased 1.7 litre (3 pint) ovenproof dish and spread the crumble evenly over. Lightly firm the surface and cook for 30–35 minutes.

LEMON CRUMBLE TOPPING: the recipe for Lemon Shortbread (*see page 124*), offers a tangy alternative topping. Follow the recipe making to the heavy crumble stage only.

Lemon Meringue Pie

This is one recipe where I prefer to use refined white caster (superfine) sugar for texture and visual effect of the meringue. However, unrefined golden caster (superfine) sugar can be used for a slightly different texture.

SERVES 6 | PREPARATION TIME – 1 HOUR PLUS 15 MINUTES FOR BAKING

pastry:

125g (4½ oz) (generous ¾ cup) rice flour

20g (¾ oz) (2 tablespoons) potato flour (farina)

20g (¾ oz) (3¾ tablespoons) soya flour

10g (½ oz) (1½ tablespoons) millet flakes

¼ teaspoon gluten-free baking powder

¼ teaspoon xanthum gum

80g (2¾ oz) (5 tablespoons) dairy-free margarine, straight from the fridge

2¼–2½ tablespoons cold water

lemon sauce:

150g (5¼ oz) (¾ cup) unrefined golden caster (superfine) sugar

25g (1 oz) (2¾ tablespoons) potato flour (farina)

140ml (5 fl oz) (½ cup plus 1 tablespoon) water

finely grated rind and juice 2 large lemons using 140ml (5 fl oz) (½ cup plus 1 tablespoon)

25g (1 oz) (1¾ tablespoons) dairy-free margarine

2 large egg yolks, reserving the whites

meringue:

2 large egg whites

85g (3 oz) (6 tablespoons) white caster (superfine) sugar

Preheat the oven to 180°C (350°F) (gas mark 4).

Sieve the flours into a mixing bowl. Add the millet flakes, baking powder and xanthum gum. Mix together, then rub in the margarine lightly with the fingertips until it resembles fine breadcrumbs. Add the water then cut and stir into the mixture with a knife until it is the consistency of soft, damp to wettish pastry. Bring together into a dough with the hands.

Flour the work surface and rolling pin with rice flour then turn the dough onto the surface. Roll out then place a 20cm (8") non-stick sponge/flan tin on the pastry and cut around the base. Cut in half and carefully lift each piece into the greased tin with a fish slice (or similar) with edges to meet. Cut strips to line the sides and make the top edge level. Line with foil and bake 'blind' for 9 minutes in the oven, remove foil then cook for a further 7 minutes. Leave to cool.

For the lemon sauce, mix the sugar, potato flour (farina) and water in a small saucepan. Add the rind and juice. Bring to the boil over a moderate heat, stirring constantly. Simmer for 1 minute, stirring. Remove from the heat. Add the margarine, stir until melted then add the egg yolks, stirring vigorously. Return to a very low heat, stirring constantly for a minute to thicken, without boiling. Remove from the heat.

For the meringue, whisk the egg whites in a basin until stiff, add the sugar and continue to whisk until the meringue is very stiff and satiny. Pour the sauce into the pastry case then spoon the meringue over the sauce to cover completely. Cook in the oven for 13–15 minutes until the meringue is lightly browned and firm on the surface. Remove from the oven. Serve hot, warm or cold.

Passion Fruit Sago Pudding

You would normally use twice as much sugar in a milk pudding but by taking advantage of the passion fruit's natural sweetness, only a tablespoon is used.

SERVES 4 | PREPARATION TIME – 20 MINUTES PLUS 25 MINUTES FOR COOKING

1.135 litres (40 fl oz) (4¾ cups) sweetened soya milk
100g (3½ oz) (⅔ cup) sago
1 tablespoon unrefined golden granulated sugar
2 teaspoons natural vanilla extract
2 large/4 small passion fruits

Preheat the oven to 200°C (400°F) (gas mark 6).

In a large saucepan, heat the milk and sago to boiling point, stirring constantly. Simmer over a very low heat for 7–9 minutes until thick and creamy. Remove from the heat, stir in the sugar until dissolved, then add the vanilla extract. Pour into a well-greased 1.7 litre (3 pint) ovenproof dish. Cook in the oven for about 25 minutes.

Halve and scoop out the passion fruit then stir into the pudding. Serve, stirring in a little more milk if desired.

Pineapple Upside-down Pudding

This classic pudding is made extra special by using fresh pineapple and cherries when in season.

SERVES 6–7 | PREPARATION TIME – 15 MINUTES (25 MINUTES FOR FRESH
PINEAPPLE) PLUS 35 MINUTES FOR COOKING

2 tablespoons maple syrup
1 rounded teaspoon finely cut fresh root ginger
4 fresh pineapple rings (or 5 tinned, reserving the juice), trimmed, cored and cut into 1cm (½") slices
9–18 fresh cherries, stoned (pitted)/9 natural coloured glacé cherries, halved
110g (4 oz) (7 tablespoons) dairy-free margarine
100g (3½ oz) (½ cup) unrefined golden caster (superfine) sugar
110g (4 oz) (¾ cup) rice flour sieved
1 rounded teaspoon gluten-free baking powder
1 teaspoon ground ginger
2 large free-range eggs

Pour the syrup over the base of a greased 20cm (8") non-stick deep sponge tin. Scatter with the ginger, then place the pineapple rings in the base. Place ½ a large fresh/glacé cherry (or 1 whole small cherry) cut side up in the centre of each ring and between rings.

Preheat the oven to 180°C (350°F) (gas mark 4).

Beat the remaining ingredients together in a mixing bowl until thick and creamy. Spread the mixture evenly over the pineapple. Cook in the oven for 30–35 minutes. Leave in the tin for a few minutes. To serve, run a plastic spatula around the tin to loosen. Place a large plate over the tin, hold in place whilst turning upside down onto the plate. Serve hot with Custard (*see page 213*), or warm to cold as a gateau with soya cream.

Quick Rice Pudding

Bananas have a high carbohydrate content in the form of three sugars – sucrose, glucose (dextrose) and fructose. They are absorbed at different rates producing a quick burst of energy, but also a sustained one (fructose being absorbed slowly).

Brown rice too is a good source of energy, B vitamins, calcium and magnesium. Of the grains it is less likely to cause intestinal gas and bowel distress. Both bananas and rice are high in fibre. This 'pudding' could also be eaten as a winter breakfast providing a warm energy boost to start the day.

SERVES 2 | PREPARATION TIME – 8 MINUTES PLUS 10 MINUTES FOR
            SIMMERING

455ml (16 fl oz) (2 cups less 1 tablespoon) rice milk
70g (2½ oz) (⅔ cup) brown rice flakes
1 medium very ripe banana
1 tablespoon soya cream

Place the rice milk and rice flakes in a small saucepan, bring to the boil and simmer uncovered for 7–9 minutes, stirring occasionally as it thickens.

Mash the banana well on a plate, stir into the cooked rice and heat briefly. Stir in the cream, adding a little more rice milk if necessary, to serve.

Rhubarb & Pear Pudding

If you choose early forced pink rhubarb it is naturally sweet and less acidic than the later maincrop variety.

SERVES 3 OR MAKES 4 'MINI PUDDINGS' IN 4 X 7.5CM (3") RAMEKIN
DISHES
PREPARATION TIME – 6 MINUTES PLUS 25 MINUTES FOR COOKING

225g (8 oz) (1¾ cups) early forced rhubarb already trimmed, peeled and cut into chunks
160g (5¾ oz) semi-ripe pear, peeled and cut into chunks (1 medium-sized pear)
1½ tablespoons water
2½ teaspoons rose water

Preheat the oven to 180°C (350°F) (gas mark 4).

Put the prepared rhubarb and pear into a small saucepan with the water. Cover and simmer for only 2–3 minutes, stirring once, until the juices just start to run. Turn into a small covered ovenproof dish with the rose water, or press down into 4 ramekins. Cook in the oven for 20–24 minutes. Serve.

Strawberry & Lime Meringue Pie

The flavours of strawberry and lime combine well to produce this unusual meringue pie.

SERVES 4 | PREPARATION TIME – 1 HOUR PLUS 15 MINUTES FOR BAKING

215g (7½ oz) (2 cups) fresh medium strawberries, hulled and halved

pastry:

125g (4½ oz) (generous ¾ cup) rice flour

20g (¾ oz) (2 tablespoons) potato flour (farina)

20g (¾ oz) (3¾ tablespoons) soya flour

10g (½ oz) (1½ tablespoons) millet flakes

¼ teaspoon gluten-free baking powder

¼ teaspoon xanthum gum

80g (2¾ oz) (5 tablespoons) dairy-free margarine, straight from the fridge

2¼–2½ tablespoons cold water

lime sauce:

130g (4½ oz) (½ cup plus 2 tablespoons) unrefined golden caster (superfine) sugar

25g (1 oz) (2¾ tablespoons) potato flour (farina)

140ml (5 fl oz) (½ cup plus 1 tablespoon) water

2 large egg yolks

finely grated rind and juice 3 limes

meringue:

2 large egg whites

80g (2¾ oz) (5 tablespoons) white caster (superfine) sugar

Preheat the oven to 180°C (350°F) (gas mark 4).

Sieve the flours into a mixing bowl. Add the millet flakes, baking powder and xanthum gum. Mix together, then rub in the margarine lightly with the fingertips until it resembles fine breadcrumbs. Add the water then cut and stir into the mixture with a knife until it is the consistency of soft, damp to wettish pastry. Bring together into a dough with the hands.

Flour the work surface and rolling pin with rice flour then turn the dough onto the surface. Roll out then place a 20cm (8") non-stick sponge/flan tin on the pastry. Cut around the base, cut pastry in half then carefully lift with two fish slices (or similar) into the greased tin with edges to meet. Cut strips to line the sides and make the top edge level. Line with foil and bake 'blind' for 9 minutes in the oven, carefully remove the foil then cook for a further 7 minutes. Leave to cool.

To make the sauce, add the sugar and potato flour (farina) to the water in a small saucepan and stir constantly over a medium heat until the sugar dissolves and the sauce thickens. As it comes to the boil, turn to low and continue to stir for 1 minute until very thick. Remove from the heat to cool slightly. Add the egg yolks, stirring vigorously. Add the lime rind and juice and return to a very low heat, stirring for a minute or so until thick, without boiling.

Place the strawberries cut side down in the pastry case. Pour the lime sauce over the strawberries.

For the meringue, whisk the egg whites until stiff, add the sugar and continue to whisk until it is very stiff and shiny. Spoon over the sauce to cover completely. Return to the oven for 12–15 minutes until the meringue is lightly browned and firm on the surface. Serve hot, warm or cold.

Warm Pineapple, Banana & Mango Salad

This warm fresh fruit salad makes a pleasant change, but for
maximum health-giving benefits enjoy it raw, perhaps laced
with a little rum. For a variation try fresh papaya instead of
mango.

SERVES 2 | PREPARATION TIME – 15 MINUTES

2 x 1cm (½") slices fresh pineapple, trimmed, cored and quartered
1 medium ripe banana, sliced lengthways and halved
2 generous slices fresh mango, peeled and sliced
10g (½ oz) (¾ tablespoon) dairy-free margarine
3 teaspoons dark rum

Melt the margarine in a large non-stick frying pan (skillet). Fry the
fruit to coat and cook for 1–1½ minutes each side until just soft. Add
rum and stir. Serve immediately, pouring over the juices.

Cold Sweets

Apple & Elderflower Jelly

This is a beautifully fresh jelly for a hot day. It is delicious
served with freshly sliced dessert apples, kiwi fruit or green and
red seedless grapes.

SERVES 4 | PREPARATION TIME – 8 MINUTES PLUS 2¼ HOURS TO SET

568ml (20 fl oz) (2⅓ cups) freshly pressed apple and elderflower juice*
11.7g (½ oz sachet) (20ml tablespoon) gelatine granules/vegetarian equivalent

**Alternatively, the jelly can be made with Apple Juice infused
with Elderflowers (see page 198).*

Heat 140ml (5 fl oz) (½ cup) of the juice in a small saucepan until
hot. Remove from the heat and sprinkle the gelatine over. Stir until
dissolved. Pour the remaining juice into the gelatine mixture, stirring
well. Pour into a wetted 568ml (20 fl oz) jelly mould and chill in the
fridge for about 2¼ hours until set.

Blackcurrant Cheesecake

The texture of the cheesecake is really soft and creamy with a
sumptuous blackcurrant and orange topping. Do remember to
bring it to room temperature at least 15 minutes before
serving, for maximum flavour.

SERVES 6 | PREPARATION TIME – 1¼ HOURS PLUS 1 HOUR FOR FINAL
CHILLING

biscuit base:

> 65g (2¼ oz) (½ cup) rice flour
>
> 40g (1½ oz) (generous ⅓ cup) gram flour
>
> 60g (2¼ oz) (3¾ tablespoons) dairy-free margarine
>
> 20g (¾ oz) (1½ tablespoons) unrefined demerara sugar
>
> 2 rounded teaspoons finely grated lemon rind

cheese layer:

> grated rind ½ large orange
>
> 5 tablespoons hot water
>
> 1 tablespoon rice flour
>
> 250g (8¾ oz) non-dairy alternative to full-fat soft cheese
>
> 285ml (10 fl oz) (1¼ cups less 1 tablespoon) plain soya yoghurt
>
> 1 tablespoon soya cream
>
> 2 tablespoons orange juice
>
> 2 rounded *and* 1 level teaspoon gelatine granules

topping:

> 80g (2¾ oz) (5 tablespoons) unrefined golden caster (superfine) sugar
>
> 1 tablespoon water
>
> 1 tablespoon orange juice
>
> ½ teaspoon finely grated orange rind
>
> 170g (6 oz) (generous 1⅓ cups) fresh blackcurrants
>
> 2 rounded teaspoons gelatine granules

Preheat the oven to 180°C (350°F) (gas mark 4).

Sieve the flours into a mixing bowl. Rub in the margarine. Mix in the sugar then the rind to bring the mixture together. Firmly press into the base of a well-greased 20cm (8") non-stick spring-form tin. Cook in the oven for 12–14 minutes until lightly coloured. Leave to cool.

Meanwhile, make the cheese layer. Simmer the orange rind in the water in a small saucepan for about 3 minutes. Stand in cold water to cool slightly. Stir in the flour and slowly return to the boil, stirring continuously. Simmer for 1 minute. Remove from the heat. Thoroughly blend in the soft cheese followed by the yoghurt and cream until smooth. Heat the orange juice in a heatproof basin placed over a saucepan of simmering water. Sprinkle over the gelatine and stir until dissolved. Remove saucepan from the heat but leave the basin resting in the saucepan whilst stirring the cheese mixture constantly into the gelatine. Pour evenly over the cooled biscuit base and chill for about 45 minutes.

For the topping, simmer the sugar and water in a small saucepan, stirring until dissolved and syrupy. Add the orange juice, rind and blackcurrants. Cook, stirring occasionally, over a low heat until just tender, with blackcurrants still whole and plump – about 3 minutes. Remove from the heat. Strain half the juice into a small heatproof basin then add the gelatine. Place over a saucepan of simmering water and stir until completely dissolved. Pour the remaining blackcurrants and juice into the gelatine mixture. Stir to combine, then stand the basin in cold water, stirring occasionally until thick and almost cool (but not setting). When the cheesecake is sufficiently set – about 45 minutes chilling, carefully pour over the blackcurrant topping.

Chill for a further ¾–1 hour. To serve, run a thin plastic spatula around the tin, release the clasp and remove the outer rim.

A creamy sheep's or goats' milk yoghurt may be used instead of soya yoghurt, if tolerated as part of a low-lactose diet.

Blueberry & Raspberry Dessert

This is a luxurious, velvety, layered dessert. To taste the full fruit flavour serve at once whilst at room temperature. Raspberries and blueberries are high in antioxidants, blueberries especially so.

Serves 2 | Preparation time – 25 minutes

85g (3 oz) (⅔ cup) fresh blueberries

40g (1½ oz) (generous ⅓ cup) fresh raspberries

3 tablespoons chilled soya cream

3 teaspoons lemon juice
8 rounded tablespoons 'fruits of the forest' soya yoghurt, chilled

In a small saucepan, gently heat 55g (2 oz) (½ cup) of the blueberries in 1 tablespoon of water. As soon as any blueberry juice escapes, lift them out with a spoon held against the side of the saucepan, allowing the water to drain back into the saucepan. Reserve 6 and divide the remainder between two stemmed glasses.

Reserve 2 raspberries for decoration. Add the remaining raspberries and blueberries to the saucepan and cover. Simmer over a low heat, stirring occasionally until soft. Press through a sieve using the back of a metal spoon. Put half a tablespoon of purée over the layer of blueberries in each glass, reserving the remainder.

In a small basin, mix the lemon juice into the cream and stir briskly until smooth. Spoon the yoghurt carefully over the cream then the reserved purée over the yoghurt. *Do not stir.*

Lift a tablespoon through the cream, yoghurt and purée layers to divide between the two glasses. Decorate with the reserved raspberries and blueberries. Serve at once or chill if preferred.

Coffee Mallow

SERVES 2 | PREPARATION TIME – 30 MINUTES PLUS 2¾ HOURS FOR CHILLING

170ml (6 fl oz) (⅔ cup) boiling water
1 lightly rounded tablespoon instant coffee granules
22 marshmallows, quartered
240ml (8½ fl oz) (1 cup) chilled soya cream
½ teaspoon natural vanilla extract
2 crushed walnuts for decoration

A variation can be made by adding a teaspoon of coffee

liqueur to each glass before carefully pouring over the coffee mallow.

Bring the water to the boil in a small saucepan. Add the coffee granules and prepared marshmallows. Stir over a very low heat until dissolved. Stand in a bowl of cold water and stir until the mixture is cool. Leave in cold water stirring occasionally, to blend the mixture until quite cold and thick, *but not setting.*

Add the vanilla extract to the cream then stir in a steady stream into the coffee mixture, blending well. Pour into sundae glasses or dishes. Chill for 2¾ hours. Decorate with the crushed walnuts to serve.

Cranberry & Raspberry Jellyoghurt

The fruit juice used here is made from American cranberries which are free from artificial colours, flavourings and sweeteners. It is rich in Vitamin C.

SERVES 4 | PREPARATION TIME – 15 MINUTES PLUS CHILLING UNTIL SET

400ml (14 fl oz) (1⅔ cups) cranberry and raspberry juice
11.7g (½ oz sachet) (20 ml tablespoon) gelatine granules
4 rounded tablespoons strawberry soya yoghurt
60g (2½ oz) (generous ½ cup) fresh/frozen and thawed raspberries

Set a 568ml (20 fl oz) heatproof basin over a saucepan of simmering water. Place 3 tablespoons of juice in the basin and sprinkle with gelatine. Stir from time to time until syrupy and gelatine dissolved. Remove basin from the saucepan.

Pour the remaining juice into the gelatine mixture stirring constantly. Pour into the yoghurt and stir until evenly blended. Pour into a wetted 568ml (20 fl oz) jelly mould. Add the raspberries. Chill until set.

Strawberry goats' milk yoghurt makes a delicious alternative to soya yoghurt if tolerated as part of a low-lactose diet.

Crème Caramel

This classic dessert works really well using soya milk and soya cream. For a more unusual variation, see mango crème caramel at the end of the recipe.

MAKES 3 | PREPARATION TIME – 25 MINUTES PLUS 40 MINUTES FOR COOKING PLUS 1½ HOURS FOR CHILLING

caramel:

50g (2 oz) (¼ cup) unrefined golden caster (superfine) sugar

1 tablespoon hot water

custard:

2 large free-range eggs

20g (¾ oz) (1½ tablespoons) unrefined light soft brown sugar

¼ teaspoon natural vanilla extract

70ml (2½ fl oz) (⅓ cup) sweetened soya milk

140ml (5 fl oz) (½ cup plus 2 tablespoons) soya cream

For the caramel, place the sugar in a small saucepan and heat slowly. Stir as it starts to darken into a syrup. Continue stirring until all of the sugar has dissolved and is smooth and syrupy. When it darkens a fraction and smokes, immediately take off the heat. Add the hot water – *but beware* – it will splutter and spit. Stir until well blended and syrupy. Pour immediately into 3 x 7.5cm (3") ramekin dishes to coat the bases.

Preheat the oven to 140°C (275°F) (gas mark 1).

For the custard, whisk the eggs, sugar and vanilla extract in a basin. Heat the milk and cream until hot, but not boiling. Pour onto the egg mixture, whisking together until blended. Divide the mixture between the ramekins and place in a large roasting dish*. Pour cold water into the dish to a depth of three quarters of the sides of the ramekins. Cook in the oven for 30–40 minutes until just set (the surface should be firm but hardly coloured). Remove from the roasting dish and leave until sufficiently cool to stand on plates in the fridge. Chill for about 1–1½ hours. To serve, run a thin knife around the edge of each caramel, place a plate or dish on top and turn upside down.

If you use a smaller roasting dish where the ramekin dishes fit quite snugly without much water to surround and separate them, they will cook a little more quickly than in a larger one.

Mango Crème Caramel:

You will need 3 very thin slices of ripe mango in addition to the above ingredients. Make the caramel as above and pour into the ramekin dishes. Cut the mango slices into small pieces and divide between the dishes to just cover the caramel. Make the custard, pour over the fruit and cook as above.

Fragrant Peach & Orange Rice

SERVES 2 | PREPARATION TIME – 15 MINUTES PLUS 15 MINUTES FOR
FINAL SIMMERING

75g (2¾ oz) (⅓ cup) pudding rice
140ml (5 fl oz) (½ cup plus 1 tablespoon) freshly squeezed orange juice
½ teaspoon orange flower water
285ml (10 fl oz) (1¼ cups less 1 tablespoon) rice milk
30g (1 oz) (2 tablespoons) unrefined golden granulated sugar
1 ripe peach, peeled, halved and stoned (pitted)
1 teaspoon soya cream (*optional*)

The sugar can be reduced to 25g (1 oz) (1½ tablespoons)

Add the rice, orange juice and flower water to a small saucepan. Bring to the boil and simmer, stirring occasionally, until the juice has just been absorbed – about 5 minutes.

Gradually stir in the milk and return to the boil. Simmer for about

14–16 minutes (uncovered), stirring from time to time until the rice is tender and the mixture thick. Stir in the sugar until dissolved. Mash the peach and mix into the rice. Stir in the cream. Serve hot or chilled.

Gooseberry & Orange Rice:

Soften 40g (1½ oz) (⅓ cup) gooseberries with half a tablespoon of water, then add to the cooked rice instead of the peach.

Fresh Fruit Salad with Pomegranate Juice

SERVES 4 | PREPARATION TIME – 10 MINUTES

20 red seedless grapes
20 green seedless grapes
20 raspberries
2 clementines, satsumas/equivalent orange segments
2 medium ripe pears, peeled, cored, sliced and diced
1–2 kiwi fruit, peeled and sliced thinly
juice from 1 pomegranate

If pomegranate is not available, use freshly squeezed orange juice.

Divide the prepared fruit between four dishes. Squeeze the pomegranate juice over the fresh fruit salads and enjoy.

Fresh Pineapple Salad

Vitamin C cannot be stored in the body and needs replenishing daily. It is essential for the formation and maintenance of bones, teeth, tissue, for healing and overall health. It is best obtained as raw energy from citrus and berry fruits, kiwi, melon and pineapple. The fruit salad is equally good made with papaya instead of mango and, if preferred, the fresh ginger can be replaced with stem, glacé or crystallised ginger.

SERVES 2 | PREPARATION TIME – 10 MINUTES

2 x 1cm (½") slices fresh pineapple rings, trimmed, cored and sliced
1 medium–large ripe banana, sliced
3 large, thick slices ripe mango, sliced
1 rounded teaspoon fresh root ginger, cut finely

Combine all the prepared fruit and mix thoroughly. Stir in the ginger. Serve immediately and enjoy.

Gooseberry Fool

Choose fresh and fragrant, creamy-white, fully open elderflower heads for this exquisitely English dessert. Some of the sweetness is provided by the flowers rather than relying on sugar alone.

SERVES 3 | PREPARATION TIME – 35 MINUTES PLUS 1¼ HOURS FOR CHILLING

400g (14¼ oz) (3 cups) fresh gooseberries
4 tablespoons water
1 rounded tablespoon unrefined golden granulated sugar
2 freshly picked large elderflower heads, rinsed, shaken and tied in a scalded muslin bag
3 large egg yolks
1 rounded tablespoon unrefined golden caster (superfine) sugar
½ teaspoon natural vanilla extract
115ml (4 fl oz) (½ cup) soya cream

If preferred, 2 egg yolks can be used, producing a paler and slightly thinner fool.

Rinse the gooseberries, top and tail and place in a medium saucepan together with the water and granulated sugar. Cover and bring to the boil, stirring occasionally. Turn down to the lowest of simmers. Add the prepared elderflowers to the liquid. Simmer for 6–12 minutes, depending on the ripeness of the fruit, stirring occasionally, until soft. Press the muslin bag with the back of a spoon to impart some of the elderflower fragrance. Stir and leave to one side, covered, for the flavours to infuse while making the custard.

Place the egg yolks and caster (superfine) sugar in a small basin. Beat with an electric whisk until light and creamy. Stir in the vanilla extract.

Bring the cream to boiling point in a small saucepan. Pour onto the egg mixture stirring. Place over a saucepan of simmering water, stirring constantly with a wooden spoon until thickened – about 7–8 minutes. Remove the saucepan immediately from the heat and the basin from the saucepan. Stir from time to time as it cools.

Place the gooseberries in a sieve and rub through into a large basin, scraping the purée from under the sieve. Squeeze the juice from the muslin bag into the gooseberry purée. Stir in the egg and cream mixture until evenly blended. Pour into individual glasses and chill for about 1¼ hours.

SERVING SUGGESTION: finely chop 18 fairly young mint leaves then crush into ¾ teaspoon unrefined golden caster (superfine) sugar to garnish, alternatively finish with a swirl of soya cream and mint leaves.

Lemon Mousse with Raspberries on a Biscuit Base

This delicate lemon mousse complements fresh raspberries to make a memorable cold sweet. The lemon curd may be replaced with Golden Curd (*see page 205*) as a variation.

SERVES 6 | PREPARATION TIME – 50 MINUTES PLUS 45 MINUTES FOR FINAL CHILLING

biscuit base:

75g (2¾ oz) (½ cup plus ½ tablespoon) rice flour, sieved

35g (1¼ oz) (2½ tablespoons) unrefined golden caster (superfine) sugar

25g (1 oz) (1¾ tablespoons) ground rice

55g (2 oz) (¼ cup) dairy-free margarine

a few drops natural lemon extract

lemon mousse:

2 tablespoons hot water

4 teaspoons gelatine granules

9 rounded tablespoons plain soya yoghurt

2½ rounded tablespoons dairy-free lemon curd

1 teaspoon lemon juice

2 tablespoons soya cream

3½–4 tablespoons dairy-free lemon curd for the base

100g (3½ oz) (generous ¾ cup) fresh raspberries

Preheat the oven to 180°C (350°F) (gas mark 4).

For the biscuit base, mix the flour, sugar and ground rice in a mixing bowl. Rub in the margarine, add the lemon extract and work into a smooth paste. Flour the work surface with rice flour. Roll out to the size of an 18cm (7") non-stick sponge/flan tin. Place the tin on the mixture and cut around the base. Cut in half and lift individually with a thin fish slice into the greased tin (filling any space between the two halves with biscuit mixture). Cook in the oven for 13–18 minutes until the base is cooked but still pale. Leave to cool.

Meanwhile, make the mousse. Place the hot water in a heatproof basin over a saucepan of simmering water. Sprinkle over the gelatine stirring from time to time until dissolved.

Mix the yoghurt and lemon curd in a separate basin, add the lemon juice and stir to evenly blend. Remove the gelatine basin from the saucepan. Pour the yoghurt and lemon curd mixture into the gelatine, stirring constantly. Whisk the cream until thick, creamy and trebled in volume, then carefully fold into the gelatine, yoghurt, lemon curd mixture.

Spread the lemon curd over the biscuit base. Arrange half of the raspberries over the curd. Pour the lemon mousse carefully over the raspberries. Chill for about 15 minutes – when it should be firm enough to arrange the remaining raspberries over the mousse. Continue to chill for about a further 45 minutes.

Bring the mousse into room temperature about 15 minutes before serving. Cut into portions and serve with a little soya cream, Sour Yoghurt (*see page 215*) or Soya Crème Fraiche (*see page 216*), as preferred.

This delicious gluten-free and dairy-free dessert can be made as a low-lactose version (if tolerated as part of a low-lactose diet), using 9 rounded tablespoons natural goats' milk yoghurt from a 360g (12¾ oz) carton.

Nectarine & Mango Milky Jelly

Enjoy a boost of vitamins A, C and E, beta-carotene and selenium for a healthy immune system with this beautiful soft-set fruit milky jelly.

SERVES 4 | PREPARATION TIME – 30 MINUTES PLUS 2 HOURS FOR CHILLING

150g (5½ oz) (¾ cup) peeled ripe nectarine
150g (5½ oz) (¾ cup) peeled ripe mango
1 teaspoon lemon juice
210ml (7½ fl oz) (¾ cup plus 1 tablespoon) freshly squeezed orange juice
4 teaspoons gelatine granules
100ml (3½ fl oz) (⅓ cup plus 1 tablespoon) unsweetened soya milk

Liquidize the nectarine and mango. Stir in the lemon juice. Reserve

3 tablespoons of the orange juice and place in a heatproof basin. Pour the remainder into the fruit purée and stir to mix well.

Place the basin of reserved orange juice over a saucepan of simmering water. Sprinkle the gelatine over the juice. Stir until dissolved. Remove the basin from the heat. Pour the combined fruit purée and orange juice into the gelatine mixture, stirring constantly. Add the milk, stirring well. Pour immediately into a wetted 568ml (20 fl oz) jelly mould. Chill until set – about 2 hours.

SERVING SUGGESTION: Nectarine Sauce (*see page 214*) poured over this dessert is a lovely accompaniment.

Orange & Chocolate Terrine

This terrine is a gluten-free and dairy-free dessert that is suitable for a special occasion (*see serving suggestion*). It is useful to have an electric mixer and 4 x 568ml (20 fl oz) basins ready before making the dessert. Use chocolate containing a minimum of 70 per cent cocoa solids for a really good flavour. The raw egg white and semi-raw yolk may pose a risk of salmonella and listeria, especially during illness or pregnancy and for vulnerable groups such as the elderly and mothers breastfeeding their babies.

SERVES 4 | PREPARATION TIME – 1 HOUR PLUS 35 MINUTES FOR
       CHILLING

orange mousse:

1 large free-range egg, separated

25g (1 oz) (2 tablespoons) unrefined golden caster (superfine) sugar

finely grated rind 1 large orange

2 drops natural orange extract

2 tablespoons orange juice

2 rounded teaspoons gelatine granules

1½ tablespoons soya cream

chocolate mousse:

1 large free-range egg, separated

10g (½ oz) (1 tablespoon) unrefined golden caster (superfine) sugar

2 tablespoons hot water

2 rounded teaspoons gelatine granules

60g (2¼ oz) gluten-free, dairy-free plain chocolate

2¾ tablespoons soya cream

extra soya cream to serve

orange segments to garnish

For the orange mousse, whisk the egg yolk, sugar and orange rind together in a small basin until pale, thick and creamy – 1½–2 minutes. Stir in the orange extract. Heat the orange juice in a heatproof basin placed over a saucepan of simmering water. Sprinkle over the gelatine and stir until dissolved. Add the whisked egg, sugar and orange mixture to the gelatine, stirring well. Remove basin from the saucepan.

Whisk the cream until trebled in volume then stir into the orange mixture until smoothly blended. Whisk the egg white until stiff and carefully fold in half at a time with a metal spoon. Pour into a greased 454g (1 lb) non-stick loaf tin. Tap the tin to level the surface. Place in the freezer while making the chocolate mousse.

For the chocolate mousse, whisk the egg yolk and sugar in a small basin until pale, thick and creamy – 1½–2 minutes. Place the water in a heatproof basin over a saucepan of simmering water. Sprinkle over the gelatine and stir until dissolved. Break the chocolate into pieces and add to the gelatine, stirring until melted and smooth. Add the whisked egg and sugar mixture, stirring well. Remove basin from the saucepan.

Whisk the cream until trebled in volume then gently stir into the mixture until evenly blended. Whisk the egg white until stiff and carefully fold in half at a time with a metal spoon. Pour the mixture over the orange mousse and chill in the fridge for 30–35 minutes.

To serve, stand the tin in hot water for a few seconds only to loosen the terrine. Place a plate over the tin and turn upside down to release onto the plate. Slice and serve with soya cream and garnish with orange segments.

SERVING SUGGESTION: for a special occasion, serve over a pool of Vanilla Brandy Cream (*see page 216*), dusted with gluten-free, dairy-free cocoa powder and orange segments arranged. The terrine can be decorated with chocolate leaves made by melting gluten-free, dairy-free plain chocolate, then brushing onto the underside of bay leaves. Chill, then carefully peel away the leaves. Decorate the plates with Vanilla Brandy Cream, chocolate leaves and orange segments.

Orange & Passion Fruit Jelly

This jelly is absolutely bursting with vitamin C because most of the orange juice is added unheated. Its flavour and goodness is infinitely superior and preferable to the artificially coloured and flavoured packet varieties.

SERVES 4 | PREPARATION TIME – 30 MINUTES PLUS 2¾ HOURS FOR CHILLING

568ml (20 fl oz) (2⅓ cups) freshly squeezed orange juice
1 large passion fruit
11.7g (½ oz sachet) (20 ml tablespoon) gelatine granules

to serve:

1 medium passion fruit, halved
satsumas/clementines/orange segments

Heat 3 tablespoons of the orange juice in a 568ml (20 fl oz) basin placed over a saucepan of simmering water. Sprinkle the gelatine over the juice and stir from time to time until thick, syrupy and dissolved.

Meanwhile, halve and scoop out the passion fruit. Place in a sieve over a basin. Rub through the sieve with the back of a spoon then pour some of the remaining orange juice through the sieve to wash through the fruit flavour. Discard the seeds. Combine the juices then pour about half into the gelatine mixture, stirring constantly. Remove the basin from the saucepan and stir in the remaining juice. Pour into a wetted 568ml (20 fl oz) jelly mould and chill until set – about 2¾ hours.

Turn out the jelly onto a serving plate, spoon the passion fruit over the jelly and surround with orange segments. Alternatively, it is superb served with soya ice cream/soya cream.

Agar flakes:

These are a natural gelling agent from seaweed extraction and can be used as an alternative to gelatine. Sprinkle 2 slightly rounded tablespoons agar flakes over 140ml (5 fl oz) (½ cup) of the orange juice in a small saucepan. Bring to a simmer over a medium heat without stirring. Simmer for 3–5 minutes, stirring occasionally, until the flakes have dissolved. Pour the remaining orange juice and passion fruit juices into the saucepan, stir well to combine then pour immediately into a wetted jelly mould. Chill. The jelly sets quickly as it cools.

Orange Yoghurt Jelly with Nectarine Sauce

The dessert is delicious when made with freshly squeezed oranges. The vitamin content is at its peak potency and flavour is superb. You will need the juice from about 5 large oranges.

SERVES 4 | PREPARATION TIME – 35 MINUTES PLUS 2¾ HOURS FOR
                        CHILLING

455ml (16 fl oz) (2 cups less 1 tablespoon) freshly squeezed orange juice
11.7g (½ oz sachet) (20 ml tablespoon) gelatine granules
125g (4½ oz) carton nectarine/peach soya yoghurt

sauce:

2 large ripe nectarines
1 teaspoon lemon juice
125g (4½ oz) carton nectarine/peach soya yoghurt – using 2 rounded tablespoons

Place 3 tablespoons of the orange juice in a 568ml (20 fl oz) basin placed over a saucepan of simmering water. Sprinkle the gelatine over the surface then stir from time to time until dissolved. Pour the remaining orange juice into the gelatine mixture, stirring constantly. Remove the basin from the saucepan and pour into the yoghurt, stirring until evenly blended. Pour into a wetted 568ml (20 fl oz) jelly mould and chill until set – about 2¾ hours.

Just before serving, make the sauce. Peel the nectarines, cut in half and remove the stones. Scrape away the redness left by the stones. Liquidize until smooth. Mix in the lemon juice then the yoghurt until evenly blended. Pour into a small jug to accompany the dessert.

Redcurrant & Strawberry Dessert

The dessert is a soft, satiny, layered combination of summer fruit purée. Serve at room temperature for maximum flavour.

SERVES 2 | PREPARATION TIME – 25 MINUTES

85g (3 oz) (¾ cup) fresh redcurrants, de-stalked
50g (2 oz) (½ cup) fresh small–medium strawberries, hulled and cut small
2 tablespoons chilled soya cream
2 teaspoons lemon juice
9 rounded tablespoons/2½ x 125g (4½ oz) pots chilled strawberry soya yoghurt

In a small saucepan gently heat 50g (2 oz) (scant ½ cup) of the redcurrants in 1 tablespoon of water. As soon as any redcurrant juice escapes, lift them out with a spoon held against the side of the saucepan, allowing the water to drain back into the saucepan. Reserve 10 redcurrants for decoration and divide the remainder between two stemmed glasses.

Reserve 2 small strawberries. Add the remaining redcurrants and strawberries to the saucepan and cover. Simmer over a low heat, stirring occasionally until soft – about 2–3 minutes. Press through a sieve using the back of a metal spoon, discarding the seeds. Put half a tablespoon of purée over the layer of redcurrants in each glass, reserving the remainder.

In a small basin, mix the lemon juice into the cream and stir briskly until smooth. Spoon the yoghurt carefully over the cream then the reserved purée over the yoghurt. *Do not stir.*

Lift a tablespoon through the cream, yoghurt and purée layers to divide between the two glasses. Decorate with the reserved redcurrants and strawberries. Serve at once or chill if preferred.

Soya Yoghurt with Brazils

Brazil nuts are one of the richest sources of the antioxidants selenium and vitamin E and therefore support the immune system. Just one or two brazil nuts provide the daily requirement of selenium. Sesame seeds are also antioxidant and have high levels of iron. Both sesame seeds and brazil nuts are good sources of omega-6 fatty acids and calcium in a dairy-free diet. Pecans also 'work' well with maple syrup and are high in potassium, vitamin A and essential fatty acids.

SERVES 2 | PREPARATION TIME – 5 MINUTES

6 rounded tablespoons plain soya yoghurt
25g (1 oz) 10 brazil nuts, sliced
1 teaspoon sesame seeds
2 tablespoons maple syrup

Spoon the yoghurt into two small dishes. Scatter the nuts and sesame seeds over the yoghurt. Drizzle the syrup over the top.

Summer Fruits Compote with Vanilla Brandy

A high-summer, rich and sumptuous dessert – you'll find a little goes a long way! It is bursting with vitamin C and antioxidants from the variety of fresh berries.

SERVES 4 | PREPARATION TIME – 20 MINUTES PLUS 1 HOUR FOR CHILLING

120g (4½ oz) (1 cup) fresh loganberries/tayberries, hulled
120g (4½ oz) (1 cup) fresh redcurrants, de-stalked
60g (2½ oz) (⅔ cup) fresh small strawberries, hulled
1 tablespoon water
10g (½ oz) (1½ tablespoons) unrefined golden icing (confectioners') sugar, sieved
120g (4½ oz) (1¼ cups) fresh raspberries
60g (2½ oz) (½ cup) fresh/frozen and thawed blueberries
1 tablespoon Vanilla Brandy*

If Vanilla Brandy is not available (see page 210), use brandy.

Place the loganberries/tayberries, redcurrants and strawberries in a medium saucepan with the water. Slowly bring to the boil and simmer over a low heat for about 3 minutes, stirring from time to time. Remove from the heat, then stir in the sugar. Mix in the raspberries and blueberries. Cool.

Stir in the vanilla brandy and pour into stemmed glasses. Chill for about 45 minutes–1 hour.

SERVING SUGGESTION: serve with Almond Biscuits (*see page 121*) or Rice Biscuits (*see page 126*) and Soya Crème Fraiche (*see page 216*) or Sour Yoghurt (*see page 215*).

Drinks

What could be more enjoyable and healthy than the vibrancy and goodness of natural fresh fruit juices? They contain a selection of crucial vitamins such as A, B, C, and E, folic acid, potassium, calcium, magnesium and zinc for healing and health. They also contribute to your daily recommended intake of fresh fruit and vegetable portions and can be used as a healthy snack or as a change from breakfast cereals. It is better to drink them immediately after making to maximise the nutrients, or as soon after chilling as possible.

Apple Juice infused with Elderflowers

Enjoy the taste of the countryside with this lovely fragrant apple drink. Only pick elderflowers which are creamy-white and fully open (but not fading) for peak freshness and flavour.

MAKES 568ML (20 FL OZ)
PREPARATION TIME — 5 MINUTES PLUS CHILLING

568ml (20 fl oz) (2 ⅓ cups) freshly pressed apple juice

3 full heads freshly picked elderflowers, rinsed

Bring the apple juice almost to boiling point in a saucepan. Remove from the heat. Tie the elderflowers in a scalded muslin bag and drop into the juice. Cover with a clean cloth. Stir occasionally until cold. Remove the muslin bag and squeeze the juices into the saucepan. Pour the juice into a jug and chill in the fridge before serving. Drink while fresh.

Cranberry, Raspberry & Pear Juice

You can buy excellent cranberry and raspberry juice, also bottled pressed pear juice, free from artificial colours, flavourings, and sweeteners, and not made from concentrates. This almost instant recipe provides a 'quick fix' healthy drink. Added passion fruit juice boosts energy levels.

MAKES 1 GLASS | PREPARATION TIME – 4 MINUTES

140ml (5 fl oz) (½ cup plus 1 tablespoon) chilled cranberry and raspberry juice

55ml (2 fl oz) (3 tablespoons) chilled freshly pressed pear juice

½ small passion fruit

Combine the two juices. Scoop out the passion fruit and rub through a sieve into the juice. Wash any remaining fruit through the sieve with the fruit juice. Discard the seeds. Enjoy.

Early Morning Restorer

Feeling a little sluggish or 'delicate' first thing in the morning? If so, try this drink for a cleansing effect. Then listen to your body and allow it time to recover!

MAKES 1 GLASS | PREPARATION TIME – 5 MINUTES

2 peeled strips unwaxed lemon rind*

½ glass water

juice from ¼ small lemon

*If waxed, scrub under hot water to remove the wax.

Add the strips of lemon rind and water to a small saucepan and bring to the boil. Remove from the heat and leave to infuse for 2–3 minutes. Strain into a glass, stir in the lemon juice and drink when cool enough.

Lime Restorer: Add 2 strips of lime rind and a peeled strip of fresh root ginger to the water, bring to the boil, remove from the heat and leave to infuse for 2–3 minutes. Strain into a glass. Add the juice from half a lime and drink when cool enough.

Mango & Passion Fruit Cooler

If the mango and milk have been stored in the fridge before-hand you'll have that ready-made 'cooler' when you really need it! This smoothie is also wonderful poured over exotic fruit salads, plain cakes, gateaux or sponge puddings as a thick sauce.

MAKES 1 GLASS | PREPARATION TIME – 6 MINUTES

50g (2 oz) (¼ cup) peeled ripe mango
½ small passion fruit, scooped out
140ml (5 fl oz) (½ cup plus 1 tablespoon) sweetened soya milk

Liquidize the mango, passion fruit and milk. Pour into a glass and enjoy.

Mango Creamy

Choose a mango with reddening to orange skin that 'gives' slightly when pressed, to ensure it is ripe. Chill the fruit and coconut milk before making so that it can be drunk immediately, retaining all of its nutrients.

MAKES 1 GLASS | PREPARATION TIME – 6 MINUTES

100g (3½ oz) (½ cup) peeled ripe mango
170ml (6 fl oz) (⅔ cup) chilled coconut milk
1 teaspoon lime juice
2–3 drops orange-flower water (*optional*)

Place the mango and coconut milk in a liquidizer. Blend until smooth and creamy. Pour into a glass and stir in the lime juice and flower water. Drink immediately.

Nectarine, Mango & Orange Smoothie

Chill the fruit before making, if possible, and drink immediately while nutrient-packed.

MAKES 1 GLASS | PREPARATION TIME – 10 MINUTES

70g (2½ oz) (⅓ cup) peeled ripe nectarine

70g (2½ oz) (⅓ cup) peeled ripe mango

100ml (3½ fl oz) (⅓ cup plus 1 tablespoon) freshly squeezed orange juice

Liquidize the nectarine and mango. Stir in the orange juice. Drink immediately or chill.

Orange Yoghurt Drink

MAKES 1 GLASS | PREPARATION TIME – 8 MINUTES

115ml (4 fl oz) (⅓ cup plus 1 tablespoon) freshly squeezed orange juice, from chilled oranges

115ml (4 fl oz) (⅓ cup plus 1 tablespoon) chilled plain soya yoghurt

Stir the orange juice into the yoghurt until well blended. Drink immediately.

Substituting naturally lower-lactose sheep's milk yoghurt makes an even nicer, creamier orange drink than soya, if tolerated as part of a low-lactose diet.

Papaya Creamy

Look for a papaya with yellowing skin to ensure it is ripe. It
makes a pretty shell-pink, creamy drink. Papaya contains
papain, a protein-digesting enzyme which aids digestion and
relieves inflammation. It may be helpful for people suffering
from gluten intolerance or wheat allergy.

MAKES 1 GLASS │ PREPARATION TIME – 8 MINUTES

100g (3½ oz) (½ cup) freshly peeled ripe papaya
200ml (7 fl oz) (¾ cup) coconut milk
1 teaspoon lime juice (*optional*)

Place the papaya and coconut milk in a liquidizer. Blend until smooth
and creamy. Pour into a glass and stir in the lime juice. Drink
immediately.

Pineapple, Mango & Passion Fruit Drink

Chill the fruit and pineapple juice before making the drink. It
also makes a beautiful fruity-flavoured sauce for pouring over
non-dairy vanilla ice cream.

MAKES 1 GLASS │ PREPARATION TIME – 8 MINUTES

100g (3½ oz) (½ cup) peeled ripe mango
1 small/½ large passion fruit
115ml (4 fl oz) (½ cup) chilled pineapple juice

Liquidize the fruit with the juice, blending until smooth. Drink
immediately.

Pineapple, Papaya & Banana Drink

This makes a long, cool fruity drink with a hint of ginger.

MAKES 2 GLASSES | PREPARATION TIME – 15 MINUTES

1 rounded teaspoon finely sliced fresh root ginger

5 tablespoons pineapple juice

125g (4½ oz) cored and trimmed ripe pineapple – about 1 large 1cm (½") slice/tinned pineapple in natural juice

50g (2 oz) (¼ cup) peeled ripe papaya, seeds removed

50g (2 oz) ½ medium peeled ripe banana

200ml (7 fl oz) (¾ cup) ginger ale

ice cubes

Simmer the ginger in the pineapple juice for 5 minutes. Leave to one side to cool. Liquidize the pineapple, papaya and banana with the cooled pineapple juice. Discard the ginger. Pour into glasses. Top up with ginger ale and stir well. Add ice cubes.

Raspberry Crush

MAKES 1 GLASS | PREPARATION TIME – 1 MINUTE

30g (1 oz) (¼ cup) fresh raspberries

185ml (6½ fl oz) (¾ cup) chilled rice milk, shaken well

2 drops natural almond extract

Liquidize the raspberries and milk. Pour into a glass, stir in the almond extract and drink immediately.

Spreads, Preserves & Curds

Chocolate Almond Spread

The spread is sufficient to sandwich an 18cm (7") sponge and complements Light Chocolate Almond Cake (*see page 152*).

see page 152

PREPARATION TIME – 10 MINUTES

45g (1½ oz) (2¾ tablespoons) dairy-free margarine
25g (1 oz) (3½ tablespoons) gluten-free, dairy-free cocoa powder, sieved
50g (1¾ oz) (½ cup) unrefined golden icing (confectioners') sugar, sieved
3 drops natural almond extract

Add the margarine, cocoa and sugar to a mixing bowl. Stir well then beat with an electric mixer until the mixture lightens in colour and texture. Add the almond extract, then stir or beat again.

Chocolate Orange Spread/Icing

This is enough spread to sandwich an 18cm (7") sponge. Double the quantity if you wish to ice a cake as well. It is a smooth spread, especially good with Dark Chocolate Orange Cake (*see page 149*).

see page 149

PREPARATION TIME – 8 MINUTES

25g (1 oz) (3½ tablespoons) gluten-free, dairy-free cocoa powder, sieved

85g (3 oz) (scant ⅔ cup) unrefined golden icing (confectioners') sugar, sieved
1 tablespoon soya cream
1 tablespoon orange juice*

Or use ½ tablespoon orange juice and ¾ teaspoon orange-flower water.

Add the cocoa and sugar to a mixing bowl. Stir in the cream and orange juice, until well mixed. Beat well with an electric mixer until smooth.

Golden Curd

Home-made curd tastes so much better than shop-bought. There is slightly less sugar in this recipe than you might expect and it has the bonus of being dairy free. It can be used for Golden Curd Tarts – a children's favourite (*see recipe for Jam Tarts on page 132*), Golden Cream (*see Lemon Cream recipe on page 213*) or Lemon Mousse with Raspberries on a Biscuit Base (*see page 188*) substituting lemon curd with golden curd.

MAKES 1 JAR – ABOUT 454g (1 lb) | PREPARATION TIME – 1 HOUR

finely grated rind and juice 1 large unwaxed orange*
finely grated rind and juice 1 medium unwaxed lemon*
110g (4 oz) (½ cup) white granulated/preserving sugar
30g (1 oz) (2 tablespoons) dairy-free margarine
2 large free-range eggs

If waxed, scrub under hot water to remove the wax.

Place the rinds, juices, sugar and margarine in the top of a double saucepan or in a basin standing over a saucepan of simmering water. Stir until the sugar has dissolved. Strain the mixture through a sieve into a clean basin, rubbing about half the rind through the sieve then adding the remaining rind back into the fruit mixture.

Beat the eggs in a separate basin then strain through the sieve into the fruit mixture. Return to cook over the simmering water, stirring frequently with a wooden spoon until the mixture thickens sufficiently to coat the back of the spoon leaving a definite layer – about 15 minutes. Cool for a few minutes. Pour into a warm, sterilized jar, cover and label. The curd will store for about 2 months refrigerated.

TO STERILIZE JARS: Place clean jars in a large pan, cover with hot water and bring to the boil. Boil rapidly for 10 minutes. Remove from pan and stand upside down to drain on a clean kitchen towel. Immerse lids in boiling water for about ½ minute. Alternatively, place jars in the oven at 170°C (325°F) (gas mark 3), for 10 minutes.

Honey Vanilla Spread

There is enough spread to sandwich an 18cm (7") sponge and it complements a Victoria Sandwich (*see page 158*).

PREPARATION TIME – 7 MINUTES

115g (4 oz) (¾ cup plus 2½ tablespoons) unrefined golden icing (confectioners') sugar, sieved
30g (1 oz) (2 tablespoons) dairy-free margarine
1 tablespoon orange-blossom honey
5 drops natural vanilla extract

Add the ingredients to a mixing bowl, stir, then beat well with an electric mixer until light and creamy.

Lemon Curd

This recipe makes a really tangy, fresh lemon curd with a slightly reduced sugar content. The sugar content can be reduced further to 215g (7½ oz) (1 cup less ¾ tablespoon) and still be tangy but not too sharp. The curd can be used to make

Lemon Curd Tarts (*see recipe for Jam Tarts on page 132*), Lemon Mousse with Raspberries on a Biscuit Base (*see page 188*) and Lemon Cream (*see page 213*).

MAKES 1 JAR – ABOUT 454G (1 LB) | PREPARATION TIME – 1 HOUR

finely grated rind 2 large unwaxed lemons*
115–140ml (4–5 fl oz) (½ cup) lemon juice
225g (8 oz) (1 cup) white granulated/preserving sugar
75g (2½ oz) (4½ tablespoons) dairy-free margarine
2 large free-range eggs

*If waxed, scrub under hot water to remove the wax.

Place the rind, juice, sugar and margarine in the top of a double saucepan or in a basin standing over a saucepan of simmering water. Stir until the sugar has dissolved. Strain the mixture through a sieve into a clean basin, rubbing the rind through the sieve.

Beat the eggs in a separate basin and strain through the sieve into the fruit mixture. Cook gently, stirring frequently with a wooden spoon until the mixture thickens sufficiently to coat the back of the spoon leaving a definite layer – about 15 minutes. Cool for a few minutes. Pour into a warm sterilized jar, cover and label. The curd will store for about 2 months refrigerated.

TO STERILIZE JARS: Place clean jars in a large pan, cover with hot water and bring to the boil. Boil rapidly for 10 minutes. Remove from pan and stand upside down to drain on a clean kitchen towel. Immerse lids in boiling water for about ½ minute. Alternatively, place jars in the oven at 170°C (325°F) (gas mark 3), for 10 minutes.

Mango & Passion Fruit Spread/Sauce

Use this spread/sauce to sandwich together a plain Victoria/whisked sponge or to pour over fresh fruit salads, non-dairy ice cream or Nectarine & Mango Milky Jelly (*see*

page 190). The quantity is ample to pour over an 18cm (7")
sponge or at least 4 cold desserts. Once prepared, eat as soon as
possible to experience its health-giving vitality and nutrients.

SERVES 4 (ABOUT 170ml/6 fl oz) | PREPARATION TIME – 5 MINUTES

175g (6½ oz) (generous ¾ cup) peeled ripe mango
1 small passion fruit
1 teaspoon lemon juice

Liquidize the mango and passion fruit. Stir in the lemon juice.

Mincemeat

Some mincemeat is incredibly sweet. This is a healthier choice,
containing about half the sugar and fat that would normally be
expected. Use for making festive Mince Pies (*see page 135*) and
tarts. If preferred, a little extra brandy or sherry may be mixed
into the mincemeat prior to using.

MAKES 1.8kg (4 lb) | PREPARATION TIME – 55 MINUTES

55g (2 oz) (⅓ cup) sun-dried/dried pear, sliced finely and diced
285g (10 oz) (2 cups) raisins
200g (7 oz) (generous 1⅓ cups) sultanas (golden raisins)
200g (7 oz) (generous 1⅓ cups) currants
55g (2 oz) (⅓ cup) mixed chopped candied peel
135g (4¾ oz) (1 cup) gluten-free shredded vegetable suet
75g (2¾ oz) (⅓ cup plus ½ tablespoon) unrefined light muscovado sugar
finely grated rind of ¾ large unwaxed lemon*
finely grated rind of ¾ large unwaxed orange*
1 teaspoon ground cinnamon

1 rounded teaspoon gluten-free mixed (pie) spice
1 teaspoon freshly grated nutmeg
200g (7 oz) (1½ cups) cooking apples, peeled, cored and sliced finely and diced
juice 1 large lemon
3 tablespoons orange juice
3 tablespoons brandy

*If waxed, scrub under hot water to remove the wax.

Add the ingredients to a large mixing bowl, stirring from time to time. Stir again thoroughly after adding the fruit juices and brandy. Pack into sterilized, cold, dry jars. Store in a cool cupboard to mature for two weeks before using. Once opened, refrigerate.

TO STERILIZE JARS: Place clean jars in a large pan, cover with hot water and bring to the boil. Boil rapidly for 10 minutes. Remove from pan and stand upside down to drain on a clean kitchen towel. Immerse lids in boiling water for about ½ minute. Alternatively, place jars in the oven at 170°C (325°F) (gas mark 3), for 10 minutes.

Tahini & Honey Spread

The flavours of tahini and honey complement each other well to make this sweet spread for Sesame Biscuits (*see page 119*), rice cakes, corn thins or Crusty White Bread (*see page 115*). The tahini (sesame seed paste) contains omega-6 and omega-9 fatty acids, iron and high levels of calcium to protect bone health, also protein, vitamins B and E, magnesium, and zinc.

PREPARATION TIME – 5 MINUTES

light tahini paste
acacia honey

Mix together equal amounts of tahini and honey to form a smooth paste.

Vanilla Brandy

Vanilla brandy is quite versatile. Use in Vanilla Brandy Cream (*see page 216*), Brandy Sauce (*see page 211*), or in desserts such as Summer Fruits Compote (*see page 197*). Drink as a liqueur or pour over plenty of ice.

PREPARATION TIME – 5 MINUTES

1 whole vanilla pod
285ml (10 fl oz) (1¼ cups) brandy

Make a lengthways slit in the vanilla pod to reveal the seeds. Press open to release the flavours. Place it in a small sterilized cooled bottle, and pour over the brandy. Seal, label and shake well. Keep in a cool dark place for three weeks, shaking the bottle from time to time, before using. This will allow the flavours to develop and it will store for about 9 months–1 year.

TO STERILIZE BOTTLE: Place in a large pan, cover with hot water and bring to the boil. Boil rapidly for 10 minutes. Remove from pan and stand upside down to drain on a clean kitchen towel. Immerse bottle top in boiling water for about ½ minute. Alternatively, place bottle in the oven at 170°C (325°F) (gas mark 3), for 10 minutes.

Sweet Sauces

Brandy Sauce

Ideal to serve with your special gluten-free and dairy-free Christmas Pudding (*see page 165*).

SERVES 4 | PREPARATION TIME – 8 MINUTES

568ml (20 fl oz) (2⅓ cups) sweetened soya milk

4 tablespoons gluten free cornflour (cornstarch)/potato flour (farina)

4 tablespoons unrefined golden granulated sugar

4 tablespoons brandy/Vanilla Brandy (*see page 210*)

3 tablespoons soya cream

Heat most of the milk in a medium saucepan. Mix the flour into the remainder until smooth, then add to the heated milk, stirring until thickened. Add the sugar, stir and simmer for 1 minute. Stir in the brandy and cream. Serve.

Butterscotch Sauce

This recipe makes a smooth sauce for pouring hot, warm or cold over sponge puddings, sliced pears or bananas, and/or non-dairy vanilla or chocolate ice cream. If you can use a pure vanilla extract, all the better.

SERVES 4 (185ml/6½ fl oz) | PREPARATION TIME – 10 MINUTES

60g (2¼ oz) (3¾ tablespoons) dairy-free margarine

1 tablespoon golden syrup (corn syrup)

50g (1¾ oz) (¼ cup) unrefined light soft brown sugar

4 tablespoons soya cream

½ teaspoon natural vanilla extract

The sauce can also be made with 1 teaspoon black strap molasses instead of golden syrup (corn syrup).

Gently melt the margarine with the syrup and sugar in a small saucepan. Stir over a low heat until the sugar has dissolved. Just bring to the boil stirring. Remove from the heat while adding the cream then stir until well blended. Return to the boil and boil rapidly for about 15 seconds. Stir in the vanilla extract. Allow to cool slightly before serving.

Chocolate/Mocha Sauce

Use as a hot or warm pouring sauce over sponges, desserts, non-dairy chocolate/vanilla ice cream and fresh pears/bananas, or cold as a mocha cream. If you prefer a plain chocolate sauce, omit the coffee.

SERVES 4 (ABOUT 170ml/6 fl oz) | PREPARATION TIME – 6 MINUTES

100g (3½ oz) gluten-free, dairy-free plain chocolate, broken

1 tablespoon hot water

½ tablespoon instant coffee granules

4 tablespoons soya cream

Set a basin over a pan of simmering water. Add the chocolate, water and coffee. Stir until melted and smooth. Remove the basin from the heat. Stir in the cream until well blended. Serve warm or reheat gently over simmering water for a hot sauce.

Custard

There is no added sugar to this custard, only fruit sugar provided by the apple juice. It is made with a percentage of water so that it is more acceptable to the non-soya drinking members of the family. A delicious sugar-free custard can also be made using powdered/liquid potato milk.

Serves 4 | Preparation time – 8 minutes

400ml (14 fl oz) (1⅔ cups) sweetened soya milk
140ml (5 fl oz) (½ cup) water
1 rounded *and* 1 level tablespoon gluten-free, dairy-free custard powder
3 tablespoons freshly pressed bottled apple juice

Freshly pressed bottled pear juice also thickens the custard quite well.

Heat the milk in a large saucepan. Mix the custard powder with the water and stir into the milk. Bring to the boil, stirring and cook over a low heat for 1 minute. Remove from the heat. Stir in the apple juice to thicken the custard further.

For a low-lactose version, make with 510ml (18 fl oz) (2 cups) goats' milk (if tolerated as part of a low-lactose diet), plus enough custard powder to thicken. Sweeten with a tablespoon of acacia honey.

Lemon Cream

The lemon curd takes the blandness from the soya yoghurt in this recipe. Sunflower seeds are a good quality source of protein, essential fatty acids, vitamins E, A, D, and B complex; the minerals zinc, iron, calcium, manganese and phosphorus. Their nutrients aid skin health and nourish and strengthen the digestive organs. Lemon cream creates a lovely dessert when poured over Lemon Syrup Cake (*see page 151*).

SERVES 1 AS A COLD SWEET OR USE TO SPOON OVER ICE CREAM, FRESH
FRUIT SALADS OR SPONGES (SUNFLOWER SEEDS *OPTIONAL*)
PREPARATION TIME – 1 MINUTE

3 rounded tablespoons plain soya yoghurt
3 rounded teaspoons dairy-free Lemon Curd (*see page 206*)
hulled sunflower seeds

Thoroughly mix the yoghurt and curd until smooth. Scatter with
sunflower seeds.

GOLDEN CREAM: replace the lemon curd with dairy-free Golden
Curd (*see page 206*) for an alternative cream.

*A creamy sheep's milk yoghurt can be used instead of soya (if
tolerated as part of a low-lactose diet).*

Nectarine Coulis

This makes a lovely fresh fruit coulis/sauce for pouring over
soya ice cream or fruit. It also doubles as a brilliant fresh fruit
drink.

SERVES 4 | PREPARATION TIME – 10 MINUTES

3 large ripe nectarines

Peel, halve and stone the nectarines. Scrape out any rough redness
from the halves, cut into quarters then liquidize.

Pear & Passion Fruit Sauce

This is a fragrant fresh fruit sauce for pouring over non-dairy
ice cream, fresh fruit salads or sponge cakes.

SERVES 4 (255ml/9 fl oz) | PREPARATION TIME – 10 MINUTES

225g (8 oz) peeled and cored ripe pears (2–3 pears)

1 teaspoon lemon juice

1 small passion fruit

Liquidize the pears. Stir in the lemon juice. Rub the passion fruit flesh through a sieve with a little of the pear purée, discarding the seeds. Combine the juices. Serve immediately or chill.

Sour Cream

Sour cream can be used for savoury or sweet dishes; it can be mixed into curries and casseroles or poured over fruit salads, cold sweets, puddings and gateaux.

SERVES 4 | PREPARATION TIME – 1 MINUTE

6 tablespoons chilled soya cream

6 teaspoons lemon juice

2 teaspoons thin honey (*optional*)

Lime juice can be used as an alternative to lemon juice.

Briskly stir the lemon juice into the cream until smooth. Stir in honey to sweeten if preferred.

Sour Yoghurt

Sour yoghurt can be used for savoury or sweet dishes as an alternative to sour cream (*see previous recipe*).

SERVES 4 | PREPARATION TIME – 1 MINUTE

6 tablespoons chilled plain soya yoghurt

4 teaspoons lemon juice

2 teaspoons thin honey (*optional*)

Lime juice can be used instead of lemon juice.

Briskly stir the lemon juice into the yoghurt until smooth. Stir in the
honey to sweeten if preferred.

Soya Crème Fraiche

Use for sweet dishes and stir in a teaspoon of thin honey to
sweeten if preferred. It is also useful as an addition to savoury
dishes.

SERVES 4 | PREPARATION TIME – 2 MINUTES

3 tablespoons chilled soya cream
3 teaspoons lemon juice
4 tablespoons chilled plain soya yoghurt

Lime juice can be used instead of lemon juice.

Briskly stir the lemon juice into the cream until smooth. Stir in the
yoghurt.

Vanilla Brandy Cream

Suitable for pouring (warm or cold) over fresh fruit, non-dairy
ice cream or as a pool of sauce under Orange & Chocolate
Terrine (*see page 191*).

SERVES 4 | PREPARATION TIME – 2 MINUTES

4 tablespoons soya cream
2 rounded teaspoons unrefined light muscovado sugar
1 teaspoon Vanilla Brandy (*see page 210*)

Heat the cream and sugar in a small saucepan stirring until dissolved.
Remove from the heat. Stir in the brandy.

Savoury Sauces, Jellies & Stuffing

'Bread' Sauce

This is a mock bread sauce but has the texture and flavour of the real McCoy. It provides a generous tablespoon per person. Serve with turkey at Christmas or Easter.

SERVES 4 | PREPARATION TIME – 30 MINUTES

55g (2 oz) (½ cup) onion, sliced and diced
70g (2½ oz) (½ cup) potatoes, peeled, sliced and diced
120g (4¼ oz) (1 cup) celeriac, peeled, sliced and diced
2 pinches sea salt
2 whole cloves
2 black peppercorns
2 tablespoons unsweetened soya milk
2 tablespoons soya cream

Add the onion, potatoes and celeriac to a medium saucepan with enough boiling water to cover. Add the salt, cloves and peppercorns. Return to the boil. Cover and simmer for about 15 minutes until vegetables are tender. Drain well. Discard the cloves and peppercorns. Mix in the milk and cream. Liquidize to obtain a 'bread' sauce with a good texture. Warm through carefully if necessary. Serve.

Dill & Caper Sauce

SERVES 4 | PREPARATION TIME – 10 MINUTES

285ml (10 fl oz) (1¼ cups less 1 tablespoon) unsweetened soya milk
285ml (10 fl oz) (1¼ cups less 1 tablespoon) vegetable water/water
2 tablespoons gluten-free cornflour (cornstarch)/potato flour (farina)
1 teaspoon dairy-free margarine
sea salt and freshly ground black pepper
1 tablespoon capers (not in malt vinegar), chopped and rinsed
2 tablespoons freshly cut dill

Mix the flour into a little of the milk until smooth. Heat the remaining milk and vegetable water/water together with the margarine in a saucepan. Pour in the flour and milk mixture. Bring to the boil, stirring. Simmer for 1 minute. Season and stir in the capers and finely cut dill. Serve.

Mayonnaise

This is a thick cooked mayonnaise suitable for use on its own, or made into Lemon Mayonnaise, Tartare/Seafood Sauce, Coleslaw or Fresh Vegetable Sauce. You will find the recipes for these after the mayonnaise recipe. The initial process of beating in a few drops of oil at a time seems laborious but is important for a successful mayonnaise. This process, however, will only take 8–10 minutes. The unused egg white could be used for meringues or Coconut Marzipan Macaroons (*see page 130*).

MAKES 210ml (7½ fl oz) | PREPARATION TIME – 25 MINUTES

140ml (5 fl oz) (½ cup plus 1 tablespoon) sunflower oil

1 tablespoon olive oil
2 large egg yolks plus 1½ tablespoons egg white*
½ clove garlic, crushed
¼ teaspoon gluten-free Dijon mustard
sea salt and freshly ground black pepper
2 teaspoons white wine vinegar

Never use eggs with cracked eggshells.

Combine the sunflower and olive oil.

Using an electric whisk, beat the egg yolks and measured egg white with the garlic, mustard and seasoning in a largish heatproof basin. Place over a small saucepan of simmering water.

Start by adding the oils a few drops at a time while beating – to avoid curdling. Continue in this way, until half of the oil has been incorporated. Do not at any time allow the mixture to boil. Add 1 teaspoon of the vinegar. Whilst beating continuously, continue to add the remaining oil in a slow trickle. Stir in the remaining teaspoon of vinegar. Immediately remove the basin from the heat and stand in a bowl of cold water. Beat for 2–3 minutes until cool. When cold, store in a covered container in the fridge.

Lemon Mayonnaise

This is ideal to serve with salads, simply grilled (broiled) fish or Salmon Parcels (*see page 52*). As variation, snipped fresh herbs such as chives, dill, lemon balm or parsley can be added to the mayonnaise.

SERVES 4

2 heaped tablespoons cooked mayonnaise
¾ teaspoon lemon juice
¾ teaspoon grated lemon rind

Add the lemon juice and rind to the mayonnaise and stir.

Tartare Sauce

SERVES 4

2 rounded tablespoons cooked mayonnaise

2 heaped teaspoons capers in white wine vinegar, rinsed and chopped

1 medium gherkin (not in malt vinegar), rinsed, sliced and diced

Mix the capers and gherkins into the mayonnaise and serve.

Seafood Sauce

SERVES 4

2 rounded tablespoons cooked mayonnaise

1 tablespoon gluten-free tomato ketchup

½ teaspoon gluten-free Worcestershire sauce

½ teaspoon whisky to taste (*optional*)

Stir the tomato ketchup into the mayonnaise until smooth, then the Worcestershire sauce and whisky. Serve.

Coleslaw

SERVES 3–4

2 rounded tablespoons cooked mayonnaise

25g (1 oz) (2 rounded tablespoons) each white cabbage shredded, carrot roughly grated and Spanish/red onion sliced finely

Mix the cabbage, carrot and onion into the mayonnaise and serve.

Fresh Vegetable Sauce

This is a fresh tasting summer sauce to accompany salads or
fish.

Serves 3–4

2 rounded tablespoons cooked mayonnaise
25g (1 oz) (2 rounded tablespoons) freshly podded peas (podded weight)
25g (1 oz) (2 rounded tablespoons) spring onions (scallions), sliced thinly (white and light green part)
25g (1 oz) (2 rounded tablespoons) cucumber, sliced thinly and diced

Mix the prepared vegetables into the mayonnaise and serve.

Parsley Sauce

Make sure the parsley is added just before serving to retain its
multivitamin content and that it is from a freshly growing
organic source, preferably. Use parsley as an edible garnish for
soups, salads, casseroles and other meals to benefit from its
restorative properties or as a seasoning for a low-sodium diet.

Serves 4 | Preparation time – 10 minutes

285ml (10 fl oz) (1¼ cups) unsweetened soya milk
140ml (5 fl oz) (½ cup) vegetable water/water
2 tablespoons gluten-free cornflour (cornstarch)/potato flour (farina)
½ tablespoon dairy-free margarine
sea salt and freshly ground black pepper
1 tablespoon soya cream
2 heaped tablespoons freshly cut parsley

Mix the flour into a little of the milk until smooth. Heat the remaining milk, vegetable water/water and the margarine in a saucepan. Pour in the flour and milk mixture. Bring to the boil, stirring, simmer for 1 minute. Season to taste. Remove from the heat. Stir in the soya cream and freshly cut parsley. Serve.

Pesto Sauce

SERVES 4–6 | PREPARATION TIME – 15 MINUTES

20g (¾ oz) fresh basil leaves
15g (½ oz) fresh parsley leaves
1 large clove garlic, flattened and peeled
50g (1¾ oz) (generous ⅓ cup) pine nut kernels
15g (½ oz) (1 rounded tablespoon) cashew nuts
15g (½ oz) 6 brazil nuts
4 tablespoons extra virgin olive oil
3½ tablespoons sunflower oil
50g (1¾ oz) (2½ tablespoons) mature cheddar-style soya cheese
1 pinch sea salt and freshly ground black pepper

Place the ingredients in a food processor and process until smooth. Use to serve with cooked pasta spirals, penne or spaghetti. Add a little olive oil to coat the cooked pasta then stir in the pesto to taste. Store any unused pesto in a sterilized jar and keep refrigerated.

SERVING SUGGESTION: serve with chargrilled wedges of fennel, red onions, peppers and courgettes, sprinkled with a little olive oil and rosemary.

Pecorino sheep's cheese (romano) can be sprinkled over the pasta and pesto, if tolerated as part of a low-lactose diet.

TO STERILIZE JARS: Place clean jars in a large pan, cover with hot water and bring to the boil. Boil rapidly for 10 minutes. Remove from pan and stand upside down to drain on a clean kitchen towel. Immerse lids in boiling water for about ½ minute. Alternatively, place jars in the oven at 170°C (325°F) (gas mark 3), for 10 minutes.

Sage Apple Jelly

This delicate flavoured jelly is used to complement Gammon & Mushrooms (*see page 70*) or cooked chicken.

Makes 3–4 small to medium jars
Preparation time – 20 minutes plus 2 hours to drain apple pulp plus 40 minutes for boiling and potting

500g (1 lb 2 oz) cooking apples/crab apples/sound windfalls
440ml (15½ fl oz) (2 cups less 1½ tablespoons) water
130ml (4½ fl oz) (½ cup plus ½ tablespoon) white wine vinegar
2 tablespoons lemon juice
2½ heaped tablespoons fresh sage leaves
preserving/white granulated sugar, about 425–455g (15–16 oz) (generous 1¾–generous 2 cups)

Wash and roughly chop the apples (including the peel and cores) into large pieces. Place them in a large saucepan with the water, wine vinegar, lemon juice and half of the sage leaves, bruised and roughly torn. Bring to the boil, cover and simmer for about 5–15 minutes, until the apples are soft and pulpy. Pour into a scalded jelly bag or a muslin lined colander, placed over a large mixing bowl and leave for a minimum of 2 hours, until the liquid has stopped dripping.

Carefully remove the jelly bag without squeezing, otherwise the jelly will become cloudy. For every 568ml (20 fl oz) (2⅓ cups) of juice use 455g (1 lb) of sugar. Return the juice plus the sugar to the clean saucepan. Place a preserving thermometer in the saucepan. Heat gently, stirring until the sugar has dissolved. Bring to boiling point and boil rapidly at setting point (105°C/220°F) for 4–5 minutes. Do the crinkle test*. If you don't have a thermometer, boil rapidly for 7–8 minutes and then do the crinkle test. If it doesn't crinkle, boil for a few minutes more and test again.

Cut the remaining sage leaves into small pieces and mix into the jelly. Allow to cool slightly so that a skin forms (this will allow the sage to be suspended evenly throughout the jelly). Pour into small, warm sterilized jars under 455g (1 lb) to ensure a good jelly set. It will store for about 1 year.

Drop a small amount of juice onto a chilled plate. Leave until it is quite cold. Push a finger through it. It will crinkle thickly if setting point has been reached.

TO STERILIZE JARS: Place clean jars in a large pan, cover with hot water and bring to the boil. Boil rapidly for 10 minutes. Remove from pan and stand upside down to drain on a clean kitchen towel. Immerse lids in boiling water for about ½ minute. Alternatively, place jars in the oven at 170°C (325°F) (gas mark 3), for 10 minutes.

Stuffing with Parsley, Sage & Thyme

A traditional recipe, ideal for stuffing a 5.9–6.8kg (13–15 lb) Christmas turkey or for shaping into forcemeat balls to accompany roast turkey, chicken or pork.

SERVES 6 | PREPARATION TIME – 10 MINUTES PLUS 30 MINUTES FOR BAKING FORCEMEAT BALLS

1cm (½") thick slice gluten-free Crusty White Bread (*see page 115*)
2 gluten-free pork sausages/equivalent pork sausagemeat
½ slice smoked/unsmoked bacon, rind and fat already removed
1 medium clove garlic
25g (1 oz) (2 rounded tablespoons) onion, sliced finely and diced
30g (1 oz) (¼ cup) hazelnuts, crushed

1 good rounded tablespoon mixed fresh parsley, sage and thyme
finely grated rind ¼ small lemon
sea salt and freshly ground black pepper

Place the ingredients into a food processor and process until the texture of breadcrumbs. Use to stuff the neck cavity of the turkey. Cook calculating the cooking time per 455g (1 lb) of turkey weight. Alternatively, when processed, shape into 6 forcemeat balls and place in a greased shallow ovenproof dish. Cook in the oven at 190°C (375°F) (gas mark 5) for about 25–30 minutes. Serve.

White Onion Sauce

For a plain white sauce omit the onions.

SERVES 4 | PREPARATION TIME – 12 MINUTES

1 onion, sliced thinly and diced
285ml (10 fl oz) (1¼ cups) unsweetened soya milk
140ml (5 fl oz) (½ cup) ham/chicken stock (bouillon)/onion water
1 teaspoon dairy-free margarine
2 tablespoons cornflour/potato flour (farina)
sea salt and freshly ground black pepper

Simmer the onion in a little lightly salted water until soft. Drain, reserving the water. Mix the flour into a little of the combined milk, meat stock/onion water until smooth. Heat the remaining liquid and the margarine in a saucepan. Pour in the flour and milk mixture. Bring to the boil, stirring. Simmer for 1 minute. Season to taste. Serve.

Breakfast Cereals

Millet Porridge

Cooked millet provides essential vitamins, minerals and amino acids to build cell tissue for healthy bones, hair, skin and nails. It makes easily digested, nutritious porridge. There is no need to add sugar – the sweetness is provided by the raisins.

MAKES 1 SERVING | PREPARATION TIME – 5 MINUTES PLUS 20–30 MINUTES FOR SIMMERING

40g (1½ oz) (4 tablespoons) millet flakes/2½ tablespoons millet whole grain
20g (¾ oz) (1 rounded tablespoon) raisins

Millet flakes:
Bring 340ml (12 fl oz) (1⅓ cups plus 1 tablespoon) water to the boil in a small saucepan. Add the millet flakes and raisins. Stir well to separate the flakes. Simmer for 20 minutes, covered, stirring from time to time (especially during the last 5 minutes of cooking) to prevent sticking. Serve.

Millet whole grain:
Bring 425ml (15 fl oz) (1¾ cups) water to the boil in a small saucepan. Add the millet and raisins. Cover and simmer for 25 minutes stirring from time to time, *then* uncover and simmer for a further 5 minutes, stirring more frequently to prevent sticking. Serve.

Muesli

The muesli mixtures can be made either with naturally sun-dried varieties of fruit (free from added sugar and preservatives), dried fruit (some containing preservative) or preserved and very sugary ready-to-eat dried glacé varieties. When eating the sun-dried variety of muesli, it is a good idea to pour the rice milk onto the muesli 2–3 minutes before eating to allow the fruit to partially rehydrate.

Makes 4 small servings | Preparation time – 10 minutes

Roasted mix:

2 tablespoons unsalted cashew nuts, halved
2 tablespoons pumpkin seeds, roughly broken
½ tablespoon sesame seeds
55g (2 oz) (4 rounded tablespoons) brown rice flakes
2 tablespoons millet flakes
2 rounded tablespoons raisins
1 piece sun-dried pear, sliced and diced

Preheat the grill (broiler) to high. Lightly roast the cashew nuts, pumpkin seeds [*beware, they are inclined to pop if left whole and toasted too long*] and sesame seeds under the grill (broiler). Leave to cool. Mix the rice flakes, millet flakes, raisins and pear. Add the nuts and mix well. Store in an airtight container. Serve with chilled rice milk.

Exotic mix:

55g (2 oz) (4 rounded tablespoons) brown rice flakes
2 tablespoons millet flakes
1 rounded tablespoon sultanas (golden raisins)
2 tablespoons sun-dried/preserved glacé papaya pieces, sliced and diced
1 sun-dried pineapple ring, sliced/1 tablespoon preserved glacé pineapple chunks, sliced and diced
½ tablespoon sun-dried banana, sliced finely and diced
1 rounded tablespoon coconut strips, cut
12 whole almonds, roughly chopped
½ tablespoon sunflower seeds

Combine all the ingredients and mix well. Store in an airtight container.

SERVING SUGGESTION: seasonal fresh fruit or non-dairy yoghurt can be added to the served muesli for variety or cooked soya/rice bran for extra fibre. A little roasted buckwheat scattered over the muesli provides extra texture and crunchiness. Serve with chilled rice milk.

Soya milk can be used, or oat/goats' milk (if tolerated respectively as part of a gluten-free and low-lactose diet).

Oat Porridge

This porridge is lovely for winter or an unseasonally cool spring/summer/autumnal day – but if coeliac, oats need to be discussed with your GP or dietician. When in season, a juicy ripe peach or nectarine makes a pleasant addition, sliced into the porridge.

1 GOOD SERVING | PREPARATION TIME – 6 MINUTES PLUS 10 MINUTES FOR SIMMERING

285ml (10 fl oz) (1¼ cups) water
40g (1½ oz) (generous ⅓ cup) porridge oats
1 pinch sea salt
6cm (2½") piece ripe banana, sliced and diced
3–4 slices ripe pear, peeled, sliced and diced
1 tablespoon sultanas (golden raisins)
2 good pinches ground cinnamon
unrefined demerara sugar/honey to sweeten
soya milk
1 rounded teaspoon sunflower seeds *(optional)*

Add the water, oats and salt to a small saucepan, then the banana, pear, sultanas (golden raisins) and cinnamon. Bring slowly to the boil, stirring. Simmer gently over a very low heat, stirring from time to time, until thickened – about 8–10 minutes. Serve. Add sugar or honey to taste and a little warm soya milk stirred into the porridge. Scatter sunflower seeds over or stirred into the porridge.

As an alternative to soya, oat/goats' milk can be used, if tolerated respectively as part of a gluten-free and low-lactose diet.

Quinoa Porridge

Quinoa porridge is very light and easily digested. The 'wonder grain' is impressively high in protein and more usable than soya or meat protein. It contains more calcium than milk, important for healthy teeth, nails, bones and cartilage.

SERVES 1 | PREPARATION TIME – 5 MINUTES PLUS 20 MINUTES FOR SIMMERING

50g (1¾ oz) (4 tablespoons) whole grain quinoa
285ml (10 fl oz) (1¼ cups) warm water/rice milk
1 pinch sea salt (*optional*)

Wash the quinoa through a sieve and drain well. Bring the seeds, water/rice milk and salt to the boil in a small saucepan. Cover and gently simmer for 18–20 minutes until the liquid has just been absorbed. Serve with a little extra warm water/rice milk to moisten if desired.

SERVING SUGGESTION: quinoa porridge is deliciously nutritious served with mixed dried fruit. Soak dried fruit overnight in water. Bring to the boil and simmer for 10–15 minutes. Serve hot or cold to accompany the porridge. Sprinkle a little sprouted quinoa on the porridge for enhanced nutrition.

Quinoa Flakes:

The porridge can also be made with 50g (1¾ oz) (½ cup) quinoa flakes to 225ml (8 fl oz) (1 cup) warm water. Stir, bring to the boil, cover and simmer for 4½–5 minutes until water just absorbed. Serve

plain or with finely sliced and diced ripe mango mixed or mashed
into the porridge.

Rice Porridge

I remember rice milk was the first alternative 'milk' I tried –
and I wasn't impressed. However, tastes change and it is now
palatable, even enjoyable. For a variation, Quick Rice Pudding
(*see page 174*) also makes a nourishing and sugar-free start to
the day.

SERVES 1 | PREPARATION TIME – 4 MINUTES PLUS 8 MINUTES FOR
SIMMERING

50g (1¾ oz) (4 rounded tablespoons) brown rice flakes
285ml (10 fl oz) (1¼ cups less 1 tablespoon) rice milk

If a slight sweetening is desired, stir in a little honey to taste.

Add the rice flakes to the milk in a small saucepan. Bring to the boil
then low simmer, covered, for about 6–8 minutes stirring occasionally as it thickens. Serve with additional rice milk if necessary.

Vinegars & Pickling

Malt vinegars contain traces of malt extract at a level that is safe for the majority of coeliacs but rice, cider and white wine vinegars make good alternatives. Rice vinegar has a robust flavour and is, for example, particularly suitable for use with fish and chips, tinned salmon or in oriental dishes. Cider and white wine vinegars are suitable for use in mayonnaise and in cooking. There is also balsamic vinegar which is pungent, dark and fruity. Balsamic, rice, cider and white wine vinegars are versatile and ideal for salad dressings, vinaigrettes, marinades, sauces, and for vegetarian, meat and fish dishes.

Rice, cider and white wine vinegars are suitable for pickling. Use a good quality vinegar of not less than 5 per cent acetic acid. Ready-spiced vinegars can be bought or made at home. If making your own, use only stainless steel, aluminium or enamel (unchipped) non-corrosive pans. All glass-lidded bottling jars and jam jars with plastic coated inner lids are suitable. The spices should be whole and fresh for the best results. For home-made cold and hot spiced vinegars, see the recipe for Pickled Onions (*see page 232*).

Pickled Beetroot

Choose succulent baby beetroot (beets) with growing tops for peak freshness. They look so attractive and give you the incentive to use them right away. Beetroot can be eaten raw or juiced for enhanced health-giving benefits. Young beetroot leaves can be eaten raw or cooked like spinach. Boiled, cooled and sliced beetroot can alternatively be used to accompany salads, or eaten sprinkled with a vinaigrette dressing.

MAKES 2 JARS AT 350g (12¼ oz)
PREPARATION TIME – 5 MINUTES PLUS ABOUT 1¼ HOURS FOR BOILING

500g (1 lb 2 oz) baby beetroot (beets), stalks ready-
   trimmed to 1cm (½")

sea salt

255ml (9 fl oz) (1 cup plus 1 tablespoon) cold/cooled hot spiced rice/cider/white wine vinegar (*see Pickled Onions below*)

2½g (⅛ oz) ready-mixed pickling spices

Wash the beetroot (beets) carefully, taking care not to damage the skins, otherwise they will 'bleed' while boiling. Place in a saucepan of boiling salted water, return to the boil and simmer, covered for about 1¼ hours – much larger beetroot may need up to 2 hours. To test when cooked, the skin should easily rub off with the thumb. Leave to cool in the liquid. Top, tail and lightly scrape off the skins. Slice thinly and place in sterilized, cold jars. Cover with cold spiced or cooled hot spiced vinegar, (*see Pickled Onions below for details*). Seal with plastic coated inner lids. They will store for about 1 year.

TO STERILIZE JARS: Place clean jars in a large pan, cover with hot water and bring to the boil. Boil rapidly for 10 minutes. Remove from pan and stand upside down to drain on a clean kitchen towel. Immerse lids in boiling water for about ½ minute. Alternatively, place jars in the oven at 170°C (325°F) (gas mark 3), for 10 minutes.

Pickled Onions

These can be made with hot or cold spiced vinegar. Read the recipes below for preparing the vinegar as the cold spiced vinegar will have to be made up to 8 weeks in advance.

MAKES 4 JARS AT 454g (1 lb) | PREPARATION TIME – 45 MINUTES

900g (2 lb) small pickling onions/shallots

brine:

75g (3 oz) (3½ tablespoons) fine sea salt

850ml (30 fl oz) (3⅔ cups) water

Place the unpeeled onions in a deep basin and pour over boiling water to loosen their skins. When cool enough to handle, minimally top and tail the onions with a stainless steel knife so that the skins peel off easily. Place them in a glass basin.

For the brine, mix the salt with the water and pour over the onions. Weight them down with a saucer or plate – so that the onions are immersed. Leave them in a cool place for 24 hours. Drain, rinse well and pat dry. Pack into sterilized, cold jars. Cover with strained cold spiced or cooled hot spiced vinegar and label. The pickles will store for about 1–1 ½ years.

Cold or Hot Spiced Vinegar:

10g (½ oz) (1½ tablespoons) whole ready-mixed pickling spices

1 litre (35 fl oz) (4 cups) rice/cider/white wine vinegar

Cold Spiced Vinegar:

This produces crunchy pickled onions. It needs to be made 4–8 weeks in advance of pickling. Place the whole mixed spices in the cold vinegar, seal the jars and allow flavours to develop – shaking occasionally during storage. Strain through double muslin before use to give a clear bright result. Pack the prepared onions (or simmered, cooled, topped and tailed, thinly sliced beetroot) into clean, sterilized jars and pour the vinegar to cover the onions. Seal with plastic coated inner lids. The flavour is medium to spicy.

Hot Spiced Vinegar:

This produces softer-bite pickled onions. Tie the whole mixed spices in a muslin bag. Place in a non-corrosive medium saucepan with the vinegar and bring to the boil. Simmer for 5 minutes, squeeze the spice bag and remove. Cool the vinegar. Pack the prepared onions (or simmered, cooled, topped and tailed, thinly sliced beetroot) into clean, sterilized jars and pour the vinegar to cover the onions. Seal with plastic coated inner lids. Leave to mature for 3–4 weeks before eating. The flavour is mild and mellow.

TO STERILIZE JARS: Place clean jars in a large pan, cover with hot water and bring to the boil. Boil rapidly for 10 minutes. Remove from pan and stand upside down to drain on a clean kitchen towel. Immerse lids in boiling water for about ½ minute. Alternatively, place jars in the oven at 170°C (325°F) (gas mark 3), for 10 minutes.

Glossary

Arrowroot powder is a starchy root, the consistency of cornflour (cornstarch) and useful as a thickening for gravies and sauces to give a clear bright finish.

Buckwheat is not related to wheat, but is a member of the rhubarb family and is a traditional food in Russia and Northern China. It is available as a natural or roasted whole grain, flakes or as flour. The grain can be used for salads and the flour can be mixed with other gluten-free flours for baking.

Carob flour is ground from the pod of the locust tree. It makes a good alternative to chocolate or cocoa for flavouring cakes, biscuits, spreads and drinks. It is caffeine free and its content of fat is lower than that of cocoa or chocolate.

Chana dhal (yellow gram) comes from whole brown peas which have been split and de-husked. They are often used in Indian and vegetarian dishes and can be added to soups and casseroles. When cooked they can be kept in the fridge for several days (in a covered container) and used in mixed grain salads.

Gram flour is made from chana dhal (yellow gram), a member of the chickpea family. It is used extensively in Indian cookery under the name of besan flour. It can also be used in gluten-free baking of flat breads, cakes, biscuits and Indian chapatis.

Millet is a small yellowish grain, grown primarily in north and west India. Millet flour can be combined with other flours for many recipes and bread making. The whole grain is used to accompany salads and other dishes, the flakes for pastry, crumbles and porridge.

Quinoa (pronounced *keenwah*) is an ancient grain (seed) originating from South America where it has grown high in the Andes since at least the time of the Incas. It can be used instead of rice, cooked for breakfast porridge, or added to rissoles and casseroles to provide a higher nutritional content. It can also be sprouted. Quinoa is available as whole natural/red seeds, puffed whole seeds, flakes and flour.

Sago is produced from the sago palm, cultivated in the warm, wet, tropical climates of Malaysia and Thailand. It can be used for hot and cold milk puddings and desserts.

Tamari is a high-quality soya sauce brewed without wheat.

Tapioca is obtained from the fleshy root of a cassava plant grown in hot, humid climates such as Malaysia. It is suitable for use in milky puddings and desserts. Also available as a flour.

Tempeh is a traditional Indonesian soya bean food. Whole soya beans are usually mixed with grains such as rice or millet and a commercial 'starter' for fermentation. This produces a dense block with a chewy texture which can be marinated, steamed, fried or grilled.

Wild rice is in fact the seed of wild aquatic grass. It can be boiled on its own or with whole grain rice. It may be combined with dried fruit, nuts and herbs for stuffing fish or poultry, to accompany main meals or used cold for salad mixtures.

Xanthum gum is produced by a fermentation process using corn or soya starch and xanthomonas campestris, a micro-organism. The starches and organism react together in a similar way to yoghurt making. The gum produced is then milled to a floury powder. It gives a gluten-like texture to gluten-free baking and is therefore useful for bread making, pastry, scones and pizza bases.

Resource Guide

Useful Addresses

United Kingdom

Action Against Allergy, PO Box 278, Twickenham,
Middlesex TW1 4QQ
Tel: 020 8892 2711 / 4949 – 9.30 a.m. to 5.00 p.m. Monday to Friday
Email: AAA@actionagainstallergyfreeserve.co.uk
www.actionagainstallergy.co.uk

Action for M.E., 3rd Floor, Canningford House, 38 Victoria Street,
Bristol BS1 6BY
Tel: 0845 1232380
Email: admin@afme.org.uk
www.afme.org.uk

Allergy UK, 3 White Oak Square, London Road, Swanley,
Kent BR8 7AG
Helpline: 01322 619898 – 9 a.m. to 5 p.m. Monday to Friday
Email: info@allergyuk.org
www.allergyuk.org for downloadable fact sheets about specific allergies

Anaphylaxis Campaign, PO Box 275, Farnborough,
Hampshire GU14 6SX
Tel: 01252 542029 – 9 a.m. to 5 p.m. Monday to Friday
Email: info@anaphylaxis.org
www.anaphylaxis.org.uk & www.allergyinschools.org.uk

Autism Unravelled, 3 Palmera Avenue, Calcot, Reading,
Berkshire RG31 7DZ
Tel: 0845 2266510
www.autism-unravelled.org

Asthma UK, Summit House, 70 Wilson Street, London EC2A 2DB
Tel: 020 7786 4900
Helpline: 0845 701 0203 – 9 a.m. to 5 p.m. Monday to Friday
www.asthma.org.uk (There is an 'email an asthma nurse service'
accessible on every web page of the website.)

Coeliac UK, PO Box 220, High Wycombe, Bucks HP11 2HY
Tel: 01494 437278
www.coeliac.co.uk

Hyperactive Children's Support Group, c/o Sally Bunday, 71 Whyke Lane, Chichester, West Sussex PO19 7PD
Tel: 01243 539966 – 10 a.m. to 1 p.m. most weekdays. Advice and Support – send SAE for details.
Email: hyperactive@hacsg.org.uk
www.hacsg.org.uk

IBS Network, Unit 5, 53 Mowbray Street, Sheffield S3 8EN
Helpline: 0114 272 3253 – 6 p.m. to 8 p.m. Monday to Friday, 10 a.m. till 12 noon Saturday

The ME Association, 4 Top Angel, Buckingham Industrial Park, Buckingham MK18 1TH
Tel: 01280 818960 / 818968 – 9 a.m. to 5 p.m. Monday to Friday
Email: enquiries@meassociation.org.uk
www.enquiries@meassociation.org.uk

National Association for Colitis & Crohn's Disease, 4 Beaumont House, Sutton Road, St Albans, Herts AL1 5HH
Information: 0845 1302233 – 10 a.m. to 1 p.m. Monday to Friday
Email: nacc@nacc.org.uk
www.nacc.org.uk

National Osteoporosis Society, Camerton, Bath BA2 OPJ
Helpline: 01761 472721 & 0845 450 0230 (local rate) – 10 a.m. to 3 p.m. Monday to Friday
www.nos.org.uk

United States

Celiac Disease Foundation, 13251 Ventura Boulevard, Suite 1, Studio City, California 91604-1838
www.celiac.org

C.F.A – USA inc. PO BOX 31700, Omaha, Nebraska 68131-0700

Food Allergy & Anaphylaxis Network (FAAN), 11781 Lee Jackson Highway, Suite 160, Fairfax, Virginia 22033-3309
Tel: 800 929 4040
Email: faan@foodallergy.org
www.foodallergy.org

The Feingold Association of the United States
554 East Main Street, Suite 301, Riverhead, New York 11901
Tel: 1 800 321 3287 (US only)
Tel: 1 631 369 9340
Email: help@feingold.org
www.feingold.org

National Osteoporosis Foundation
1232 22nd Street N.W. Washington DC 20037-1292
Tel: (202) 223 2226
www.nof.org

Canada

Anaphylaxis Canada, 416 Moore Avenue, Suite 306, Toronto, Ontario
M4G 1C9
Tel: 416 785 0458
Email: info@anaphylaxis.ca
www.anaphylaxis.org

Dr Janice Joneja, Health Service Inc. Vickerstaff, 2016 High Canada
Place, Camloops, British Columbia V2E 2ES
Tel: 250 3723246

Mail Order Suppliers of Gluten-free and Dairy-free Products

Dietary Needs Direct
Tel/Fax: 01527 579 086
www.dietaryneedsdirect.co.uk

Gluten Free Foods Direct, PO Box 156, Selby YO8 6WA
Tel: 01757 630725
www.glutenfreefoodsdirect.co.uk

Gluten Free Foods Ltd., Unit 270, Centennial Park, Elstree,
Herts WD6 3SS. For a full list of gluten-free & dairy-free products
contact the company direct.
Tel: 020 8953 4444
Email: info@glutenfree-foods.co.uk
www.glutenfree-foods.co.uk

Lifestyle Healthcare Ltd., Centenary Business Park, Henley-on-Thames,
Oxon RG9 1DS. For a full list of gluten-free & dairy-free products
contact the company direct.
Tel: 01491 570000
Email: sales@gfdiet.com
www.gfdiet.com

Potters Herbal Medicines Ltd., Leyland Mill Lane, Wigan WN1 2SB
Apply direct for a full list of gluten-free products.
Tel: 01942 405100
Email: info@pottersherbals.co.uk
www.pottersherbals.co.uk

Index